Rock Hardware

The Instruments, Equipment and Technology of Rock

Rock Hardware

The Instruments, Equipment and Technology of Rock
Edited by Tony Bacon

HARMONY BOOKS
NEW YORK

Consultant Editor
Tony Bacon

Contributors
Ken Achard•Josh Benn•Richard Burgess•Gary Cooper•Dave Crombie
Ben Duncan•Mel Lambert•Roger Phillips•Adam Sweeting

A QUILL BOOK

First United States edition published by
Harmony Books, a division of Crown Publishers,
One Park Avenue, New York, New York, 10016.
Harmony Books is a registered trademark of
Crown Publishers, Inc.

Published simultaneously in Canada by General
Publishing Company Limited.

Copyright © 1981 by Quill Publishing Ltd.

Library of Congress Cataloging in Publication Data
Main entry under title:
Rock hardware
Bibliography: p.
Discography: p.
Includes index
1. Musical instruments – Handbooks, manuals, etc.
2. Rock music – Handbooks, manuals, etc. I. Bacon, Tony
ML460.R62 784.5′4 81-1473
ISBN 0-517-54521 7 (bound) AACR2
ISBN 0-517-54520 9 (pbk.)
10 9 8 7 6 5 4 3 2 1

First Edition
ISBN: 0-517-545217 (cloth)
0-517-545209 (paper)

This book was designed and produced by
Quill Publishing Ltd.
32 Kingly Court, London W1

Art director James Marks
Production director Nigel Osborne
Editorial director Jeremy Harwood
Senior editor Liz Wilhide
Editorial research Sue Steward
Designer Paul Cooper
Illustrators Ray Brown, Paul Cooper, David Weeks
Photographers Tim Bishop, Clive Bowden, Dave Crombie, Roger Phillips, David Weeks
Picture research Mary Frampton, Sue Steward
Devised by Nigel Osborne

Back jacket photograph by London Features International
Filmset in Great Britain by Text Filmsetters Ltd., Orpington, Kent
Color origination by Hong Kong Graphic Arts, Hong Kong
Printed in Hong Kong

Quill would like to extend special thanks to Gwen Alexander and Jim Wilmer at Rose-Morris, Barry Answorth at Mobile One, Cornelia Bach at Time Out, Noel Bell at Studio Sound, Howard Braine at Argent's Keyboards, Alan Brown at EMI, Peter Cook, Paul Day, Elliot Easton of The Cars, Mike Fine Silver at Pathway, Dave Green of Roland (UK), all the staff at Guitar Man, Henrit's Drum Store, John Hill at CBS-Arbiter, Ed Jones at the London Rock Shop, Max Kay at EFR, Robb Lawrence, Faye Levine at Electro-Harmonix, Fred Mead of Brodr Jorgan, Dominic Milano at Contemporary Keyboard, Barry Mitchell at Wing Amplification, Trevor Newman and Jim Porter at Rosetti Ltd, Tim Page at Guitar World, Val Podlasinski at Moog Music Inc, Hugh Portnow at Phoenix Studios, David Rivett at Scenic Sound, John Smallwood at Quarto New York, Scott Thompson at Colac, Jenny Torring at Trident, Andrew Wallace at Fender Soundhouse, Malcolm Ward and Roger Horrobin at Premier Drum Company, Charlie Watkins at WEM, Liall Watson at CBS Musical Instruments, Tom Wheeler at Guitar Player.

CONTENTS

INTRODUCTION

Rock music has come a long way since the basic two guitars, bass and drums setup of the early 1960s, when minimal playing technique and little technical knowledge were necessary for contemporary musicians. Much has happened in the meantime. Amplification systems have alternately grown and shrunk as fashions in power and size have changed, while many keyboard players have considered electronics evening classes in an attempt to understand the inner workings of the newest synthesizer. Guitarists have seen the introduction of plastic production materials, while bass players have dealt with fretless necks and active electronics. Even drummers have had to come to terms with the increasing use of drum synthesizers and drum machines and have benefited from general improvements made to the stability of their acoustic kits. Altogether, the modern rock band is an amalgam of so many diverse technological parts that to generalize is to trivialize. In a business superficially crowned with fashion and surprise one thing is reasonably certain: all modern rock players rely on rock hardware, the very driving force of the music.

Rock itself embraces many individual music forms. It is affected by a sweeping range of influences and parallels and absorbs other modern phenomena like technological innovation

Left One of the most successful singer-songwriters to arise out of the folk movement, Paul Simon began his musical career as one half of Simon And Garfunkel. Following the worldwide hit album of 1970, *Bridge Over Troubled Water*, Simon went on to pursue a solo career and eventually won critical acclaim for his later work which showed a maturing of his talent.

and cultural diversification along the way. These factors are drawn into sharp focus by rock music's interaction with technology, the science of the industrial arts. Rock as Art or Rock as Spectacle, the musical source is usually a combination of voice, guitar, bass, keyboard and drums, or variations on this basic theme.

Rock music's close relationship with technology is based on the dichotomy of science and art. Throughout rock's history (and some would date its birth as late as the appearance of The Beatles in 1963), rock musicians have treated their instruments, amplification, recording

Left As bass player with Sly And The Family Stone, Larry Graham pioneered the popping percussive style later copied by many funk and disco players. Graham left the group in 1972 to form his own band, Graham Central Station, whose music is based around the same funk rhythms that made his work with Sly so distinctive.
Below From their beginnings as aggressive representatives of Mod culture, The Who have established themselves as one of the most durable rock and roll bands. Violence on stage – smashing guitars, microphones and attacking drumkits – was their early hallmark; their success took on a new dimension with the release of the hit album *Tommy*, a rock opera which was later made into a film.
Bottom Santana were relatively unknown when they caused a sensation at Woodstock in 1969 with their original blend of Latin music and African and blues rhythms. Soon after, the group recorded their first album; their second, *Abraxas*, (1970) defined Latin rock.

methods and sound reinforcement as tools of the trade. They also seem to accept grudgingly, even if indirectly, that the hardware at least *makes* the message in this particular medium.

❝ Well, I'm not really much of a musician anyway. I approach the piano or the keyboard as a guitar player. My brother took piano lessons and he said that all my fingers are wrong. Apparently you have to use certain fingers for certain notes. Well, I don't know none of that (*laughs*). I'm very much limited to a one-finger motion, two at the most. To be honest, I'm not that good a player at all. I can get quite nice sounds. I know what the dials do on a Minimoog. I know what the gadgets are and can work them quite well.**

Gary Numan 1980

** Credibility was more important than anything (when The Police first started) because let's face it, the music was very low-key. Another thing was that we could actually play our instruments. To be absolutely cruel about it, there wasn't much playing going on. It was bang-crash-bang with a few chords thrown in here and there. I could sing which was also regarded as a bit suspect because it was the time of shouting down microphones.**

Andy Summers, The Police 1980

Playing ability is largely a self-taught skill in rock, and players themselves argue about the relative merits and demerits of instrumental dexterity: one camp says that it is not important which instrument you play, the feeling is what counts; the other that technique is all, and that the newest toys that technology can offer should be exploited to the hilt. Between these two exaggerated stances lies the average musician's attitude: a balance between technical knowledge and strong emotions.

Rock and technology are more closely linked than this argument would allow: rock produces its own technology, even if the derivations of that technology were evident long before rock's putative birth date of 1963. It was in the 1920s and the 1930s that musicians, primarily guitarists, began to wonder how the emerging amplification systems could be used to boost their fading sound. Guitarists at that time had to contend with increasingly louder instruments drowning out their contributions – a trumpet in the left ear, some saxophones in the right, with little of the guitar reaching the listening audience. Many of these players in the United States were using Gibson guitars. An engineer and musician who worked at that company, Lloyd Loar, began to experiment with pickups, electromagnetic devices which converted the vibrations of the guitar strings into electrical energy.

The same innovation that made these early amplifers possible – the thermionic tube – was also used to produce a few essentially "electric" instruments, most of which were rather obscure and experimental in nature. One that survived was the Theremin, a strange device with two antennae developed by a Russian inventor, Leon Theremin, which eventually was used by The

Above The king of rock and roll, Elvis Presley, in 1957, two years after the release of *Heartbreak Hotel* transformed popular music.

Below Joe Zawinul played with Miles Davis in the late 1960s before becoming the keyboard player for the jazz-rock group Weather Report, whose fusion of jazz and rock styles is popular in both musical areas.

Beach Boys to produce the wailing sounds at the close of *Good Vibrations* in 1966.

Back in the 1930s, the electric guitar had begun its slow birth; the early developments were varied in both success and method. These included Adolph Rickenbacker's Frying Pans (that's what they looked like) and the first commercial Gibson electric-acoustic guitar of 1935, the ES150, with its now-famous pickup, the Charlie Christian model (named after the famous jazz guitarist who used the device).

The Hammond organ was first patented in 1934, and paved the way for other electric keyboards that eventually provided rock musicians with all the tone colors required to create exciting, dynamic and textured music. Laurens Hammond's first production electric organ, the Model A, made its debut in New York at an Arts exposition a few months before the outbreak of the Second World War. At about the same time, a guitarist called Les Paul was experimenting with solid electric guitar designs based on his working model, affectionately known as the Log – which is more or less what it was, along with some pickups, switches, strings and wiring. After the war another guitarist, Merle Travis, explored solid electric guitar construction with engineer Paul Bigsby and Harold Rhodes developed the Rhodes electric piano, although it did not go into production until the mid-1960s.

In the late 1940s, Leo Fender, a Californian who was to have a profound effect upon the shape and sound of rock music, began to produce his first amplifiers and, more importantly, in

Left Early on, the legendary Rolling Stones cultivated a dark satanic image which suited both their violent, blues-based music and the charismatic live performances of Mick Jagger, an image which seemed tragically appropriate when a fan was killed by Hell's Angels during a concert at Altamont in 1970. The Stones remain one of the all-time classic rock bands; their record sales and sell-out concerts testify to the perennial fascination they hold for many rock fans.

1948 put into production the world's first commercial solid electric guitar, the Fender Broadcaster (soon renamed the Fender Telecaster). Fender followed this innovation with a masterstroke. In 1951, he introduced the first electric bass guitar, the Fender Precision bass. At the Gibson factory in Kalamazoo, Michigan, an endorsement deal with guitarist and inventor, Les Paul, saw the issue of the first Gibson Les Paul solid electric guitar in 1952. The Fender Stratocaster, a glorious example of 1950s' engineering that still epitomizes all that is stylish about the rock guitar, emerged from the Fender workshops in 1954. In the same year, work was progressing in the United States on the forerunner of the synthesizer, the RCA Music Synthesizer, developed by Dr. Harry Olsen.

The arsenal of instruments which would fire the Beat boom was almost complete. In the middle of the Beatlemania year of 1964, Robert Moog announced his prototype synthesizer using voltage control, which went into production by 1966. The drumkit began to grow tougher: individual drums became bigger and louder and natural drum heads eventually gave way to the plastic head, based on drummers' desires for increased volume to match all the electrification of the rest of the band. Rock's basic technology was poised for action: electric guitar and electric bass; loud, tough drums; electric pianos and organs; growing amplification power; and the promise of synthesizers.

❝ We realized anyway it wasn't the easiest thing in the world to break through into the disc big-time. We'd been knocked out when we first got the Parlophone contract but probably it was a good thing that we didn't zoom straight to the top. Back in the New Year of twelve months ago we were doing ordinary engagements in the Liverpool area, where we were known but managed to appear without having the whole police force called out to look after us. ❞
John Lennon, The Beatles 1964

❝ Jimi Hendrix always seemed like a very glamorous guy to me until I met him, and he was a sad, very unhappy guy, very unhappy. Spending months on the road – as a truck driver, or as a musician – is, for me, a very painful way to lead a life... you never get to know anybody, and it causes no end of strife, one way or another. Performers like Elton John can afford to be a little more glamorous, but Little Feat is a long way from being that kind of financial success. ❞
Lowell George, Little Feat 1976

Far left Buggles' 1980 international hit *Video Killed The Radio Star* was the product of hours spent in the studio using a vast range of advanced technology to capture the original sound of the demo. The record was released with an accompanying video.
Left The two members of Buggles, Trevor Horn and Geoff Downes, joined Yes for a short period just before the group's final breakup in 1981. Yes was originally formed in 1968 but did not come to widespread recognition until 1971 when Steve Howe joined as lead guitarist. Howe's arrival and the addition of Rick Wakeman on keyboards coincided with the beginning of the group's popularity as the foremost exponents of "technorock".

Left The Swedish group Abba began their international career after winning the Eurovision Song Contest in 1974. Their carefully crafted hits, sung in English and distinguished by close harmonies and dynamic studio production have made them Sweden's largest export. Vocalists Anni-Frid Lyngstad-Fredriksson and Agnetha Ulvaeus are shown here rehearsing in the studio.

Rock music manifests itself in two main forms: live performance and recorded music. At first, successful and influential groups and artists originated largely as live performance phenomena. While the British Beat boom bands of the early 1960s achieved their initial success at home by playing live, their wider international successes relied heavily on recorded music – and primarily singles. For the really big group, success usually means diminishing returns from live performances, as the venues need to be larger to accommodate the fans and contact with the audience drifts away. This merry-go-round was largely to blame for The Beatles quitting live performances in 1966 to concentrate on recording.

George Martin was the person who was adept at maneuvering The Beatles' sound on to magnetic tape. He became a producer of note due to his skills and technical association with the new, popular music. Martin worked with groups other than The Beatles, including another Liverpudlian outfit, Gerry And The Pacemakers, whom he spotted at a gig in Birkenhead in 1962. In the winter of late 1964 a typical session took place at EMI's Abbey Road studios in northwest London, and it gives some idea of the sort of loose collaboration between musicians and recording personnel that was slowly beginning to develop.

At this session, Gerry And The Pacemakers were scheduled to record the title track for the film *Ferry Across The Mersey*. Under Martin's direction, the session for the title song ran efficiently. Engineer Peter Bown had the basic track down in four takes – Gerry Marsden's vocal balanced against his guitar, Les Chadwick's bass and Freddie Marden's simple three drum setup. (Both guitarists used Selmer amplifiers). The Pacemakers' pianist, Les Maguire, then dubbed on his instrument to finish the group's contribution, and George Martin brought in an orchestra, dubbing on strings and french horns. During the final playback later in the day, everyone decided that *Ferry Across The Mersey* would be the group's next release (in fact, it was their last top ten single in Britain).

Contrast that scene of relative simplicity against the kind of recording gymnastics taking place in studios today, and the effect of technology on rock recording is instantly highlighted. For example, the Buggles' huge international hit of 1980, *Video Killed The Radio Star*, needed a massive amount of overdubbing and remixing to coax into hit mode. Buggles Trevor Horn and Geoff Downes (Downes was a session bassist and Horn a jingle composer and producer; both went on to join Yes) found it difficult to capture the deceptively straightforward sounds of their demo on the final recording. A session singer eventually matched Tina Charles' backing vocal performance on the demo after three days of mis-takes, although use of a device called the Aphex Aural Exciter (a studio box invented by Swedish engineer Curt Knoppel that adds clarity and brilliance to recordings) posed further problems when the tape came to the disc-cutting stage.

The lead voice on the demo, nicknamed "Harry" by Downes and Horn during the sessions, also proved difficult to recapture. It took four long mixing sessions to perfect the sound at different studios, with the right combination eventually emerging only five minutes before the end of the last mix at Sarm Studio in London. The final mix included drumkit, dry and flanged electric bass guitar, acoustic piano, Yamaha electric grand piano, glockenspiel, acoustic and electric guitars, various synthesizers including a Moog Polymoog and a Sequential Circuits Prophet 5, vocals and effects. But the work was worthwhile; *Radio Star* was a huge hit in over 15 countries.

Record sales are considered by some players to be much more important than live performances, and much time is consequently spent in the recording process. As a result, some groups persist in treating live performances as exercises in the on-stage reproduction of a popular recorded sound. Technological trickery has encouraged this attitude; as recording techniques have developed, live sound paraphernalia has been quick to follow. Not all modern groups record in such a complex manner as the Buggles example above, but these innovations also mean that better technical quality is now available further down the recording ladder and new bands are able to record more cheaply.

66 Liverpool is home to us. It's where we started. Liverpool fans helped to get us where we are today and we'll always be grateful to them for that. We developed our act at places like the Litherland town hall and believe me, that's a very good place to learn. But, of course, we can't let our London fans down either, or for that matter any fans anywhere in the country, so we're going to divide our time as fairly as possible.99
Ringo Starr, The Beatles 1963

66 The show is a special thing, that's a life to itself. See, I would like to have shows that were funkier where there were areas of annoyance where the audience would want to get up and walk around. Go to the lobby or the washroom or

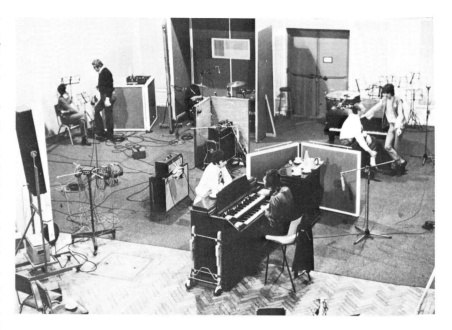

Above The Beatles in Studio 2, Abbey Road, EMI's recording studios in London. The photograph shows all the members of the group, including John Lennon playing a Hammond organ and George Martin at the piano with George Harrison. Recording techniques have altered dramatically since the days when the Beatles recorded *Sergeant Pepper* using four-track machines.

something, and just have chaos on stage. A lot of electronic noise, and I'd like to have video areas ... I really enjoy myself in shows but I know I could enjoy myself even more if the show was more fragmented and if I could ad lib more. The way that we structure our shows doesn't permit me to get loose or talk. I'd just like to have freakier things happening, I'd like to have people standing around on the stage for some reason. I'd just like to try different things now.99
Deborah Harry, Blondie 1980

Despite the arguments extolling the importance of recorded music, there are few doubts that the true excitement of rock music is reserved for live performance where the spontaneity and energy of rock can thrive. In its infancy, live sound had been boosted merely by utilizing inefficient systems designed for crackling, tinny announcements at football stadiums. Gradually PA (Public Address) has adopted "bin-and-horn" speaker systems, originally designed for cinema use. These horn-loaded loudspeakers are designed to couple more efficiently with the surrounding air and modern rock PAs exploit this principle by assigning different frequency bands of sound to each horn or group of horns. Most systems can now achieve relatively high quality sound.

While earlier rock groups used crude amplifier and column speaker setups to amplify the vocals, gradually the trend turned to "miking up"–putting microphones in front of the instruments' speaker cabinets and feeding these microphone signals via a mixer to, at first, crude amp-and-columns combinations, and later to power amplifiers feeding the bin-and-horn speaker systems. In 1971, John Robson, sound engineer with the British supergroup, Emerson, Lake And Palmer, fitted his band up with four new cinema-type speaker cabinets, each with 10-foot folded horns and twin 15-inch loudspeakers for the bass frequencies, plus four Vitavox horns and two American JBL horns for the higher frequencies, all driven by the group's Crown power amplifiers.

Rock musicians have always had to contend with all manner of innovation, technical wizardry, electronic scheming and, on some occasions, a good deal of nonsense. Musical instrument and amplification manufacturers aiming at the rock market are trying to update and replace older models – some of this is well-meaning research intended to offer players more realistic solutions to sound problems, but a small proportion is only inspired by marketing.

Many rock musicians collect instruments, and not only because early and rare examples are worth a great deal of money. Instruments vary widely in tone and quality; a player who wants to experiment with different musical styles may need a range of different instruments to achieve different types of sound.
Right Steve Howe's guitar collection features six Les Pauls, including a Les Paul Recording, Les Paul Special and Les Paul Junior, and four mandolins.
Below Suzi Quatro with her bass guitar collection. She is holding a B. C. Rich; the others include a Gibson Triumph, Fender Precisions and a Gibson Thunderbird.

Below Andy Powell's collection includes *(left to right)*: a 1959 Flying-V; a Fender Telecaster from the early 1950s; a 1963 Flying-V; Schecter Telecaster, fitted with a Stratocaster neck; and the 1958 Flying-V

Right Andy Powell of Wishbone Ash with his 1958 Flying-V. Gibson introduced the Flying-V in 1957 – its odd, arrow-shaped body was originally designed for a Red Indian cabaret duo but failed to find favor with rock players of the time. The Flying-V was reintroduced in 1964; Johnny Winter has a collection of these unusual guitars.

Left Elliot Easton's (The Cars) left-handed guitar collection. Left-handed guitars are reversed versions of the normal right-handed models. Well-known left-handed players include Jimi Hendrix and Paul McCartney.

Right Gary Grainger, guitarist with Rod Stewart's band, is shown here with his valuable 1960 Gibson Les Paul Standard. The guitar has a fine tigerstripe finish.
Inset An immaculate example of why this 1956 Gibson Les Paul Custom is nicknamed the "Black Beauty".

66 Ibanez... keep sending me these experimental models. They don't take the same one away and modify it; they just build another one and send it. So I've got hundreds of Japanese men standing outside my front door with these black cases (*laughs*)! The Japanese are fantastic – so efficient and ready to please, and they can build you anything you want. They'll do that here (the United States) too, but the Japanese are fantastic. So I've got a lot of Ibanez guitars at home. I still collect a few Fenders. 99
Jeff Beck 1980

66 I was given (a drum synthesizer) actually, other than that I don't think I would have gone into the world of electronic drumming at all. 99
Terry Chambers, XTC 1980

66 Wayne Yentis and I worked together on the design of (the Clavitar, a keyboard worn round the player's neck like a guitar) – now this shows you how science can come together with musicians! Like he had a little knob, he says for the pitchbend, I said no, no, no, put a *wheel* in there. I said to him, "I tell you the wheel's a great invention, look at the automobile." I said put that wheel in there, and it gave him a lot of trouble for a while to find something small enough to fit in a guitar neck, but he found something. And man, it made a big difference! 99
George Duke 1979

Rock players themselves often influence the types of instrument produced – after all, who could be better qualified to recommend improvements to a guitar's design and performance than a guitarist? This can result in the sort of deal where a player "endorses" a particular product by actually being involved in the design process. American jazz-rock drummer Billy Cobham, for example, works closely with the Japanese drum manufacturer Tama, often as a codesigner. He also appears at drum "clinics" for the company, where demonstrations and question-and-answer sessions are held for younger, up-and-coming drummers. This two-way endorsement arrangement often benefits both parties: the company gets help from a musician who is well-known, and who knows the instrument inside-out, and the player gets ideas put into practice by a company drawing on wide manufacturing expertise.

Sometimes, endorsement deals are signed with musicians who regularly play a particular instrument anyway – manufacturers merely move in to exploit the association. An early

Above Keith Emerson's wild antics on stage first drew attention when he was the keyboard player with The Nice. With Emerson, Lake And Palmer, Emerson also was renowned for throwing knives at his Hammond organ, wheeling it around the stage and hurling it to the floor – tricks which not only provided a spectacle for the audience but also enabled Emerson to exploit feedback and other unusual sounds that resulted from this treatment.

example of this was John Lennon and the Rickenbacker guitar company, who advertised his continuing use of the three-pickup 1996 model semi-acoustic electric guitar. "For a long time now John and his Rickenbacker have been inseparable," ran a 1965 ad.

The extent to which a top group using a particular brand of equipment in the late 1960s could accelerate sales for the lucky company concerned was shown when Reg Clark of Jennings Musical Industries (who made Vox amplifiers and guitars in Dartford, England) issued a public statement after Keith Richard and Mick Jagger had been found guilty at West Sussex Quarter Sessions on drug charges in June 1967. Richard and Jagger were given what seemed like harsh jail sentences as a result.

Above The technical brilliance and virtuoso playing of John McLaughlin had a major influence on the scope of rock music in the 1970s. McLaughlin played on the seminal *Bitches' Brew* (1970) with Miles Davis and went on to form the Mahavishnu Orchestra, one of the first jazz-rock groups, which drew its musical influences from a wide range of musical styles including Eastern music. Almost a school for jazz-rock players, the Orchestra went through many personnel changes in the 1970s: Jan Hammer, Ralphe Armstrong, Billy Cobham, and Jean-Luc Ponty are among the musicians who worked with McLaughlin in this period.
Left Brian May, lead guitarist with Queen, has remained rooted in the sound of the 1970s. Influenced by Jimi Hendrix, May still uses a stack of Vox amplifiers and plays his guitar with a sixpence instead of a plectrum. Queen have been successful in bringing the sound of heavy rock to a wider audience.

❝These sentences are bound to have an effect on Britain's thriving pop industry. For the past three years the Rolling Stones have travelled all over the world using our equipment. The result has been that they have played a vital part in obtaining export orders for 72 different countries for amplifiers, radio microphones and electronic (*sic*) guitars similar to those used by the group. In many cases we can trace our export achievements directly to the Rolling Stones. When The Beatles gave up touring the world, the Stones became their natural successors. What the Stones used as equipment, the beat groups in Malaya, Venezuela and East Berlin wanted. Nobody can take that away from them.❞
Reg Clark, general sales manager, JMI 1967

It is clear that Clark regarded the Stones virtually as travelling salesmen for Vox, packing up their wares each night to take on to some new, untrodden market where local fans would soon be striking up Mick Jagger poses in front of a gleaming new Vox AC30 (**export** model). The Stones doubtless got their side of the bargain too; after all, they presumably chose Vox amps originally because they liked the sound.

Since then, many manufacturers have used endorsees in ads, handouts and promotional material. Keyboard players have not escaped the attentions of ads designed to promote the "If I use instrument X, I will sound like my hero Y" theory. ARP, one of the top synthesizer producers in the United States, pictured players like Stevie Wonder and Joe Zawinul of Weather Report in their press advertisements of the late 1970s; others have pressed flexi-discs to promote their product and give an instant demonstration of how the equipment sounds. "Herbie Hancock demonstrates the Rhodes Piano" is a 1973 example.

Guitar makers seem particularly keen on naming instruments after their endorsees. This phenomenon, usually restricted to the electric guitar, dates from Gibson's Les Paul model of 1952; since then players have had to choose between such exotica as the Burns Marvin, the Guild Duane Eddy, the Ibanez Bob Weir and the Aria Gerry Cott. Endorsees tend not to get free equipment these days, but might pay lower

prices for their gear. If money is offered, the company is paying for the musician's instrumental expertise and promotional potential – no more and no less. There has certainly been a decrease in the type of situation where ads claim that a certain musician uses so-and-so's new Wonder Guitar, while it is common knowledge that on stage the musician in question always plays a trusty Strat. Players and manufacturers appear to be helping each other in a more positive way in the 1980s. It is becoming increasingly difficult to decide whether or not all the new hardware that is being introduced is of any positive value. In the 1980s, the rock musician is spoilt for choice by the sheer range of musical instruments, sound modifying devises, amplification systems, recording paraphernalia and live sound equipment available.

Guitarists find that the instruments offered today essentially resemble the designs of 20 or more years ago, yet the variations on this basic theme are numerous. The two biggest producers

Left The British instrumentalist Bert Weedon with Bo Diddley. Weedon is holding Bo Diddley's Gretsch; Bo Diddley designs and hand-carves many of his own guitars but Gretsch have also made a number to his specifications. Bo Diddley, together with Chuck Berry, was one of the key figures in the development of early rock music. His powerful, hypnotic rhythms inspired many of the Beat groups of the early 1960s.

of electric guitars are the United States, nurturing a craft heritage that has embraced rock innovation, and Japan, a nation whose guitar makers have copied and learnt, and then gone on to produce their own commercially successful designs.

❛❛ The first reaction (of other guitar companies) to our solid body guitars was to make a lot of fun of them. But, you know, I believe that eventually, our dollar volume put us into the number one position in the whole world. But those other companies, they laughed at us at first – thought we were real amusing. (*Pauses, then laughs out loud.*) Maybe they've changed their minds by now.❜❜
Leo Fender 1978

❛❛ Over 40 years ago the acoustic guitar became the electric guitar – in almost 40 years, no change. But musicians have improved their playing technique, and drawn almost all the possibilities from the electric guitar. So musicians improve and develop new sounds... acoustic to electric; electric to electronic; it's a very natural step.❜❜
Ikutaroo Kakehashi, president of the Roland Corporation, Japan 1978

Above left Jimi Hendrix probably influenced more guitarists than any other rock player. He was the first rock musician to explore the potential offered by pure electric music. His playing style was equally striking: he played his guitar with his teeth and set fire to it on stage.

Above The late 1960s and early 1970s saw the emergence of the lead guitarist as the focal point of rock bands. Guitarists who came to the forefront during this period include Eric Clapton, shown here flanked by Ron Wood and Pete Townshend, whose first commercial success came with Cream. His fame as the world's guitar hero rests on his solo work, however, particularly the 1970 album, *Layla*. He has also played with many of rock's greatest names including George Harrison, Steven Stills, John Lennon, Pete Townshend and Duane Allman.

Today's player, whatever guitar he or she uses, is tempted by bolt-on bits and pieces, designed to glitter in the stage lights and sing to the amplifiers; a brass bridge, for example, is both a musical and visual plus, according to popular opinion. The guitarist keen to keep up with current trends now pays more for add-on accessories since the brass bridge was first introduced.

The manufacturers' concentration on accessories hides an otherwise evident fact: development in the design of electric guitars has virtually halted. There almost seems nothing left to improve. The guitar's electronics have been developed, and now the guitar's sonic range can be extended by converting its pitch – the strings' vibrations – into the synthesizer's driving force, voltage. Guitar synthesists are a new breed of player, although they have not yet appeared in any great numbers.

❛❛ I've always thought that the quality which defines a guitar sound is the attack and decay configuration – the attack reflects the percussion aspect of hitting the note, the decay of the note fading away afterwards. With (the guitar synthesizer) you can eliminate and modify both of those, you can get a very square wave sustain and the actual percussion doesn't need to be there. Plus you can play chords; so really you

have the ability to modulate everything you ever tied into the guitar, in one machine."
Steve Hackett 1978

"In fact, the synthesizers I use are very, very simple indeed. What I really use is the control room. I just set all the synthesizers up and link them straight into the desk so that any instrument can, at the turn of a switch, be fed straight through my synthesizer. That way I can alter the sound in any way I want. I have a high regard for the synthesizer as a part of the whole complex. The whole control room is my synthesizer, but the synthesizers I own are the most modest synthesizers you can get."
Brian Eno 1978

The synthesizer has invaded electric keyboards; rock keyboard players of today have far more to deal with than the electric pianos and electric organs of their predecessors. The original synthesizer manufacturer, Moog, together with another American, ARP, captured most of the initial keyboard synthesizer sales; more recently, Korg and Roland from Japan and Sequential

Above By the mid-1970s The Eagles had become the leading American country-rock group, playing their particular blend of West Coast, country-inspired music to huge audiences around the world.
Right The Pirates play in one of London's "pub rock" venues, the Hope and Anchor. The Pirates reformed in 1976; they were originally Johnny Kidd And The Pirates.

Circuits and Oberheim from the United States have extended the range of instruments further, taking the keyboard synthesizer beyond its original role as imitator, into innovation and diversity. Digital machines like the Australian Fairlight CMI (Computer Music Instrument) are paving the way for synthesizers which will control both compositional and production facilities, along with possessing nearly infinite powers of sound construction.

Electronics could also mean the end of acoustic drummers. The early "drum machine" was basically any device which would produce semi-rhythmic thumps in a hesitant four-to-the-bar bash but these have given way to vastly superior units in both programming versatility and sound reproduction: one of today's slickest drum machines has digitally recorded drums played by a top American session drummer as its basis. However, top drummers still retain traditional acoustic drums and metal cymbals in an environment of electronic overkill. Drum synthesizers exist, but have been used mainly on disco records – the bass drum, floor tom, hanging toms, snare, hihat and cymbals are still basic equipment for the majority of rock drummers. Again, the Japanese manufacturers have copied the key American and European originals, and then designed for themselves: the Japanese are largely to be thanked for making drum hardware and fittings more resilient and robust, following drummers' frequent requests.

In the early 1970s, there suddenly seemed to be a place for the electric bass as a prominent, melodic rock instrument. The dominance of the instruments made by the bass' inventor, Fender, has receded to reveal today's crowded electric bass marketplace with, predictably, the main competition existing between the United States makers and the Japanese makers.

❛❛ I've tried various different speakers in the cabinets but I couldn't tell you what's in them now. I don't know if they're JBLs or Altecs or what. The (Hiwatt amps) I use are actually four-input amplifiers; each one with its own volume control and master volume at the end and they've only got treble and bass controls. They're really basic valve amps. I use the input full up to get the distortion and then turn the guitar down to control the amount of distortion from the guitar. And the master volume about half up. They're only rated at 95 watts but they're really good and reliable. I rarely get any trouble on stage. ❜❜
Pete Townshend 1979

❛❛ Now we're using someone out front so I can concentrate more on what I'm doing. I used to have two Mavis mixers, a tape mixer, echo units on both systems and I really had to be like an octopus. It was getting a bit out of hand for me, and I felt as though I was cheating The Who, because someone must go out front. This is the first tour we've had someone out front, and it's working out really well, because I can concentrate on my own mixing. ❜❜
Bob Pridden, The Who's monitor mix sound engineer 1975

Amplification communicates all the musical instruments to the audience, be it backline (the personal instrument amplifiers used behind each player on stage) or PA (the sound reinforcement equipment, the loudspeaker cabinets of which are stacked either side of the stage). Both

Left Billy Cobham set a trend for bigger and more elaborate drumkits incorporating percussion instruments from different musical cultures. Cobham endorses the Japanese manufacturer, Tama's equipment and runs "drum clinics", teaching sessions for young and aspiring drummers.

backline and PA have been through changes of internal and external structure, fashion often dictating the type, size and power of the components used. In the recording studio, too, musicians face new techniques, with the digital system promising a future of crystal-clear, perfect reproduction. At home, players are offered ever more comprehensive and creative recording equipment at relatively decreasing prices.

Despite all these technological benefits and opportunities, rock musicians will survive on their own wits, on their own strengths and on their own traditions. They will need wit to select the tools of their trade carefully. They will need strength to survive invention and experimentation (not to mention record companies). And they will need to remember their traditions in order to fuel and influence new directions.

❛❛Music's meant to be fun, not like some crass music machine... that's not what we care about at all. We care a damn lot about music but, like, so what if you mess up a couple of chords? Big deal. The point is you tried, and that's what counts.❜❜
Johnny Rotten, The Sex Pistols 1977

❛❛Another day will pass before we're through with the vocals, and the next day we start to mix. I would like to point out that although this seems to proceed very slowly, it is not because of any lack of energy. The whole time-consuming business is created because everything – I mean everything – is tried out. The group can arrange and record full four-part harmonies, double track them and, if it doesn't come out right, erase them and start over again!❜❜
Michael Tretow, Abba's recording engineer 1980

Rock remains good fun. From the little clubs where new talent bursts with vibrant, creative energy to the most expensive show ever staged, complete with flashing lights, lasers, video, and the sequencer bashing out the digits for the opening synthesized bass line, rock music continues to maintain its relationship with rock hardware. This relationship goes both ways. The technology which gives rise to new instruments inadvertently brings about new music, while the dreams and aspirations of musicians provide the stimulus for the development of the instruments needed to realize them: an exhilarating and productive exchange.

Below Orchestral Manoeuvres In The Dark follow on in the tradition of electronic music begun by the German synthesizer bands Kraftwerk and Can, who in turn were influenced by the German composer Stockhausen.

THE ACOUSTIC GUITAR

The acoustic guitar in rock is popularly associated with the singer-songwriter, that breed of folk-based composer which sprang to prominence in the late 1960s. Suitably constructed from natural materials, acoustic guitars accompanied the ballads of such artists as Joni Mitchell, James Taylor, Paul Simon and Judy Collins. The fact that today Joni Mitchell or Paul Simon is just as likely to play an electric guitar (an Ibanez George Benson or a Gibson Les Paul, respectively) is an indication of the acoustic guitar's recent neglect, even in folk-derived areas of rock.

Nonetheless, the acoustic guitar still finds many creative applications in rock – in the hands of an instrumentalist such as Leo Kottke; in the ethnic mixture of Ry Cooder's music; or as the percussive rhythm machine behind Joan Armatrading's powerful songs. In the recording studio, where it can be mixed more easily with its amplified counterparts, the acoustic guitar has on many occasions reached the peak of its potential, often artfully incorporated both as a percussive and melodic instrument. Today, an American company called Ovation has done much to maintain the use of acoustic guitars on stage by rock musicians.

In the early days of rock, the acoustic guitar often was used merely as a prop for the up-front performer – it hardly mattered that Elvis Presley's acoustic, slung low at pelvis level, was barely heard. But the acoustic guitar is rock's major link with the history of a traditional guitar-shaped instrument which has been in existence for many hundreds of years in various guises and under many different names.

Early Guitars

The development of the guitar makes a confused story but the instrument proper can be traced back with some certainty to the *guitara latina* which turned up in Spain in or around the thirteenth century, to another distant relative of today's acoustic guitar, the *vihuela*, and to the lute family in general. A connection can be traced back even further to the Middle Ages, to instruments whose relationship to the guitar is a little more strained. The *lyra* (a kind of lyre, like a mini-harp) and the *kithara* (a heavier version of the lyre, often with more strings) are the obvious links.

Initially, around the sixteenth century, the guitar, shaped more or less as we know it today, was strung with four "courses" (pairs of strings, tuned in unison), and these were tuned C F A D, as the *vihuela* had often been. A fifth course was added some time later in the sixteenth century (the usual tuning was A D G B E), and in the latter part of the 1700s the courses were replaced with single strings, a sixth lower-tuned string being added around 1790 to give the existing standard tuning of E A D G B E.

Also in the eighteenth century, the tied-on gut frets were replaced with metal or ivory frets, while the nineteenth century saw the guitar's body become broader and shallower and metal screws rather than wooden tuning pegs were adopted.

Many of the innovations and changes that brought the steel-strung acoustic guitar (the acoustic instrument used primarily in rock) to its present shape, size and construction were made by American guitar manufacturers in the twentieth century.

Basic Anatomy

Acoustic guitars can generally be allocated to one of three categories: the nylon-strung "classical" guitar, the nylon-strung or steel-strung "folk" guitar, or the larger steel-strung "Dreadnought" or "Jumbo" guitar.

Classical acoustics are rarely used in rock, except by the odd classically trained player who may choose to use the instrument in a rock setting – the obvious example is John Williams of Sky. The more traditional narrow-waisted folk shape is generally more suited to the few rock guitarists who have developed finger-style playing and who need the folk acoustic's treble response and balanced sound. The Dreadnought guitar is the one most used in rock, and the shape was introduced originally to provide a bassier sound and a deeper tone which singers were demanding from their instruments, and which in rock lends itself well to plectrum strummers.

Above The acoustic guitar as we know it today has many varied ancestors, like this highly decorated Spanish guitar dating from the eighteenth century.

Right Leo Kottke with a Bozo acoustic guitar. Kottke came to prominence in 1971 with his *Six And Twelve String Guitar* LP recorded after he had sent tapes to another fine acoustic guitar instrumentalist, John Fahey. Georgia-born Kottke's melodic ability on the acoustic guitar has made him a steadily successful musician.

The most common acoustic is the six-string type, although 12-string models, with six courses, have been popular at various times. Most makers offer 12-string versions of their more successful six-string guitars. Strings are anchored at the bridge on the body, traveling over a single-piece saddle which gives reasonably accurate intonation. The ball ends of the strings are pushed into holes behind the saddle and are held in place with bridge pins (usually plastic). Up at the headstock, the strings travel over the nut to the machine heads which enable the player to tune the guitar. There is usually some form of scratchplate around the soundhole to prevent too much damage to the wooden top.

Materials

Various standardizations have occurred in the methods and materials of construction over the years. A general pattern has emerged which gives some clues to the sound that acoustic guitar players demand from today's instruments. Tops are usually made from spruce on middle range and more expensive guitars, although a rarer wood found on premier instrument tops is cedar; the back and sides are most often made from mahogany or rosewood; the fingerboard is frequently of rosewood, with more expensive instruments featuring denser,

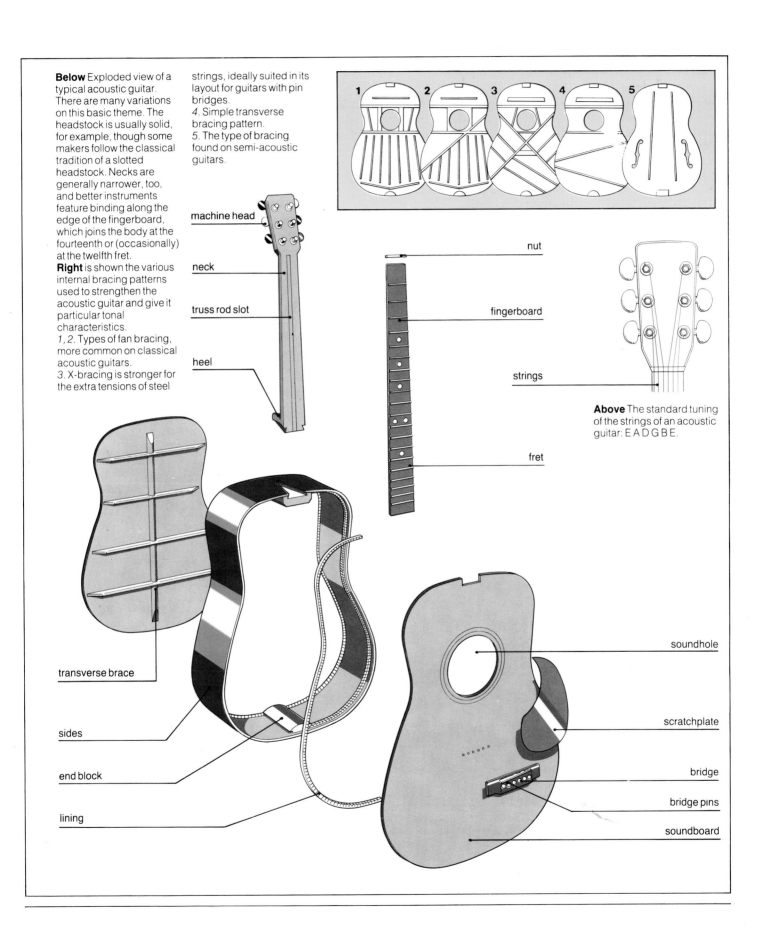

Below Exploded view of a typical acoustic guitar. There are many variations on this basic theme. The headstock is usually solid, for example, though some makers follow the classical tradition of a slotted headstock. Necks are generally narrower, too, and better instruments feature binding along the edge of the fingerboard, which joins the body at the fourteenth or (occasionally) at the twelfth fret.

Right is shown the various internal bracing patterns used to strengthen the acoustic guitar and give it particular tonal characteristics.

1, 2. Types of fan bracing, more common on classical acoustic guitars.

3. X-bracing is stronger for the extra tensions of steel strings, ideally suited in its layout for guitars with pin bridges.

4. Simple transverse bracing pattern.

5. The type of bracing found on semi-acoustic guitars.

machine head

neck

truss rod slot

heel

nut

fingerboard

strings

fret

transverse brace

sides

end block

lining

soundhole

scratchplate

bridge

bridge pins

soundboard

Above The standard tuning of the strings of an acoustic guitar: E A D G B E.

harder ebony; the neck of an acoustic guitar is most usually made of mahogany, with some cheaper instruments making use of maple. Less expensive instruments often have a laminated wood top, which does not develop the "aged" sound quality of solid-topped (and therefore more desirable) guitars.

Variations on these general guidelines do occur. Some makers have produced guitars from unusual or exotic woods, and these are usually expensive, or else they are from families of wood offering much the same qualities as the commoner types referred to above. The Daion acoustics, for example, recent products of Japan, feature *ovoncol* sides and back, and a *nato* neck.

Martin

The Martin Guitar Company was founded soon after Christian Frederick Martin emigrated to New York from Germany in 1833, moving to its present home in Nazareth, Pennsylvania in 1839. A few steel-strung acoustic guitars were made by the company as early as 1900, but these were one-off specials, not production models. Steel strings first appeared as a regular feature on the Martin 2-17, which was redesigned to take the strings in 1922. By the late 1920s, most models were available braced for steel strings, and in the mid-1940s the bracing design was strengthened to allow for heavier strings still.

Martin's famous Dreadnought model, named after the British battleship of the time and

Right Emmylou Harris strums a big Gibson J200 acoustic guitar. Born in Alabama in 1947, Harris initially collaborated with Gram Parsons and almost joined the Flying Burrito Brothers just before they split. After Parsons' death she started recording her own work, beginning with *Pieces Of The Sky* in 1975. Her backing group, the Hot Band, has included musicians of the caliber of guitarist Albert Lee.

Above Christian Frederick Martin (1796-1873), founder of C. F. Martin & Co, the top American manufacturer of acoustic guitars. The family company has produced many types and variations of guitar, and is renowned as the inventor of the Dreadnought-style acoustic, designed by F. H Martin and Harry L. Hunt. Two of the popular Martin types are the D-0018 (right) first introduced in 1935 and the D45 (far right) introduced in 1938.

Left Willie Nelson with a very well-used acoustic guitar, the primary instrument for many country musicians.

characterized by a wide-waisted, narrow-shouldered body, was designed in 1916-7 by Harry L. Hunt, manager of the Ditson Company music store in New York City, and Frank Henry Martin, of the Martin Guitar Company. The bassier sound quality of the Dreadnought has become a favorite in folk, country and western and most kinds of popular music from that time onward – in rock, the Dreadnought's sound has lent itself well to the strumming, plectrum-style so prevalent among today's rock exponents. The shape and dimensions of the Dreadnought have been copied by most acoustic guitar makers at one time or another.

Originally, the Ditson Company sold the early Dreadnoughts exclusively in its store, but when the store went out of business in the late 1920s, Martin, who had been making the guitars for Ditson, went on to experiment with the basic design. He made a few D1 and D2 models in the 1930s which eventually developed into the archetypal Dreadnought acoustic guitars – the D18 and D28, first listed in Martin's catalog for 1935. Martin went on to issue a range of different-sized guitars, including the famous D45, which was reissued in 1968 due to demand. Other folk-size Martins have been used less widely although the 00 and 000 sizes occur here and there. Martin acoustic guitars are expensive, but in quality they are second to none.

Guild

Perhaps the next most impressive acoustic guitar name is Guild. The company was formed in 1952 by Alfred Dronge who took on some Epiphone craftsmen, luthiers who specialized in carved-top jazz guitars. Initially, Dronge was mainly interested in making this type of instrument.

The rise of the folk strummers in the 1960s was paralleled by Guild's entry into the flat-top guitar field, and from that time on the Guild name has been virtually synonymous with good folk/pop/rock acoustic guitars. The folk-shaped (narrow-waisted) F40 and F50 were the first Guild flat-tops to appear, along with the cheaper F20 and M20. Guild's first Dreadnought-shaped acoustics, the D40 and D50, were issued in 1963 and established a success in this area that continues to this day.

The acquisition of Guild in 1966 by a large conglomerate did not affect the company's skills in flat-top production. Models introduced since then, such as the D25 and D35 (cheaper versions of the D40 style), the D40C (a D40 with a florentine cutaway – a deep incision into the lower part of the body to allow the player easier access to the upper frets), or the G312 and G212

12-string Dreadnoughts, have all found favor at various times with performing acoustic guitarists.

Gibson

Electric guitar manufacturers do not necessarily succeed in acoustic guitar building: Fender acoustic guitars, for example, have never been terribly successful. Gibson's acoustics have been used from time to time in rock, although most players would be quicker to identify Gibson with electric guitars. Gibson are also more directly concerned with producing carved-top guitars rather than with flat-topped acoustics. This stems from the company's early history when its founder, Orville Gibson, brought his skills as a woodcarver (and a musician) to guitar building.

Gibson's first Dreadnought-shaped acoustic appeared in the late 1930s following Martin's innovation and was called the Jumbo, which has since become the other common name for

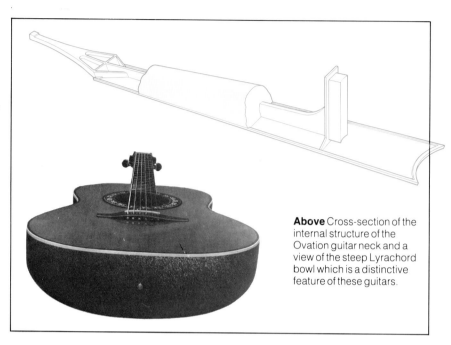

Above Cross-section of the internal structure of the Ovation guitar neck and a view of the steep Lyrachord bowl which is a distinctive feature of these guitars.

Right The Ovation electric-acoustic guitars were based on two new design concepts, the round back made of a fiberglass-like material called Lyrachord, and the pickup system mounted directly into the bridge (below).

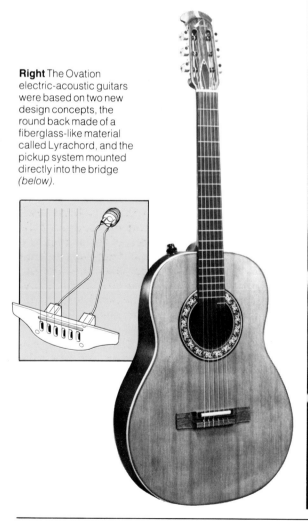

Dreadnought-shaped acoustics. Perhaps the most famous of the Gibson acoustics, the J45 (cherry sunburst finish) and the J50 (natural finish), were first issued in 1956, while the J200, whose basic design dates from 1936, is still going strong as an upmarket but popular model. Throughout the 1960s, Gibson produced some odd and some useful instruments: in 1962 the Everly Brothers model was produced after a pair specially built for Don and Phil aroused wider interest. This is a rare example of a named-and-endorsed acoustic guitar, a practice more common among electric models. In 1965, the Heritage acoustic joined two inlaid and decorated models introduced in 1962, the Dove and the Hummingbird. Of these, the Hummingbird is the premier instrument.

Gibson's reputation in the acoustic field could not have been enhanced by the failure of the Mark range issued in 1977. These guitars were based largely on scientific measurement and analysis of structure and materials, researched by a team which included a chemical physicist, an acoustic physicist and Gibson's top luthier. The major changes suggested concerned alterations to the internal bracing of the instrument, and four guitars appeared: the 35, 53, 72 and 81. The guitars were not popular with players and did not sell well. Cynics were heard to mutter that science and music do not mix.

Ovation

Nevertheless, science *has* merged with music to produce one of the most crucial developments for the continuing use of acoustic guitar in rock music – the Ovation acoustics. Charles Kaman of the Kaman Corporation, which manufactured helicopter rotor-blades in the 1960s together with other aircraft-related products, became interested in researching the acoustic properties of guitars; this was an extension of similar research that Kaman, as an aeronautical engineer, had undertaken concerning the vibrational and acoustical physics of rotor-blades. Rigorous tests throughout the mid-1960s resulted in the appearance of the first series of Ovation acoustic guitars in 1966. These were the Balladeer six-string and the Pacemaker 12-string, both with the famous rounded back of the instrument made from a fiberglass substance called Lyrachord.

Efficient sound reflection and strength were Lyrachord's major contributions to the Ovation's distinct tonal qualities, and the guitars rapidly became popular. Other models were added in the later 1960s, and two sizes of bowl depth and various bracing patterns emerged.

Ovation's most important innovation was the addition of a built-in transducer to the successful projectional qualities of the Lyrachord bowl. A small pickup, mounted under the saddle on the bridge, senses the vibrations of the strings and the top of the guitar. These transducers (first offered on the Artist, Pacemaker and Legend instruments in 1969) connect to a small preamplifier mounted inside the bowl, and the instruments feature a volume control mounted near the heel of the neck.

The sound of these "amplified acoustic" Ovations appealed to many rock players who wanted the traditional shape and qualities of an acoustic guitar combined with the potential for amplification. The Ovation electric-acoustics now grace many a rock stage and have assured the acoustic guitar a continuing place in live rock. The up-market Ovation Adamas uses even more outlandish technology, including a sandwich of graphite fibres and woods for the guitar's top and "scientifically repositioned" soundholes. The result of all this lengthy (and expen-

Left John Williams pictured playing at a Together For Children benefit concert with his Ovation Classic guitar. Williams has taken his classical guitar training and adapted it for use with his amplified group Sky who play a mixture of classical and pseudo-classical music.

sive) work in the laboratory is a price for the acoustic version double that of any other top quality instruments. One of the few people you'll see using an Adamas is Denny Laine (ex-Wings), but he also has a Martin D28.

Other Manufacturers

Japan

The Japanese have made wide inroads into the guitar market generally in the last ten years or so, and the acoustic sector has seen similar activity. Yamaha acoustic guitars were particularly popular in the late 1960s and the 1970s, when their various ranges (both folk and Dreadnought varieties) were used widely in many rock contexts. Yamaha also offer a more exclusive and expensive handmade range of acoustics – Bert Jansch is one of the British folk-based acoustic guitarists who have used Yamaha guitars to good effect. Japan now also produces the Epiphone acoustics, Gibson having ceased to make Epiphones some ten years after acquiring the name in the late 1950s.

Europe

European acoustics had some success in the early 1960s. The Levin Goliath (Swedish) was much used in the folk boom, while John Lennon could be seen in early Beatles poses with a Hawk

Above Steve Howe is a keen guitar collector and is seen here with a selection of his Martin acoustic guitars.
Right David Byrne of Talking Heads is known as an electric guitarist but is shown here with an acoustic 12-string guitar which has a pickup added – the lead to the amplifier can be seen trailing out of the guitar's soundhole.

Left Two members of
Lindisfarne playing
mandolins – the band used
the instruments to add a folk
quality to their music. A
mandolin can be heard
prominently on their 1970 hit,
Lady Eleanor.

acoustic (German). The omnipresent Eko
guitars hail from Italy. These good, budget-
priced instruments are widely used – Martin
Barre of Jethro Tull still uses his battered Eko to
write songs. More recent activity has been
limited to the sporadic success of the excellent
Fylde acoustics guitars (British), used by such
guitarists as American fusionist Al DiMeola.

Use in Rock

The acoustic guitar, like many other acoustic
instruments adapted for use in electric rock, is
used more in recording studios than on the
stage. On record its role is extremely varied,
although very often it is the instrument's particular percussive qualities which are exploited.
Played with a plectrum and with a little
equalization to emphasize the higher frequencies, the acoustic guitar can be an effective and
incisive instrument in rock music.

Some good examples of this loom from the
1960s: then, both the Rolling Stones and The
Who used the acoustic guitar in this manner.
Pete Townshend's acoustic guitar *tour de force*
throughout *Pinball Wizard* is still a shining example of the way the instrument's rhythmic
qualities can be exaggerated to good effect. More
recently, the acoustic guitar seems less in
fashion in rock.

Above The dobro uses a
vibrating metal plate on top
to increase the instrument's
volume and projectional
qualities.

On stage, the problem which afflicts the
acoustic guitar is the same one that afflicts all
acoustic instruments adapted for rock – the
difficulty of achieving loud and accurate amplification. Most acoustic guitar manufacturers
have for many years offered models with built-in
pickups and associated volume and tone controls and these, along with acoustic guitars with
owner-installed pickups, offer one solution. This
has often been found to be unsatisfactory,
however. The drawback to acoustic guitars with
attached pickups is that, when amplified, they
rarely produce the sound of a louder acoustic
guitar – the sound is usually more like a thin-
sounding electric guitar. The reason for this is
due to the fact that the sound of an acoustic
guitar is based on both the sound of the strings
vibrating and on the sympathetic vibrations of
the wood of the guitar's body.

Ovation instruments have become very popular with musicians seeking to use acoustic guitar
on stage. Opinion differs as to how "real" the
Ovation electric-acoustic guitar sounds, but
small transducers mounted on the body to pick
up the string vibrations and the body vibrations
are often claimed to give a more accurate sound
of an amplified acoustic guitar. On the Ovations,
the transducer is in the bridge, underneath the
string saddles. Other makers such as FRAP and
Barcus Berry offer transducers to mount near or
on the bridge.

With the electric guitar so firmly placed at the
heart of the rock sound, acoustic players tend to
be found on the peripheries of rock – these instruments are second nature to a vast army of
singer-songwriters from John Denver to Bob
Dylan. Other musicians have stressed the rhythmic potential of the instrument: the energetic
Richie Havens or Joan Armatrading.

The Guitar Family
The Dobro

The dobro, more correctly termed the ampli-
phonic resonator guitar, originated in the
United States in the mid-1920s. The Dopyrea
brothers were instrumental in developing the
dobro when guitarists of the time called for
louder instruments. The Dobro Company was
formed in 1928, and their instruments were
based upon the theory that a resonating metal
disk on the top of the guitar's body will substantially increase volume. The other major American maker, National, merged with Dobro in
1934. The instruments are rarely used in rock:
Ronnie Lane has used them with The Faces and
since; more recently, Dire Straits' talented
guitarist Mark Knopfler has indulged in their
projective qualities.

The Mandolin

A descendant of the lute, the mandolin did not appear in its modern form until at least the late seventeenth century. Its angular back is built up by internal ribs, and the fretted neck sits under four pairs of "courses" played with a plectrum. The instrument is occasionally used in rock where a folk quality is required. Examples include many of the tracks recorded by the English folk-rock group Lindisfarne.

The Sitar

The Sitar is an Eastern descendant of the long-necked lute, and dates back well into the Middle Ages. Modern instruments usually have from four to seven strings attached to variously angled tuning pegs. The frets are movable to allow the player to experiment with scales. The tuning of a modern four-string sitar is normally GCFC, and the melody is played on only one string, the others providing drones and harmonic sympathy. The sitar is closely linked to some of the psychedelic music of the late 1960s – George Harrison's songs *Love You Too* and *Within You Without You* from this period demonstrate relatively pure sitar sounds in rock. Attempts have been made to blend the sitar's sound into rock, such as Denny Dias' electric sitar solo on Steely Dan's *Do It Again* (1972).

The Banjo

The banjo has a tambourine-shaped body consisting of a frame with a parchment-like membrane stretched over the front. Four strings plus a thumb-string are common; the thumb-string ends halfway up the fretted neck at its own machine head, separate from the four on the headstock. The instrument is played either with a plectrum or with the fingers, and is occasionally used to add an "ethnic" quality to rock recordings, for example on Crosby, Stills, Nash And Young albums.

Below The banjo comes in two main styles, long neck or tenor, with a rare larger size, the bass banjo, reserved for use in banjo bands.

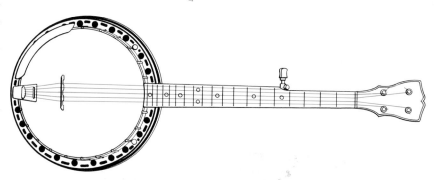

Left Steve Howe using the steel in straight rock – an unusual occurrence as the instrument is more readily adaptable to country-rock. The pedal steel guitar is largely associated with country music and, as an electric instrument, blends well into amplified country-rock. Various footpedals and knee levers – as many as eight of the former – alter tuning and other parameters. The steel itself is a thick metal bar which the player slides against the strings to produce notes in much the same way as a bottleneck is used on conventional guitars.

THE ELECTRIC GUITAR

Jimi Hendrix took what is arguably the most popular rock guitar, the Fender Stratocaster, and literally turned it on its head. Using an inverted right-handed guitar, restrung and with the controls on top, he produced some of the most inspired music ever played through the electric guitar, that peculiar assemblage of wood, metal, magnets and plastic. The electric guitar is still the heart of rock music. Its close identification with this key area of modern culture belies its relatively long history, a timespan from which three major dates loom: 1931, 1948 and 1952.

It was in 1931 that the first commercial electric guitars were sold, the Rickenbacker A Models, since nicknamed the "frying pans". Leo Fender brought out the Fender Broadcaster electric guitar in 1948, the world's first commercial solid electric guitar, still selling widely today as the Fender Telecaster. And in 1952 the Gibson Les Paul model was introduced, one of rock's most frequently used solid electric guitars.

Electric guitars may originate from solitary makers crafting one instrument a year or from huge factories churning out thousands of units per annum. But despite differences in manufacture and style, they are all designed to make music, a function only limited by each player's imagination. The electric guitar gives instant sound to the competent guitarist; to a gifted player such as Hendrix it offered far more. Today, the electric guitar is found in a variety of different styles and makes. Technology now proffers electronic advantages that early makers could not envision, scientists concoct artificial materials for guitar manufacture, and the player can only benefit from a wider choice than ever before.

Basic Anatomy

The electric guitar is in essence a simple device: vibrating strings plucked or picked by the player are transferred into electrical energy by the pickup; this energy is processed and sent out of the guitar to the amplifier.

An electric guitar is termed either solid or semi-acoustic: the body of a solid electric guitar is usually made of solid or laminated wood, most often maple, alder, mahogany or ash. An electric semi-acoustic guitar's body is hollow – as the name implies, this guitar is a combination of acoustic and electric properties. However, the most popular electric guitar for rock music is the solid variety, the Fender Stratocaster and the Gibson Les Paul being the most common designs and shapes.

The neck of the electric guitar is either bolted to the body as in the Stratocaster, glued to the body as in the Les Paul, or forms an integral part of the body, as in the design of some recent guitars. Necks are usually wooden – most often they are of maple or mahogany. A few production instruments use necks of metal, or a metal and wood combination.

Metal frets, by which the player stops the open strings to produce certain notes, are either sunk into the face of the neck itself, as on most Fender guitars, or else a thin fretboard with frets is joined to the face of the neck. The most common woods for the fretboard are rosewood or ebony – ebony is denser and more resilient, but more expensive than rosewood.

Most makers of electric guitars insert what is known as a truss rod into the necks of their instruments. The truss rod is a long, narrow, steel rod that effectively strengthens the neck and reduces the possibility of it becoming warped or bent due to the load exerted by the strings (up to 200 pounds/440 kg of pressure). The most common type of truss rod is inserted into a tube running the length of the neck. One end of the rod is attached to the neck, the other is adjustable. On the Stratocaster, for example, the rod can be adjusted at the "bullet" where the neck meets the headstock; on some other guitars this is under a cover on the headstock. When tightened, the rod is levered against the pull of the strings. The guitar repairer can use the truss rod to correct bows or warps in the guitar's neck.

At the top of the instrument where the neck joins the headstock is the nut, a small piece of bone, ivory, plastic or brass with slots cut into it. These slots accommodate the strings which pass at this point from the neck to the headstock's machine heads. The machine heads, one for each string, are metal peg-and-gear devices with which the player tunes the strings. The nut

"stops" the strings at the headstock end of the fingerboard before they reach the machine heads.

The bridge is the device that anchors the strings at the body end and offers, depending on the particular model, various degrees of control for improving and adjusting the intonation of the individual strings: many bridges allow the player to adjust the effective string length by the horizontal movement of the string saddle along the string. The guitarist can also adjust the string's height at the bridge, and thus its height in relation to the fretboard (called the "action"). Some bridges have a handle attached which drops the pitch of the strings and then, thanks to a spring mechanism, returns them to pitch. This handle is usually called a tremolo arm but is more accurately a device for introducing vibrato effects.

The body houses the heart of the electric guitar – the pickups and associated controls. The operation of a pickup relies on a simple fact: if a magnetic field is disturbed by vibrations, a current will be induced in a coil situated in that field. A basic single-coil pickup has a central magnetic core surrounded by a coil of wire. The pickup sits immediately under the strings and the coil generates a signal of electrical current as strings are plucked and vibrated. This signal is passed to the amplifier via the guitar's controls. Humbucking, or hum-cancelling, pickups con-

Below left The ("pot") or potentiometer controls the volume and tone of electric guitars: a volume pot regulates current output; a tone pot has a capacitor to regulate the output of high frequencies. When the knob on top of the guitar body is turned, the shaft to which it is attached revolves and a metal protrusion sweeps around a resistance contact, providing the variable resistance function. The pot is wired to the pickup and the jack plug socket.

Right The pickup is an essentially simple mechanism based on the fact that vibrating strings in a magnetic field will induce a current in a coil in that field. The pickup converts string vibration into electrical energy, usually by means of a permanent magnet, or six magnetic polepieces, surrounded by a wire coil. There are two basic types of pickup: single-coil (based around one coil) (1) and humbucking (based around two coils) (2).

Above The functions of the machine head ("machine") is to tighten or loosen the string tension gradually, so the string can be tuned accurately. This is achieved by means of a gear mechanism. In open machine heads (1) the mechanism is exposed; in closed machine heads (2) the mechanism is enclosed.

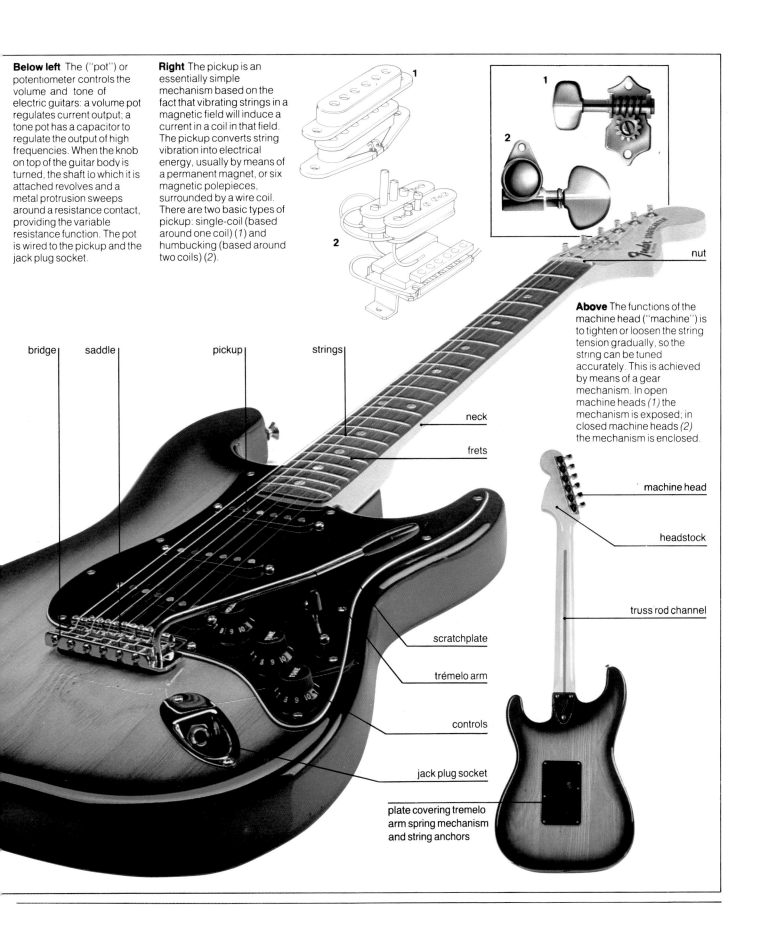

bridge   saddle   pickup   strings

nut

neck

frets

machine head

headstock

truss rod channel

scratchplate

trémelo arm

controls

jack plug socket

plate covering tremelo arm spring mechanism and string anchors

sist of two coils wound in opposite directions to cancel out each other's hum. Single-coil pickups tend to sound trebly; humbucking pickups sound warmer.

The controls, seen as plastic knobs or metal switches on top of the body, affect such things as volume, tone, pickup selection on guitars with more than one pickup, phase and coil selection of pickups, preselected tone settings, and sometimes even an on-board preamplifier. These knobs and switches are generally attached to a plastic scratchplate which, when removed from the guitar's body, reveals on its underside the actual control components and the connections between them. On other instruments the control components and wiring are housed in a recess in the wooden body covered by the scratchplate.

The pickups are wired to the potentiometers (or "pots") which the volume and tone knobs operate, with further wiring leading to the guitar's jack plug socket which is where the jack-to-jack cord (lead) is plugged in to connect the guitar with the amplifier.

Early Developments

In the 1920s, Lloyd Loar was a leading figure in the Gibson Guitar Company of Michigan. Orville Gibson had founded the company towards the end of the nineteenth century, and by this time it was well-known for its carved-top guitars. Loar had been responsible for introducing several innovations to Gibson instruments such as the neck truss rod and the adjustable bridge, but he was also interested in the new art

Below Two excellent examples of attractive wood finishes on Les Paul Standard 80 models. These guitars were introduced by Gibson in 1980 and were intended to provide a "vintage-style" Les Paul as a new instrument. The beautiful body woods used were Tigerstripe *(above)* and Flame *(below)*.

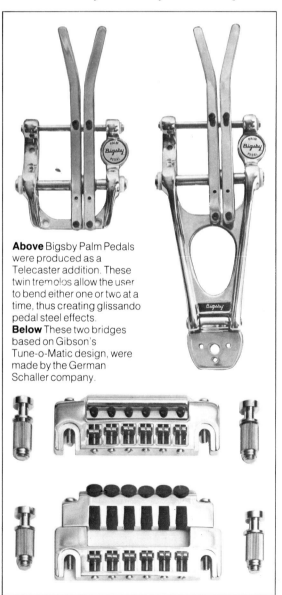

Above Bigsby Palm Pedals were produced as a Telecaster addition. These twin tremolos allow the user to bend either one or two at a time, thus creating glissando pedal steel effects.
Below These two bridges based on Gibson's Tune-o-Matic design, were made by the German Schaller company.

Left Tony Zemaitis represents the personalizing custom-builder. Zemaitis' early reputation grew from Ron Wood and Keith Richard's trade, particularly Richard's five-string, inlaid with mother-of-pearl daggers. He is seen with a shell-inlaid model for James Honeyman-Scott.
Below left In the Fender spray room at the Fender factory, racks of sanded bodies await application of final sealer and polyester lacquer.
Right The final inspection in the Fender factory involves two thorough playings of the tuned instruments.

of amplification and electrification of musical instruments. He experimented with crude magnetic coils to develop a pickup for instruments and soon left Gibson to form his own Vivi-Tone company.

At the same time, several other people in the United States were following parallel paths, developing ideas for instrument pickups. In 1931 Horace Rowe, an engineer, and Mr. DeArmond, a musician, were among the first few into production with a guitar pickup. The first pickup they offered to guitar makers coincided with the formation of the Rowe-DeArmond company which is still a respected name in this field today.

Also during this period, George Beauchamp and Paul Barth were employed by the National

Small-scale guitar makers are able to select their wood from freshly sawn logs at David Dyke's Sussex woodyard, which continues the tradition of made-to-measure wood cutting. Dyke cuts down a log to rough strips for the finger-board *(1)*. The strips are cut to an exact size *(2)* and fed through a machine which planes and fixes the exact thickness *(3)*. The wood is stored in loose bundles, according to size, in the drying room *(4,5)* – a converted chapel.

Far right Peter Cook's custom-made guitars are built from wood cut at David Dyke's woodyard. Cook, who works from a small shed in his garden, is seen using a caliper to check the neck's final dimensions, prior to gluing it to the body.
Inset Once the body has been sprayed and lacquered, the final stage is wiring up the circuitry by soldering the pickups to the "pots".

1

4

5

2

3

company in California and were keenly experimenting with instrument pickups. Adolph Rickenbacker, a Los Angeles-based machine and engineering contractor, was approached by National to make the metal bodies for their resonator guitars, and through this connection met Beauchamp and Barth. Together, the three men formed the Electro String Company which produced the first commercial electric guitars in 1931. These Rickenbacker A22 and A25 models were cast-aluminum lap steel instruments, and became affectionately known as "frying pans" due to their shape. The twin horseshoe-shaped magnet structure around the pickup coil was a feature of the early Rickenbacker guitars which survived through to some recent models. The first commercially produced electric "Spanish" guitar is credited to the National company soon after Rickenbacker's first instrument.

In Kalamazoo, Gibson were not slow to react to the interest in electric instruments, and their semi-acoustic ES150 model made its debut in 1935 after the company had already produced some electric steel guitars. The ES150 incorporated what is now known as the Charlie Christian pickup; Christian was a pioneer among pre-war electric guitar players, and the ES150 enjoyed considerable popularity, partly because of his use of the guitar. The Gibson Charlie Christian pickup consists of a mild steel core or pole-piece bolted to two strong magnets underneath

Far left Adolf Rickenbacker exhibiting his "frying pan" – an aluminum lap-held Hawaiian guitar made in 1931, the first to incorporate an electric pickup which transformed the sound of a vibrating string and registered the beginning of the age of the electric guitar.
Left Leo Fender's development of the solid-bodied guitar in the late 1940s dispelled hum and distortion problems suffered with amplified hollow-bodied instruments, and in effect created a new instrument.

Below Extract from patent for a Fender guitar pickup dated 1951.

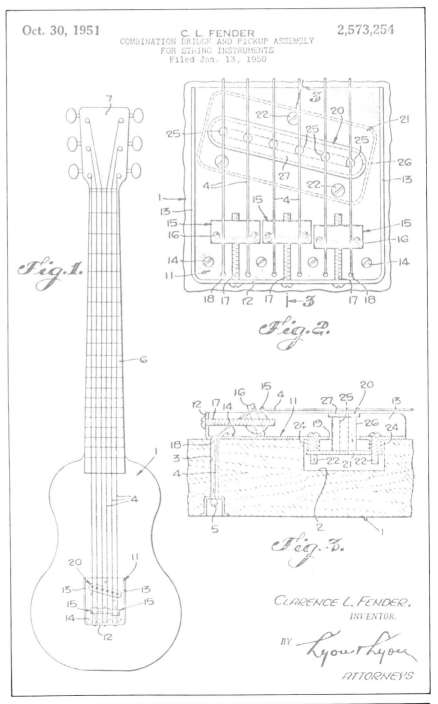

the top of the body. The core protrudes through the top and is covered by a copper wirewound coil in a distinctive black-and-cream angled bakelite mounting.

Throughout the prewar years there continued to be a good deal of development work and experimentation in electric guitar design. Les Paul, a well-known player of the time, was meddling with a solid-core guitar in the early 1940s – his so-called "log" was a cello guitar with the middle section sawn through and replaced by a solid piece of wood on which were mounted the electrics and bridge hardware. Paul Bigsby also made solid guitars in the late 1940s – in collaboration with a popular country guitarist, Merle Travis. An example of their work currently resides at the country music Hall Of Fame in Nashville.

In 1948 the big breakthrough in electric instruments came in the shape of Leo Fender's Broadcaster model, the world's first commercially produced solid electric guitar. It had an ash body with a detachable, solid maple neck into which the frets were directly sunk. There

Left The early days of guitar mass production, seen in these 1923 interior views of Orville Gibson's factory at Kalamazoo, Michigan, reprinted from Gibson's catalog of that year.

Below Lloyd Loar brought his skills as a musician and acoustic engineer to the Gibson company in 1920, but his plans for electric amplification were much more advanced than Gibson's and he left. Loar is pictured here with the Loar F5 mandolin, featuring characteristic Loar bound edges to the hand-carved body and a scrolling effect on the upper right side.

Gibson

Gibson is a magical name for many players. Gibson themselves claim to have made electric guitars since 1924 – the 1935 ES150 semi-acoustic guitar was Gibson's first commercial electric model, and it continued alone in production until the 1940s when it was joined by other ES models.

Gibson's first solid electric guitar appeared in 1952 and was known as the Les Paul model, Les Paul lending his name to the instrument via an endorsement deal. This first Gibson Les Paul solid electric guitar had two cream-colored single-coil pickups designated P90 types, and came with a trapeze tailpiece and bridge combination. The guitar had a gold luster-finished top which was carved into a shallow arch, and had distinctive trapezoid-shaped pearl position markers in the rosewood fingerboard. Most of the Les Paul guitars made since 1952 have been based on the original single-cutaway design and specifications. Like Fender's Telecaster and Stratocaster, the Gibson Les Paul remains one of the most popular designs today, and is almost certainly the design most imitated by other makers, whether directly or indirectly.

Flat-topped, uncarved versions of the Les Paul were introduced in 1954, with two pickups (the Les Paul Special) or a single pickup (the Les Paul Junior). These guitars, like all early Les Pauls, were inexpensive at the time of issue but command high prices today. Perhaps the most highly prized Les Paul among players and collectors is the original Les Paul Standard, made between 1958 and 1960, and affectionately known as "the sunburst" due to its fine cherry sunburst-finished, flame maple top. The original had two of the new humbucking pickups set in cream mounting rings; some gold-top Les Pauls were made a year earlier with these new pickups. The humbucking, or hum-cancelling, pickup was an important new development and showed up in the late 1950s on several new Gibson models.

The problems of feedback and hum were the most difficult to eliminate of those facing players using early pickups, and the humbucking pickup was a major improvement. In 1956 Seth Lover and Ted McCarty were finalizing their ideas at Gibson in order to put into production a twin-coil hum-cancelling pickup, based on the relatively simple concept that two coils placed next to each other, wound in opposite directions and wired in parallel with opposing magnetic poles, will cancel each other's hum. The humbuckers on the early Les Pauls were marked "Patent Applied For", and are now known as PAF types.

The futuristic Flying-V and Explorer guitars

were two single-coil pickups on the Broadcaster, one smaller unit sitting near the neck, the other sloping and built into the bridge. Two brass knobs controlled volume and tone, and a selector switch on the same control plate offered three distinctive pickup selections (front, both, and back). Although Fender's first instruments were without truss rods, these were fitted as standard soon after.

Leo Fender named the Broadcaster after his business interests in radio, but had to change the guitar's name to Telecaster in 1950 after the Gretsch company pointed out the use of the name on their Broadcaster drumkits. The design of Fender's first solid electric guitar was simple yet functional, and today's ever-popular Telecaster, more than 30 years later, is almost identical to the original.

Undoubtedly, Leo Fender's 1948 design paved the way for the development of the electric guitar – almost 15 years before the instrument was to become the catalyst that provoked the "Beatboom" and eventually led to the emergence of rock music generally.

Above Vivi-Tone was set up by Lloyd Loar and two ex-Gibson employees. Some of their guitars, such as this one, had f-holes in the back and a soundhole under the bridge – reminiscent of violin and acoustic guitar designs.

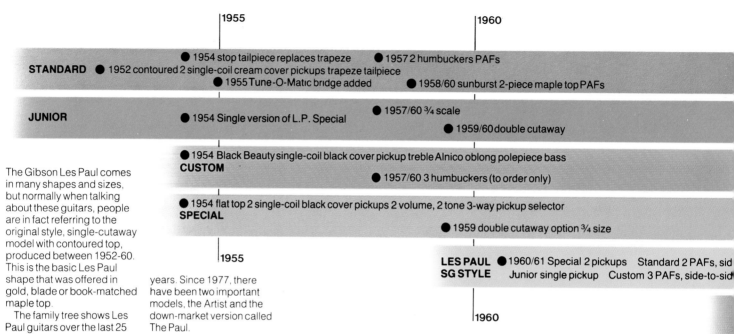

	1955		1960	

STANDARD ● 1954 stop tailpiece replaces trapeze ● 1957 2 humbuckers PAFs
● 1952 contoured 2 single-coil cream cover pickups trapeze tailpiece
● 1955 Tune-O-Matic bridge added ● 1958/60 sunburst 2-piece maple top PAFs

JUNIOR ● 1954 Single version of L.P. Special ● 1957/60 ¾ scale
● 1959/60 double cutaway

CUSTOM ● 1954 Black Beauty single-coil black cover pickup treble Alnico oblong polepiece bass
● 1957/60 3 humbuckers (to order only)

SPECIAL ● 1954 flat top 2 single-coil black cover pickups 2 volume, 2 tone 3-way pickup selector
● 1959 double cutaway option ¾ size

LES PAUL SG STYLE ● 1960/61 Special 2 pickups   Standard 2 PAFs, sid
Junior single pickup   Custom 3 PAFs, side-to-sid

The Gibson Les Paul comes in many shapes and sizes, but normally when talking about these guitars, people are in fact referring to the original style, single-cutaway model with contoured top, produced between 1952-60. This is the basic Les Paul shape that was offered in gold, blade or book-matched maple top.

The family tree shows Les Paul guitars over the last 25 years. Since 1977, there have been two important models, the Artist and the down-market version called The Paul.

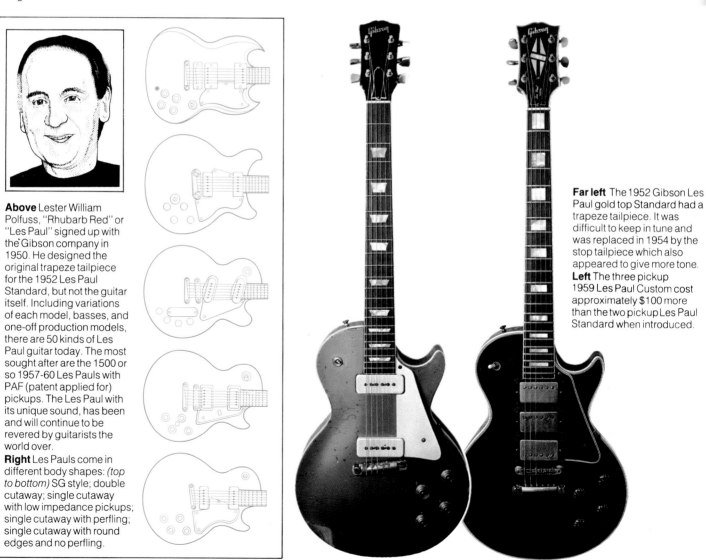

Above Lester William Polfuss, "Rhubarb Red" or "Les Paul" signed up with the Gibson company in 1950. He designed the original trapeze tailpiece for the 1952 Les Paul Standard, but not the guitar itself. Including variations of each model, basses, and one-off production models, there are 50 kinds of Les Paul guitar today. The most sought after are the 1500 or so 1957-60 Les Pauls with PAF (patent applied for) pickups. The Les Paul with its unique sound, has been and will continue to be revered by guitarists the world over.

Right Les Pauls come in different body shapes: *(top to bottom)* SG style; double cutaway; single cutaway with low impedance pickups; single cutaway with perfling; single cutaway with round edges and no perfling.

Far left The 1952 Gibson Les Paul gold top Standard had a trapeze tailpiece. It was difficult to keep in tune and was replaced in 1954 by the stop tailpiece which also appeared to give more tone.
Left The three pickup 1959 Les Paul Custom cost approximately $100 more than the two pickup Les Paul Standard when introduced.

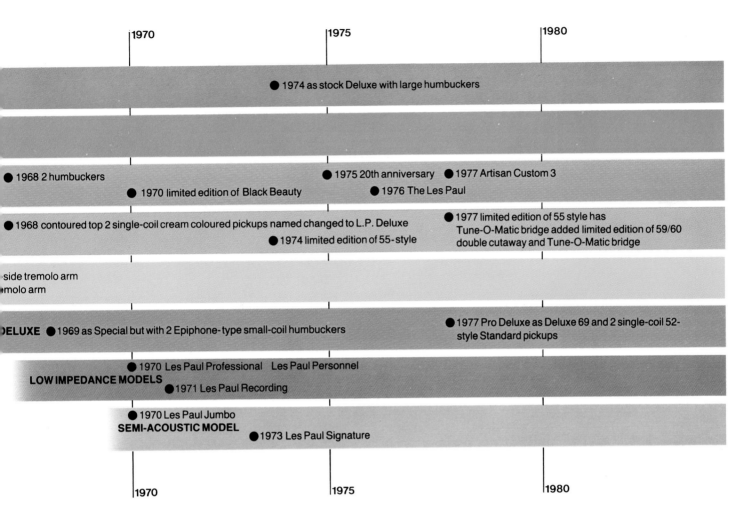

1974 as stock Deluxe with large humbuckers

1968 2 humbuckers

1970 limited edition of Black Beauty

1975 20th anniversary

1976 The Les Paul

1977 Artisan Custom 3

1968 contoured top 2 single-coil cream coloured pickups named changed to L.P. Deluxe

1974 limited edition of 55-style

1977 limited edition of 55 style has Tune-O-Matic bridge added limited edition of 59/60 double cutaway and Tune-O-Matic bridge

side tremolo arm
emolo arm

DELUXE · 1969 as Special but with 2 Epiphone-type small-coil humbuckers

1977 Pro Deluxe as Deluxe 69 and 2 single-coil 52-style Standard pickups

1970 Les Paul Professional   Les Paul Personnel
LOW IMPEDANCE MODELS
1971 Les Paul Recording

1970 Les Paul Jumbo
SEMI-ACOUSTIC MODEL
1973 Les Paul Signature

1970   1975   1980

made in small numbers in 1958 by Gibson have become more popular over the years. Just over 100 Flying-V guitars were originally made in 1958 and 1959 period after two prototype arrow-shaped instruments had been specially built for a red Indian cabaret duo. Only 38 examples of the angular Explorer were originally made in 1958 and these, like the original Flying-Vs, are naturally very rare instruments. In the late 1950s, too, the Les Paul Special and Les Paul Junior were redesigned with a double-cutaway shape, and were later properly designated the SG Series. The first twin-necked Gibson guitars were also produced at this time, and users have ranged from John Witney of late 1960s/early 1970s progressive rock group Family to the jazz-influenced player, John McLaughlin.

In the mid-1960s the popularity of the Gibson Les Paul waned, with other American makers like Gretsch becoming common in the Beat bands of the time. The older Les Pauls had been designed with dance combos and their restrained amplification in mind. Cranked up through the new 100-watt tube amplifiers which were introduced in this period, the guitars were now used by blues-rock players – especially

Above Jeff Beck has been loyal to Gibson Les Paul Standards throughout his career – from The Yardbirds – through to recent jazzy rock adventures. The guitar is always embellished by his use of pedals and electronic effects.

white British guitarists like Peter Green, Jeff Beck and Eric Clapton – who found that the sound of the Les Paul and the steaming tube amp was just the combination they were after: a sort of sweet distortion at the edge of controlled feedback. The new demand became so great that in 1967 Gibson reissued the Les Paul as the Les Paul Deluxe, with twin Epiphone-style humbuckers. Since then, many new issues and numerous reissues of older models have appeared. The Les Paul design continues to be one of the all-time classics.

The odd "upside-down" Gibson Firebird models appeared in 1963, but the off-center design was not popular until the 1970s when the Firebirds were used by such guitarists as Steve Stills and Johnny Winter.

Gibson's electric guitars were poor in design and quality in the early 1970s (other writers have determined the down-period more precisely as 1967 to 1971), but came back strongly later in the decade with some reissues of original models and with some enterprising new designs and new uses of technology. Collaboration with synthesizer inventor Robert Moog resulted in the RD Series guitars issued originally in 1977 and incorporating active electronics – in this case, an on-board circuitry system enabling the player to control "expansion" and "compression" and therefore to shape more accurately the sound of the notes being played. The long-scale neck 1977 model was joined by a conventionally scaled guitar in 1979. The essentially experimental nature of the RD guitars coupled with their slightly eccentric shape make them a rare sight on the rock stage.

Among the few "new" solid electric guitars to appear from Gibson in this period are the 335S Series instruments, supposedly solid versions of the popular ES335 semi-acoustic guitar. Gibson's semi-acoustics have enjoyed wide appeal in all areas of rock and related music forms: from the jazz-rock users of the ES335 like Larry Carlton, through such blues players as B. B. King whose "Lucille" is a specially-built version of an ES335, to the heavy rock player Ted Nugent who, surprisingly, because of semi-acoustics' inherent tendency to feed back at high volumes, uses an ES330. The solid 335S range, issued in

Below The Gibson Flying-V is always dwarfed against Albert King's giant frame. He plays a custom copy – upside down, not restrung, but obtaining a uniquely "singing" sound from retuning the low notes and playing mainly the top three strings. Under the influence of the blues note-bender, T-Bone Walker, Albert King developed a unique sound playing technique and uses feedback and sustain like the white rock and rollers who learned from him. He calls his technique "string squeezing".

Bottom John McLaughlin pioneered the playing of a double-necked guitar with a custom-made Rex Bogue model. Its capacity for almost indefinite note sustain is harnessed to McLaughlin's unsurpassed speed-of-light technique to create some breathless solos particularly in his Mahavishnu Orchestra work.

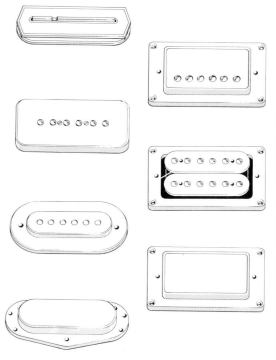

Right Gibson pickups: (top to bottom) The Charlie Christian pickup was used originally on Gibson's first commercial electric guitar, the ES150 of 1931. A mild steel core is bolted to two magnets, and the pickup's position relative to the strings can be altered by adjusting three screws. The standard 1952-style single-coil pickup was used on the original Gibson Les Paul. The single-coil pickup was featured on early 1960s Melody Makers. The low impedance pickup was used on the Les Paul Recording guitar and the associated Triumph bass introduced in 1971.

Far right A selection of more recent Gibson pickups: (top to bottom) the Super humbucking, the Dirty Fingers and the True Blues. Gibson now make over 25 kinds of humbucking pickups.

Left Frank Zappa is an unusual kind of guitar collector. He chooses an instrument for its sound qualities and according to his musical needs of the moment. "A Strat has a drier, more acute and exact sound; I use a Gibson for a sweat-hog type of sound". Zappa is seen here playing a Gibson SG Special made between 1966 and 1970 with the tremelo arm removed. He is one of the well-known players of this particular Gibson range.

Below David Byrne, guitarist, singer and writer with Talking Heads, the New York-based group whose textured, artful music became popular in the late 1970s and early 1980s. Byrne is playing a Fender Musicmaster, a cheap guitar first issued in 1958, to which he has added a second pickup.

giving relatively accurate intonation. The Stratocaster has a contoured body which was more comfortable to play than most solid "planks", and was an instant success.

The sound of the Stratocaster has always guaranteed its success with guitarists and like most good ideas it is basically simple. The front and middle pickups have a tone control each, the rear pickup having its tonal characteristic pre-set, and a single volume pot controls all three pickups. These three controls are angled away in a line below the rear pickup, and in front of them is the pickup selector switch. On production models it is a three-position switch – front, middle or rear – but players quickly discovered two distinctive out-of-phase sounds when the switch was lodged between positions 1 and 2 or 2 and 3. Thus replacement switches were soon offered with five definite switching positions.

Early players exploited the range and tone of the Stratocaster, and one musician who did much to make the Stratocaster visible and audible in the music of the late 1950s was Buddy Holly. Hank Marvin of The Shadows is credited as the first person to bring the Stratocaster to Britain at this time. Perhaps the most famous exponent of the Stratocaster was Jimi Hendrix, but the guitar has been used by countless thousands of rock guitarists throughout the world, and probably always will be.

Although the Telecaster and the Stratocaster made Fender's name, a few minor models have been intermittently fashionable, enjoying limited use as a result. The later 1950s saw the issue of the Fender Jazzmaster guitar, intended as a jazz player's solid alternative to the rock 'n'

1980, look more like double-cutaway Les Pauls and are still awaiting wide use.

It was also in the early 1980s that Gibson introduced their first plastic-bodied electric guitars. Called the Sonex Series, the body of these instruments consists of a wooden core surrounded by a manmade material which Gibson choose to call Resonwood. Gibson seem to have realized that they can no longer succeed merely by resting on their past performance. Their recent bouts of experimentation and low-key innovation point to a bright future for them.

Fender

Leo Fender's brilliant design concepts continued to be influential during the 1950s after his innovation of the solid electric guitar in the late 1940s. 1954 saw the introduction of a guitar destined for classic status, the Fender Stratocaster. It was the first solid electric guitar with three pickups, and featured its own built-in tremolo unit, a floating design which attempted to overcome players' problems with other units that often failed to return the strings to accurate tuning after use. The bridge, too, was a player's dream, being adjustable in every direction and

roll Stratocaster. It boasted an offset body shape and a floating tremolo unit. Later, in 1961, an updated version called the Fender Jaguar was put on the market with similar styling but with the addition of various pushbuttons and switches for tone presets and pickup selection, and became Fender's most switchable solid electric. The use of the guitar by Elvis Costello in the late 1970s ensured it a new lease of life – previously, its popularity had centered on the early 1960s surf-music groups in the United States.

In the 1970s, Fender's dominance (with Gibson) of the electric guitar market became diluted by a deluge of new makers and designs, not least those emanating from Japan. The giant CBS Corporation had taken over Fender in 1965, and little valuable development has taken place since then, apart from a couple of solids issued in the late 1970s called the Lead I and Lead II, and the issue in 1980 of a slightly modified and cosmetically improved version of the Stratocaster, called The Strat (which, confusingly, is what most players call the Stratocaster anyway). CBS seem quite confident that Leo Fender's original designs are utterly timeless.

Below left The changing face of *the* rock guitar: the Fender Stratocaster. In 1954 Leo Fender and Fred Tavares revolutionized the sound possibilities for guitar players with the development of this two-tone, maple neck sunburst solid electric *(1)*. The special features, apart from its modern shape, were three staggered-height pickups and the debut of the Strat tremolo unit, which allowed the wah-ing and note-bending taken to extremes by Jimi Hendrix. This 1963 red metal flake model *(2)* has a rosewood fingerboard and Hank Marvin was in the spotlight with his single note, echoed style of playing using such a model. 1981 saw the launch of "The Strat", finished in candy-apple red or Lake Placid blue *(3)*.

Below This exploded diagram of a composite Fender electric guitar shows the interconnection and construction of the instrument, featuring elements of all the popular Fender six-strings with their insistence on the bolt-on neck and general simplicity.

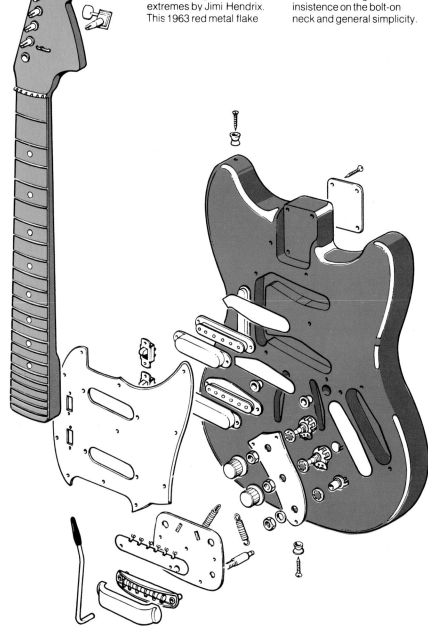

Above Eric Clapton was responsible for establishing the trend of extended electric guitar solos during his work with the Yardbirds and particularly Cream. Clapton was faithful to Gibson guitars, often playing the angular Explorer; in Derek And The Dominoes, he switched to a Fender Strat, which he has since referred to as his "basic stage guitar".

Other American Makers

The Guild guitar company was conceived and founded by Alfred Dronge in 1952 when he opened a workshop in Manhattan to make jazz guitars. In the late 1950s, Dronge moved Guild to Hoboken in New Jersey where they were soon making electric versions of their arched-top cello acoustics and these became popular with some of the rock'n'roll players of the time, most notably the young twanging guitar star, Duane Eddy. A model was made bearing his name, and in England a similar model was endorsed by another guitar instrumentalist of the time, Bert Weedon.

Guild's first solid electric models arrived in 1963 and, in keeping with the style of the Gibson Firebird and other contemporary designs, were

Above A surprising deviation from the Fenders and Gibsons, Lou Reed is seen playing a transparent plastic guitar, custom-built by the imaginative New York company, Guitar Man. **Above right** Guitar Man make conventional wooden-bodied instruments as well.

of unusual body styling. The Guild Jet Star (single pickup), Polara (two pickups) and Thunderbird models (deluxe, two pickups) were all fitted with a unique folding stand in the back of the body which was scooped out at the bottom to form two "legs" of a tripod with the folded stand. Later, the Guild solids were to become very similar to Gibson's SG series, and the Guild Starfire range of single and double cutaway models proved to be very popular among players in the 1960s. Later in the 1970s Guild experimented with active electronics, and currently continues to sell steadily its small, well-made range of guitars.

Gretsch were producing jazz guitars in established workshops long before Guild was started, and by the mid-1950s they were making solid

Above The Gibson Sonex guitar was introduced in 1980 and marked the company's entry into experimentation with non-wood materials – the body consists of a maple core surrounded by a fiberglass-like material called Resonwood.

Far right Paul Hamer who, along with partner Joel Dantzig, makes Hamer guitars in Illinois, demonstrates the Floyd Rose tremolo system on one of his guitars.

Right (top to bottom) Peavey too have made prototype guitars from non-wood materials; the T60 is a conventional production model. B.C. Rich guitars are made by Bernardo Rico and boast some of the more outlandish features of modern electrics. Kramer's DMZ1000 is an example of the company's neck design with its T-section of aluminum supposedly giving extra sustain potential. Despite Ovation's popular acoustics, they also make solid electric guitars like the Breadwinner. Travis Bean was the first maker to put aluminum-necked guitars into commercial production.

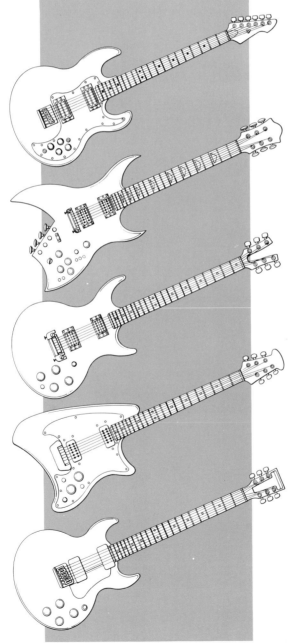

electric guitars of single cutaway, arched-top design, in a similar style to the Gibson Les Paul. Four models were listed in the 1955 catalog differing only in color option: the Duo Jet was black, the Silver Jet silver, the Jet Firebird red and the Round Up brown. The company became best known, however, for its association with Chet Atkins, then a rising star among country guitar pickers. For some time this took most Gretsch guitars away from the rock area.

In the 1960s Gretsch regained much of its rock reputation, particularly when players like George Harrison were seen with Gretsch instruments. The company also made a special Monkee model for the TV bubblegum group in the later 1960s. The Gretsch White Falcon had become the world's most expensive guitar when it was issued in the late 1950s, overflowing with tone toggle switches and offering optional stereo wiring, but became especially popular when used by Steve Stills in the late 1960s and early 1970s. More recently, Gretsch instruments have once again dwindled in popularity and are rarely seen on the rock stage.

Several American guitar makers no longer in business are worth mentioning here: Danelectro, who became famous for their long-horn lyre-shaped solid guitar, just visible in the drawing on the cover of The Youngbloods' 1969 album *Elephant Mountain*; Mosrite, who came to prominence when their guitars were used by 1960s' American guitar-instrumental group, The Ventures; Ampeg, with their guitars designed by Dan Armstrong, made of transparent

"plexiglass" and featured occasionally by Keith Richard; and Harmony, who were at one time the world's largest producers of guitars.

After their innovations in the 1930s, Rickenbacker came back during the 1960s with the arrival of The Beatles. John Lennon's short-scale semi-acoustic caused a lot of guitarists to take notice of Rickenbacker once again, and Roger McGuinn's use of the 360-12 electric 12-string model at the heart of The Byrd's unique sound sustained this interest. Paul Weller of The Jam is one of the more recent of a continuing line of guitarists who use semi-acoustic Rickenbacker guitars in rock music.

Epiphone have been linked closely with Gibson since their acquisition by the Kalamazoo-based company in the late 1950s, and most of the electric guitars produced with the Epiphone name parallel models in the Gibson range. Up to their acquisition, Epiphone were known mainly for their jazz guitars, but the first solid electric guitars from Epiphone appeared at around the same time as the Gibson SG series in the early 1960s. Single-sided headstocks were featured on some later models, and this was a distinct break-away from the usual Gibson factory practice. In the early 1970s, Epiphone production was halted in the United States and moved to a Japanese factory.

The Veleno guitar enjoyed brief popularity in the mid-1970s as an all-aluminum guitar, and the metal was also used at this time by Travis Bean in the first commercially available metal-necked instruments. The Travis Bean guitar was put on the market because of some players' need to get more sustain from their electric guitars. Jerry Garcia used a Travis Bean guitar for some time in the 1970s. Criticisms from players concerned mainly the lack of stability of the guitar's tuning. The guitar's neck and its body's central core were made of aluminum, with the head-stock, bridge, neck and tailpiece forming one aluminum structure on which the strings vibrate freely, and a conventional guitar body was crafted around it from exotic woods.

Kramer capitalized on the aluminum idea with their own range of instruments with aluminum T-section necks, but even Kramer began to offer wooden-necked guitars early in the 1980s. The use of new materials both as substitutes for diminishing world resources and as an exercise in cost reduction has recently marked one of the most interesting aspects of electric guitar evolution. Alongside the work done with metals, plastics have been exploited for their experimental potential, and so far three American companies have pioneered this work: Ovation, Peavey and Gibson.

Above The Jam's Paul Weller is a notable player of the Rickenbacker 330 which originated in the 1960s. It is a semi-acoustic guitar, with volume and tone control for each pickup, plus a tone filter mixing knob behind these four controls. The scimitar-shaped soundhole, unique to Rickenbacker, was first featured on their instruments of the 1930s designed by luthier Roger Rossmeisl.
Left Bo Diddley, a self-taught guitarist, designed many strangely shaped instruments, including his famous oblong "block of wood" model, built by Gretsch. Diddley's rhythmic playing style, heard on his first single Bo Diddley (1955) infuses r'n'b with his original "jungle rhythms".

Ovation's main innovations in the materials field have occurred in their distinctive round-backed acoustic and electric-acoustic guitars. Peavey have built on the success of their T60 guitar, issued in 1978, using computer-controlled production equipment, by identifying the need to look to other areas as wood prices rocket. Mississippi-based Peavey developed prototypes of their T25 guitar later in the 1970s with a moldable plastic body, patented "Sustanite" and designed to have the same resonant and structural characteristics as wood. But it looks as though production models of the Peavey T25 may well end up with wooden bodies, due mainly to the escalation in price of oil-based plastics in the early 1980s. Gibson's plastic experiments resulted in the Sonex range introduced in 1980, with their Resonwood bodies.

As well as materials experiments, the guitar's electronics went through an explosive growth in the 1970s. Players always want to increase their instrument's versatility, and continue to listen for new ways to modify amplified sound. Active electronics consists of an on-board preamplifier,

Above Joni Mitchell has forsaken the simplicity of her early folk singer/acoustic guitarist style for fuller, electric productions. She is playing an Ibanez George Benson here – a small, handy guitar similar to Gibson's jazz model, the ES175.

Left Carlos Santana with a Yamaha SG2000 customized for him. Santana, a Mexican, moved to San Francisco in the mid-1960s and merged his Latin roots with rock music – to give a strong percussion section fronted by his lyrical guitar solos.

usually powered by batteries but occasionally by mains, that enables the player to cut and boost the settings of the instrument. On standard, "passive" guitars, it is only possible to cut the tone settings. Active electronics gives a more powerful, aggressive and wide-ranging sound, but although this system is increasingly being incorporated into guitar designs and offered to guitarists, bass players seem more at home with the increased tonal ranges made available.

The emergence of the Integrated Circuit (IC) and the general miniaturization of electronic components have enabled makers to expand their sounds and to hope that players will be attracted: the Alembic company, a small high quality custom builder in California, pioneered many active electronics techniques. Gibson's RD Series issued in 1977 used the facility, and Leo Fender's reemergence as a guitar designer and maker with Music Man in the late 1970s also resulted in his use of active circuitry. However,

Above In the late 1960s many copies of the Gibson Les Paul were made by Japanese manufacturers who put Western-sounding names on the headstock, like this Eros.

Left Japanese guitar production. Sawn timber is left to season in an open-weather yard.
Inset Fret slots are cut direct into the fretboard, then the metal frets are hammered into them for an exact, tight fit.

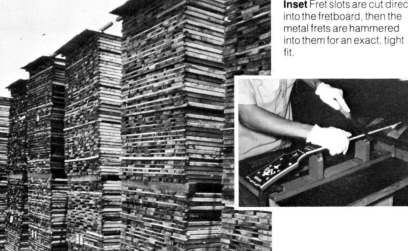

when his first G & L guitars appeared in 1981, they were without active electronics – an indication of the lack of general interest displayed by guitarists. Players seem to have decided that this particular form of sound expansion does not suit the six-string guitar at all.

Japan

The reissue in the late 1960s of Gibson's Les Paul solid electric guitars was provoked not only by players' interest in the sound of older instruments, but by an invasion of Western guitar markets by inexpensive Japanese replicas. The Orient has been active in electric guitar production since the early 1960s.

Most of the earliest Japanese guitars were crude in comparison to their European and American counterparts of the 1960s, but they offered the only financial alternative for many first-time players. This development took place at the start of the Beat boom; the Japanese shrewdly moved into a market that was to see millions of electric guitars sold throughout the 1960s. Brand names like Broadway, Guyatone and Zenon were seen on the headstocks of these early Oriental efforts, but the later generation of "copy guitars", the generic name given to guitars which copy a well-known design of another famous make, were to have a marked effect upon the electric guitar market. The Japanese were quick to capitalize on many star guitarists' use of obsolete Les Pauls in the late 1960s by churning out thousands of copies which were in many cases excellent facsimiles. They went on to produce a plethora of copies, mostly Fender and Gibson designs.

The Japanese opted for a two-stage attack on the market, as they have done in other industries. The first stage was the "copying" phase, introduced, as mentioned previously, in the late 1960s and early 1970s. This involved taking apart all the popular and successful designs, copying them, and presumably learning much in the process about how a guitar works as a homogenous unit. Later in the 1970s the second stage began in earnest: the introduction of original designs. Gibson had indulged in some legal activity over the use of their designs, but the knowledge gained by the Japanese makers in stage one gave them a firm foundation from which to experiment. Several Japanese companies have emerged from this period of transition as particularly fine guitar makers with their own original ideas.

These second stage makers all dabbled in copying before rising to their current status: the Yamaha company, for example, has long been in existence and its early Les Paul copies were as good as most. But Yamaha decided to design a firm competitor for the Les Paul, rather than continue to produce its mirror image. In 1976 they launched the SG2000 as the top of their solid guitar SG range, loosely based on the Les Paul design despite its double-cutaway shape, and boasting all the class and craftsmanship of top American instruments. Several leading guitarists have chosen to use the Yamaha SG2000 – perhaps the best known is Carlos Santana whose soaring, swooping, sustained guitar lines entirely suit the Yamaha. Now the SG2000 is part of a large Yamaha electric guitar range, and does much for the Hamamatsu-based company's reputation as both a maker and designer of electric guitars.

Arai produce Aria guitars, which owe a lot of their original success to the excellence of their Pro II PE1000 guitars, beautifully carved and crafted instruments first put on the market in 1977. Many Aria designs and ranges have followed these originals. Aria's marketing skills were highlighted by their early endorsement deal with Gerry Cott, guitarist with the then fledgling British group, the Boomtown Rats. The relationship resulted in the issue of a modified PE1000, sprayed blue and with active electronics, called the Aria Gerry Cott.

Ibanez has had a relatively long history for a Japanese guitar manufacturer, including, like Aria, the obligatory period of Gibson and Fender copying. They have fared better with their original design guitars and have been active in opening up market opportunities by offering a very wide range of guitars indeed, and by sign-

Center B. B. ("Blues Boy") King's raw-edged brilliance was an undisputed influence on all players who brought the blues into their music.
Below left Ry Cooder's distinctive bottleneck playing reflects his long interest in blues and Hawaiian music. After years of dissatisfaction with Fenders, Cooder has settled for a cheap Strat copy which he revitalized to do exactly what he wants.
Above right For Jimmy Page, with a Gibson Les Paul Standard (Tigerstripe), the sound of the blues is never far away.
Right Keith Levine, formerly the guitarist in The Clash's original lineup, plays today with PIL (Public Image Limited). Noted for his sparse, minimalist playing, Levine has recently been feeding his guitar through synthesizers.
Below right Keith Richard uses a wide variety of guitars with the Rolling Stones – favorites include Fender Telecasters and Strats, Gibson Les Pauls and Zemaitis custom-built guitars. He occasionally uses a five-string guitar, which evolved from an open G five-string tuning for slide playing.

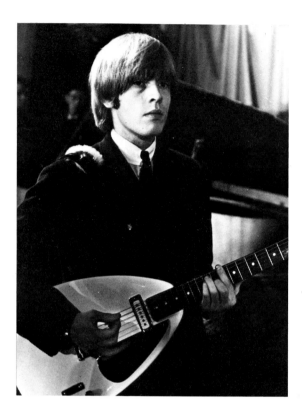

Above left Brian Jones of the Rolling Stones played a distinctive peardrop-shaped Vox Phantom.
Above Pete Townshend has recently taken to using a Telecaster style guitar composed of parts made by Schecter.
Left Hank Marvin was long associated with British guitar-maker Burns before moving on to the inevitable Strat.

ing endorsement agreements with many top players. Steve Miller, George Benson and Bob Weir are among American guitarists associated with the marque; Weir, for example, prompted Ibanez to launch its Bob Weir "autograph" range in 1978, based on the previous Ibanez Artist guitar (another Japanese success with a double-cutaway Les Paul-inspired format). Ibanez continue to introduce new instruments, have experimented with active electronics, and supply the guitars for fellow Japanese company Roland's guitar synthesizers.

Some American brand names, Epiphone and Washburn for example, are now manufactured by factories in Japan. Epiphone guitars had been made at Gibson's Kalamazoo factory for some time, but in the early 1970s production there was phased out and Norlin, the company which owns Gibson, decided to make a new range of inexpensive Epiphone solid electrics in a Japanese factory, with the more recent double-cutaway Les Paul-type Epiphone Genesis being a good example of their work.

The Washburn brand shows just how attitudes to Japanese guitar makers have changed since their first unfortunate attempts at the art in the early 1960s. Washburn began as an American company, founded by George Washburn in Chicago in 1876. A century later, Washburn guitars are being designed in the United States and built in Japan.

The United States and Japan are currently the two biggest producers of electric guitars in the world. The United States' industry is based upon a heritage which expanded rapidly in the 1960s and 1970s. The Japanese industry reacted to that expansion, and has expanded as well. At present, the most successful Japanese makers are Ibanez, Yamaha and Aria, probably in that order. They, like other guitar makers, will have to remain responsive to players' needs and continue to innovate to maintain their positions.

Britain's only other commercial guitar maker is Jack Golder's Shergold company. Today Shergold produce high quality, reasonably priced instruments, having survived changes of ownership from the Hayman origins.

Elsewhere in Europe, Hofner (in Germany) and Hagstrom (in Sweden) have been among the most prolific electric guitar makers. Karl Hofner's company was one of the early imitators (although not direct copiers) of American models, using tremolo arms, single-sided headstocks and similar body stylings. The Hofner V3 of the early 1960s and the later Galaxie were obvious attempts to offer alternatives to the three-pickup Stratocaster design.

Albin Hagstrom's company produced a garish guitar in the late 1950s called the De Luxe which continued in production in the early 1960s and featured a complex (for the time) switching panel. A Hagstrom De Luxe is featured on the inside of the sleeve of Roxy Music's first album. Later Hagstrom players include the talented Jan Akkerman, at one time with Focus, who often uses a Hagstrom Swede, first introduced in 1971. Hagstrom ceased guitar production in the early 1980s.

Europe

The early 1960s supported a very active guitar-making industry in Europe before the cheaper imports, mainly from the East, began to attract players and caused many European companies to fail. In Britain, several companies were producing a large quantity of good quality guitars, though most of them did not seem to catch the popular mood or attract major endorsements.

One of these British companies was Vox who, while well-known for their amplifiers, never made a large impact with their electric guitars. The company experimented with on-board electronics and touch-activated frets on the Guitar-Organ in the mid-1960s; they also issued several unusual instruments – the pear-shaped Phantom guitars were used originally by players like Brian Jones of the Rolling Stones, and more recently by two-tone band The Beat's guitarist Dave Wakeling. Vox guitars eventually ceased production in the early 1970s.

The other British maker of note is Burns. Jim Ormston Burns' early Trisonic and Duosonic guitars are now classics of 1960s guitar design, and models like the Black Bison, the Vibrasonic and the TR2 were popular in the company's heyday. Later, Burns secured an endorsement deal with Hank B. Marvin of The Shadows, and produced a Burns Marvin model. After various unsuccessful ventures, Burns was back in business, and in 1981 reissued the Burns Marvin.

Above British electric guitars have never enjoyed great success when compared to their American and Japanese counterparts, although Burns (Black Bison, *left*) have enjoyed sporadic popularity. The Shergold company (Meteor, *center*) was founded by Jack Golder and Trevor Houlder in the 1960s and is still going strong, producing well made, good value instruments including oddities like 12-string guitars, twin-necks, and six-string and eight-string basses. Repairman and guitar maker Dick Knight (an example of his work is shown *right*) does work for many top players.

Guitar Hardware

Electric guitar hardware has developed at an unprecedented rate in recent years. Customizing has become important for players who seek to individualize their instruments or to improve the looks and often the performance of their guitars, and for manufacturers who have largely run out of ideas for new electric guitars. The ultimate for a few players is to have their instrument made totally to their own specifications. These are made by custom guitar makers, luthiers who will produce one-off models for the demanding guitarist. Most guitarists, however, are content to add various bits and pieces to their stock instrument.

The metal-neck experiments of Travis Bean and Kramer in the mid-1970s led many guitarists and makers to think about the sustaining qualities of dense metal hardware, and eventually brass became the material especially favored by guitarists as a sustaining agent. Makers have offered replacement brass bridges for popular models, and the fad culminated in a whole host of add-on brass bric-a-brac ranging from strap-buttons to scratchplates, nuts to control knobs. Most discerning guitarists now accept that the sustaining qualities of their guitars will only be enhanced by brass saddles on the bridge – the rest is purely decorative.

Some custom-parts manufacturers, such as Schecter and Mighty Mite, now offer all the components that players need to make their own instruments – Pete Townshend, for example, can often be seen using a black Schecter Telecaster. Larry DiMarzio, head of the New York-based DiMarzio company, is particularly responsible for the bolt-on craze, originating with his replacement pickups which became steadily popular throughout the 1970s. One of the most-used replacement pickups today is the DiMarzio PAF-type, designed to reproduce the sound of the early Gibson "Patent Applied For" humbuckers.

The electric guitar has given birth to several novel hardware inventions, some of which were made to add on to existing instruments, others to be built into an original design. The tremolo arm was one of the earlier add-on innovations, having been developed by Paul Bigsby in the late 1940s. A tremolo arm alters the pitch of the produced note or notes by raising or lowering a mechanical device to which the strings are attached. Bigsby's device worked by wrapping the ball-end (the metal "stop" at the end of the

Above A vast array of add-on paraphernalia faces the guitarist today. Some of the pickups include units from DiMarzio, Bill Lawrence, Mighty Mite, and Schecter. **Left** Guitar hardware made by Mighty Mite.

string which is usually secured to the bridge) around a roller which was attached to the tremolo arm by a hefty spring. When the player depressed the Bigsby arm the tension on the strings was released, thus lowering the note(s); when the arm was pulled up the tension on the strings was increased, thus raising the pitch.

One prime disadvantage of early tremolo units was the tendency of the springs not to return to the same position each time after use, thus making the guitar go out of tune. A solid spring-leaf type mechanism was used in the Gibson Vibrola and the Rickenbacker Ac'cent units, but perhaps the most effective and most popular tremolo is Fender's unit, built into the original 1954 Stratocaster design.

The Stratocaster tremolo anchors the strings to a cast block under the tailpiece assembly, and this is allowed to pivot by a lever, the tension being maintained by five large springs underneath a plate on the back of the instrument. These springs can be tensioned individually to compensate for the intonation of each string and to allow for various gauges of string to be used. Other tremolo units produced since the 1950s have been variations on these mechanical themes, for example, Leo Fender's new tremolo arm design for his G & L guitars introduced in the early 1980s. Virtually any Jimi Hendrix track gives an indication of the Strat tremolo's versatility; earlier, Hank Marvin had made prodigious use of its twanging possibilities. More recently, the tremolo seems less in favor.

Most basic bridge designs were also settled upon early in the electric guitar's history. Many bridges are combined with tailpieces (or string anchors) on solid instruments, and once again it was Leo Fender who set the pace with his original Broadcaster (Telecaster) design in the late 1940s. The bridges on these instruments gave limited intonation adjustment on three separate saddles, each carrying two strings, but his ultimate Stratocaster design of 1954 with six individual saddles, each adjustable for height, camber and intonation, is often imitated. Gibson soon developed their Tune-o-Matic bridge which has been used on many of their electric guitars, both solid and semi-acoustic, and while adjustable for intonation (length), height can only be altered at each side of the Tune-o-Matic bridge. A recent development, yet to be widely used, is the Tripp Suspension Bridge which literally suspends the strings in midair at the bridge – the strings never pass over saddles. The Tripp bridge is used on some of the more recent guitars made by Rick Turner, a guitar maker who left the Californian Alembic company to start on his own in 1977.

THE ELECTRIC BASS GUITAR

Even if Leo Fender's only invention had been the bass guitar, he would still be one of the legendary figures of rock history. The fact that he is generally cited as the father of the electric solid six-string guitar too, attests to his even wider importance. The bass guitar has had a profound effect on the inherent sound of rock; indeed, some have argued that rock music would not exist in its present form, would not have developed as it has, had the bass guitar not been introduced in the early 1950s by Leo Fender.

At that time, the bass player in a band would be stuck with the bulky, cumbersome and often barely audible double bass – an instrument that Leo Fender remembers as "the doghouse". This instrument was criticized for hindering, amongst other things, the bassists' natural desires for choreography and general perambulation. Ironically enough, later electric bass players, particularly John Entwistle, became famous for their impassive, stationary stage style. The players themselves were after a louder, portable instrument and one that would allow them to execute their rhythmic passages in a precise melodic fashion.

The answer was Fender's Precision bass guitar, launched in 1951 and based largely on Fender's already successful solid six-string guitar, the Telecaster. From Fender's early innovations, the bass guitar developed into something much more than the instrument at one stage thought fit only to be given to the worst guitarist in the band, based on the assumption that four strings will automatically pose fewer problems for the slow learner than six. Bassists quickly outgrew such criticisms from their fellow musicians and have evolved their own styles of playing.

Fender

Fender's Precision bass was an ash-bodied, maple-necked instrument, with four strings tuned E A D G like the double bass, but otherwise guitar-styled. It was revolutionary. A simple four-pole pickup was controlled by a pair of knobs governing volume and tone, and the bridge boasted a feature that today's bassists have at long last decided to endorse whole-heartedly: brass saddles. The saddles are the portion of the bridge against which the strings actually rest, and therefore the place where the greatest benefit can be gained from the metal's more resonant and sustaining qualities.

This overall design was to remain largely intact until 1957, when the Precision was re-designed to look as it does today. The headstock was restyled more along Stratocaster lines and a distinctive "split" pickup design was installed. One portion of a staggered two-section pickup is placed under the lower-pitched strings (E and A), the other half under the higher strings (D and G). This arrangement gives a greater clarity of sound because each string has two polepieces rather than one (the polepiece is the part of the pickup which "senses" the sound). Today, bassists still value these early redesigned Precisions of the late 1950s for their intense bass punch and drive.

Important players in the early development of the electric bass guitar were "Duck" Dunn, Carol Kaye and James Jamerson. "Duck" Dunn, closely associated with the early development of the Fender bass, was an inventive early electric bassist, drawing rhythmic bottom lines into the rhythm and blues flavored instrumentals of Booker T And The MGs, including the timeless *Green Onions*. Carol Kaye became a session player in the late 1950s, first on guitar, then switching to Fender bass in 1964. She appeared on countless hits such as the Beach Boys' *Good Vibrations* and a string of Motown tunes from such artists as Martha Reeves and Stevie Wonder. James Jamerson was another Motown session player, joining the company in 1959, touring with the Miracles in 1963, and staying studio-bound from 1964 until 1973. Another Fender fan, Jamerson turns up on stacks of Motown hits – The Four Tops' *Reach Out* is a perfect example of his simple, driving style.

While bass players' abilities and techniques improved through the early and middle 1960s, their choice of instruments seemed to remain as narrow as ever. Fender continued to dominate the market thanks to the ever-popular Precision, and the new Jazz bass, introduced in 1960. The Jazz bass was distinguished by its offset body shape akin to its contemporary, the Fender Jazz-

Right Bill Haley and his Comets had three massive hits in the mid-1950s with *Shake Rattle And Roll, Rock Around The Clock* and *See You Later Alligator*. The upright bass was not the best instrument to be used in active rock and roll stage shows, despite the Comets athletic efforts shown here. Gradually, the large acoustic instrument gave way to Leo Fender's electric Precision bass which had been introduced in 1951.

master six-string electric guitar. The Jazz bass is larger than the Precision with relatively wide string spacing in the playing position, and boasts more tonal variation with its three knobs (two volume controls and one tone control). Players consider it a slightly harder instrument to control, but the Jazz bass has gained much respect, often from players who work in more complex areas of rock. However, the Precision remains the standard bass guitar, and it is heard constantly on a huge number of rock albums and rock stages across the world. On record sleeves, "Fender bass" often appears as a generic term for the electric bass guitar.

Gibson

Playing styles developed dramatically in the late 1960s and there was a greater acceptance of other manufacturers' instruments. Gibson had introduced their EB1 bass in 1953. This original "violin bass" was made more popular by the German maker Hofner who copied the general

Below John Entwistle's static stage presence with The Who belies his powerful bass sound. He was responsible in the 1960s for converting the dull sound of the bass guitar to an almost piano-like twang thanks largely to his innovative use of roundwound strings. Entwistle is shown here with one of his many Alembic basses – he is a keen collector of bass guitars, and has over 75 instruments.

Above The hidden face of the bass belongs to Carol Kaye, who has been for the past two decades one of the West Coast's most prolific session bassists. Her contributions include early Motown hits, Beach Boys' *Good Vibrations*, Glen Campbell's *Wichita Lineman* and numerous film scores.

Left The Fender Precision Special with active electronics and brass hardware, introduced 1980. **Below** Original Fender Precision of early 1950s vintage, Fender Musicmaster beginner's bass; Fender Jazz bass, and Fender Telecaster bass, styled closely to the original Precision.

design in the early 1960s; the Hofner Violin bass's widespread popularity was instantly assured when it was adopted by a very talented bass player, Paul McCartney.

Gibson's own brief period of popularity as a maker of bass guitars came about when Jack Bruce of Cream used an EB3. Bruce's rich, thick, dirty sound relied heavily on the intrinsic merits of the Gibson's uncompromising lack of subtlety. The EB3 had been introduced in 1960 as a two-pickup version of the previous year's SG guitar-styled EBO (Andy Fraser of Free is a noted bassist who played an EBO.) The EB3's small

humbucking pickup mounted near the bridge provided a wider, denser sound via the rather clumsy-looking four-way rotary pickup/tone selector knob mounted on the front of the instrument near the normal volume and tone knobs.

McCartney and Bruce represented the two distinct rock bass sounds in Britain in the late 1960s. McCartney preferred a melodic, surging style that can be heard on almost any Beatles track, though 1966's *Taxman, Rain* and *Paperback Writer* are worth special mention. Bruce's viscous bass lines were spaced out below the increasingly improvised but blues-based music

Right Twin-neck guitars are used sparingly in rock, primarily because they are very heavy to wear for an hour or so on stage, even though they are essentially performance instruments anyway – in the studio the player would simply use two different guitars for the separate parts. Various twin-neck combinations exist, the type shown being a copy of Gibson's bass and guitar version. The other common type is the six-string/12-string version.
Far right Kramer bass guitars, with their aluminum necks, come with a variety of fingerboard options for the fretless player: *(left to right)* traditional fretless neck with no markings at all; fretless neck with "dot" position markers only;

fretless neck with "dot" position markers and white lines indicating conventional fret positions; "half fretless" neck – fretted to the D position, the remainder being fretless with white line fret markers.

of Cream, and his playing can be heard at its best on tracks like *Politician*. That riff became many fledgling bassists' first exercise on the instrument.

In the United States, innovative playing during this period came primarily from soul and funk players. Larry Graham, then of Sly And The Family Stone, developed a slapping, popping percussive technique which had a marked effect on playing styles. This sound can be heard at an early stage on the classic Sly album *There's A Riot Going On* (1971), and to greater effect on Graham's later albums with his own group, Graham Central Station.

Alembic

Toward the end of the decade, a Californian company called Alembic began to emerge as an exclusive but high quality maker, closely collaborating with the West Coast's premier groups of the time, Jefferson Airplane and The Grateful Dead. Alembic modified and re-equipped their instruments and equipment, especially the Guild bass of the Airplane's bass player Jack Casady. Later, Alembic coopted luthier Rick Turner and began to develop their own models which became the Rolls Royces of bass guitars for discerning (and rich) bassists of the 1970s. Players from all areas of rock have utilized these luxurious, expensive instruments: John McVie of Fleetwood Mac, Marvin

Right Stanley Clarke's name has become synonymous with top class bass playing via Chick Corea's Return To Forever group, and his own set of finely wrought, skilfully played solo albums of which the first, simply titled *Stanley Clarke*, made many fellow players envious. His funky thumb-slapping style coupled with the wide tonal range available from the Alembic basses which he plays combine to give a musicianly sound that many have emulated.

Isley of The Isley Brothers, John Entwistle and Stanley Clarke have all used Alembic electric basses to impressive effect.

The Alembic basses are made of first-class woods, including exotic ones like peroba rosa for decorative inlays and laminates, and feature brass and gold-plated fittings, Light Emitting Diodes (LEDs) as fingerboard-edge position markers and active circuitry. Active circuitry (active electronics) allows the player, by means of an on-guitar preamp powered by batteries or mains, to boost or cut tone settings over a much wider range than that offered by a normal, or passive, bass.

The Rickenbacker Series

Another player in Britain who influenced many of his peers in the early 1970s was Chris Squire, then of Yes, who was closely associated with the Rickenbacker 4000 Series bass guitars and the powerful trebly, clanking sound that he achieved with such instruments. Adolph Rickenbacker, who had produced the first electric guitars back in the 1930s with George Beauchamp and Paul Barth, founded a company which produced its first 4000 Series bass in the late 1950s. The famous 4001 model followed a decade later. It features a large body with an outsize upper "horn" and a distinctive white scratchplate stretching from the pickup surrounds down to the controls section. The Stereo model allows the player to route the sound from the two pickups to two different amplifiers giving a wide range of tone colors. The "Ricky", as it is affectionately known, with its huge chrome pickup cover and triangular position markers on the fingerboard, is, if not particularly pleasant to look at, one of the most popular bass

guitars on the market. Squire used one from his early days with Yes right through the band's popular period in the early to mid-1970s. He can be heard in fine form on most Yes recordings, especially on *The Yes Album* from 1971.

Right Jaco Pastorius' fluid fretless bass sound can be heard with Weather Report and on recent Joni Mitchell recordings. He originally removed the frets from his Fender Jazz bass himself.

Below Jack Bruce epitomised creative 1960s bass playing when his growling guitar was heard at the heart of Cream's three-man sound. Associated then with the Gibson EB3 bass, he has used many instruments since, including this Dan Armstrong model and, more recently, the Japanese Aria basses.

Fretless Basses

Fretless bass playing became a big trend in the later 1970s. One player instrumental in popularizing the fretless bass was Ralphe Armstrong, who played at the time with John McLaughlin's Mahavishnu Orchestra. Armstrong's bass is prominently displayed on the sleeve of the Orchestra's *Visions Of The Emerald Beyond* (1975). But Jaco Pastorius is undoubtedly the best known exponent of fretless playing. His languid, hollow-sounding bass lines trace effortlessly through the tight mesh of Weather Report's later records, while a more robust style is evident on the successful *Birdland*, from the group's *Heavy Weather* album. Pastorius originally removed the frets from his ailing Fender Jazz himself even though several different fretless basses were available on the market – Fender had been producing a fretless version of their Precision bass since 1970. Most large guitar producers have followed suit over the past few years, offering fretless models to players keen to achieve that distinctive but technically tricky sound.

The obvious drawback of playing fretless is that the bassist cannot use the absent frets to obtain precise intonation. This is balanced, however, by distinct gains in the quality of the sound. The characteristics of individual notes' attack and decay vary considerably from those played on a fretted bass. On the fretless bass the

Right John Entwistle holds the handiwork of British guitar maker Peter Cook *(right)*. Players often feel that they will be able to get nearer to their ideal instrument by hiring a guitar maker to produce a guitar or bass to their precise requirements, and most countries have a small network of these specialist luthiers.

Left These Wal basses are made by British luthier Ian Waller, who started out by making one-off, customized instruments. He then began to offer production-line models some years ago, and is now back to crafting personal instruments based on an overall design policy aimed to give first class guitars to professional bassists. He has an enviable reputation among the top British session players.

smooth fingerboard is more curved across its width, consequently, notes executed on these instruments seem to "growl", to *increase* in volume after they are plucked instead of gradually dying away as they do on a fretted bass guitar. Jaco Pastorius' *Continuum* on his solo album provides a good example of the singing, fluid sound the fretless bass can achieve. Stanley Clarke and Jack Bruce have also been known to play the fretless bass. With a fretless bass, a player can often obtain a much more expressive, open style of playing, but it is best left to the technically adept.

Left The Rickenbacker 4001's clanking tone has made it one of the more popular electric bass guitars on the market today, although its uncompromising sound is not to every player's taste. Perhaps the best-known player to exploit its sound was Chris Squire when with Yes.

Left The genius behind Chic comes from their two co-producers: guitarist Nile Rogers *(left)* and bassist Bernard Edwards *(right)*. Their musical assertion that disco success revolves around a tight bass-and-drum sound is not particularly revolutionary in itself but when it is coupled with the staggering bass guitar dynamics employed by Edwards then Chic move into a class by themselves. Precise playing and repetitive structures define Edwards' sound, which is placed at the very front of Chic's overall mix and thus dominates the music.

Left The Fender Precision bass must be the most popular electric bass in the world. It is seen here used by Bruce Foxton of The Jam. The Precision's popularity stems from its inherent design sense, embodying the premise that simplest is best.

Active Electronics

Bass guitar experimentation continued in the 1970s, with active electronics introduced primarily by Alembic. Gibson's RD Series bass, issued in 1977, made use of the technical expertise of synthesizer experts Moog to create a system of expansion and compression (cutting and boosting the signal), which lent itself to diverse bass sounds. Despite this development, and Gibson's later Ripper and Grabber basses, styled more closely to the Fender models, Gibson's basses are still largely shunned by players, who complain that they seem "cold" or "stiff".

Fender acknowledged the existence and uses of active electronics when they launched their Precision Special in 1980, after a long spell when they produced few new basses apart from the Mustang and the Musicmaster "budget" models. The Precision Special was a significant addition to the Fender range, in that it offered the first Fender-authorized modification to the Precision's electrics for many years. This bass presents players with the wider tonal potential of active electronics, plus a slightly narrower (and consequently more "playable") neck, along with the benefits of brass hardware.

Recent Developments

Other companies continue to develop new models and ranges. Japanese manufacturers switched from their wholesale copying of the early bass shapes to produce their own designs to their own specifications in the 1970s. Aria's SB1000 is an excellent up-market active bass with distinct Alembic leanings, while Ibanez produce some superb bass guitars in fretless, fretted, active, passive, expensive and budget styles. Yamaha have yet to be quite so convincing with original designs, but their Precision-based BB1200 finds favor with a good many players.

American basses continue in popularity too. The Guild B301 is a long-standing favorite with its "scooped-out" body shape and straightforward electrics. Kramer build on their experiments with aluminum neck-sections to produce some responsive instruments, especially toward the top of the range where there is strong competition from makers like B. C. Rich, who produce some particularly exotic and odd-looking guitars and basses. In Britain, Ian Waller continues to sell his high quality Wal basses, mostly to studio session players at whom many of the instruments' facilities are directly aimed; and the Shergold company under the aegis of Jack Golder produces some excellent value-for-money instruments. These include a good range of four-, six- and eight-string basses, along with double-neck instruments, one of which they have built for Genesis bassist Mike Rutherford.

Playing styles, too, continue to evolve. Reggae bassists exploit the deep range of the instrument while being experts on effective use of the pause; examples are Family Man Barrett on any of the Wailers' records or top Jamaican session bassist Robbie Shakespeare who appears on many reggae records, including Peter Tosh's albums.

Below Paul McCartney started out as a guitarist with The Beatles when their bass player was Stu Sutcliffe, and he first used a Zenith six-string guitar, followed by a Rosetti solid electric which he used throughout the very early Cavern days. When the group went to Hamburg for the first time the Rosetti was damaged and McCartney became the piano player for a few weeks. But when Sutcliffe left, McCartney switched to bass and revitalized the group's sound with his Hofner Violin bass – he bought the first one in 1962 and had it revarnished and rewired at London's Sound City repair shop. More recently, McCartney has experimented with other basses like the Yamaha.

Jazz-influenced bass playing can also be invigorating. Virtually any record by Stanley Clarke or Alphonso Johnson is recommended for sheer musicianship, while Robert Popwell is superb with The Crusaders in the late 1970s and Colin Hodgkinson is master of the fretboard on the now-defunct Back Door's records. Straight rock casts a wide net, but John Wetton (Family, Roxy Music, King Crimson), Neil Murray (National Health, Whitesnake), Bruce Thomas (Quiver, Elvis Costello And The Attractions), Tina Weymouth (Talking Heads), Rick Danko (The Band), Phil Chen (Rod Stewart Band), and George Murray (with David Bowie) are all worth a mention.

The remarkable king of the disco bassists is Bernard Edwards of Chic, whose voluptuous bass lines, pushed right up-front and dominating the mix (Edward is Chic's co-producer), go some way toward realizing every bassist's dream – pure bass guitar music.

DRUMS AND PERCUSSION

When rock and roll was born in the mid-1950s, it inherited the drumkit from jazz. By this time, the drumkit (set) had been distilled to the essence: bass drum, snare drum, two tom toms, ride cymbal, crash cymbal and hihat cymbals. This basic setup, which originated in the jazz bands of the late 1920s and early 1930s, remained much the same right up until the mid-1960s; Ringo Starr was playing with this type of kit as late as 1966.

As rock got louder, drummers had to rely on sheer brawn to project their drumming over the electric and bass guitar amplification. The inherited kit began to crumble under the strain. Stands and fittings had to be seriously reinforced, heads needed to be improved, cymbals had to be tougher and brighter sounding. Bigger drums, with increased volume, were in demand.

The major drum manufacturers responded by producing larger drums, stronger fittings and louder plastic heads which were impervious to atmospheric change. Led Zeppelin's drummer, John Bonham, was playing the basic rock drumkit in the mid-1970s, but each drum was much larger than it had been ten years earlier.

From that point on, changes in drum design have mainly been subtle refinements aimed at producing louder, stronger drums. Despite the recent emergence of electronic drums, there will always be a place in rock music for what are basically the simplest musical instruments of all.

Principles of Design

Drum design has not changed very much since the end of the nineteenth century, and the underlying principles have remained the same since the earliest log and skin drums of stone age times. These drums were hollow logs; wet animal skins were stretched across the open ends, tied tightly and left to dry.

There are three basic components to the sound produced by a drum: the tap produced when the stick hits the head, the sound of a large volume of air being moved and the resonance (which corresponds to the pitch) created by the whole drum vibrating.

When struck, a stretched membrane will vibrate at a frequency proportional to the product of its tension and mass. The tighter the membrane or head is stretched, the higher the resulting note will be. The thickness of the head will also affect the apparent pitch of the note. A thin skin will produce more upper partials (higher sounds) than a thick skin.

The note produced by a tightly stretched skin is not in itself very loud: it must be amplified, and this is the role of the shell. At some point it was discovered that logs of certain volumes and proportions rang or resonated in sympathy with the note produced by the head. If the head is tensioned (tuned) to the resonant frequency of the shell, the drum will realize its maximum potential volume.

Above left The basic rock drumkit includes a bass drum, two tom toms, snare drum, hihat, crash and ride cymbals. This kit, manufactured by Ludwig, also includes a floor tom. The metal snare drum is seamless; the stands are all heavy duty, designed for rock. Drumkits manufactured today are stronger than their predecessors.
Above This larger Ludwig kit has five tom toms, two of which are mounted on a special floor stand and a floor tom. With the range of sizes and flexibility of stands now available, kits can be assembled according to drummers' individual requirements.

The Basic Rock Drumkit

The major drum manufacturers include Ludwig, Rogers, Gretsch and Slingerland (American); Premier (British); Sonor (German); and the Japanese companies Pearl, Tama and Yamaha. Drummers sometimes build up their drumkits with drums from different manufacturers; in extreme cases, some drumkits used in recording sessions feature a snare drum, bass drum, tom toms, stands and pedals all by different makers. For live performances, however, when some consistency in appearance is important, it is more usual just to find that the snare drum (a personal piece of equipment) and perhaps the stands are the only items that differ.

The drums discussed in this chapter are acoustic, but in 1980, a totally new type of drum emerged, the Simmons SDS V electronic drumkit. This system differs from early drum synthesizers in that it can be convincingly substituted for an acoustic kit. It is extremely touch-

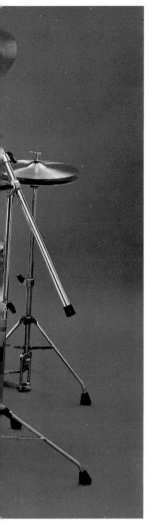

Left Sticks are made from a variety of different woods, but the close-grained hardwood hickory is widely used. Shapes also vary; some tips are made of nylon.

Below Modern cymbal stands are robust and stable. This boom stand from Tama allows the cymbal to be positioned close to the drummer.

Below The Police's drummer, Stuart Copeland, using a Tama setup. One of the groups who have been increasingly successful in recent years, The Police base their music on a mixture of reggae, African and white rock rhythms.

sensitive, giving the player great control and can also be controlled by computer.

The Bass Drum

The largest drum in the kit is the bass drum. This ranges in diameter from the 18-inch jazz drum, through the popular stage and studio sizes of 20 and 22 inches, to the 24- and 26-inch heavy rock variety. The depth also varies from 14 to 17 inches. Only ten years ago the larger drums were only available on special order. The bass drum is operated by a foot pedal clamped to the hoop. Pressing this pedal swings a beater made of wood, cork or felt that hits the center of the drumhead. The drum rests on its side and is balanced by two legs; it sometimes supports one or two tom toms on top.

The Snare Drum

The snare drum is the drum which is used for the downbeat. It gives a sharp, cracking sound that can cut through the sounds made by the rest of the band. This sound is the product of the snares, parallel strands of crinkled wire (or gut) which are stretched across the thin bottom head or snare head and attached at either side to strainers. The top head of the snare drum is thicker and is known as the batter head.

The snare drum is usually 14 inches in diameter, but a constant search for new sounds has led to many different depths being made available. Snare drums were originally only sold in five-inch or five-and-a-half-inch depths (except for the very shallow piccolo drums popularized by Tony Meehan of The Shadows in the late 1950s), but now are available in six-and-a-half-inch, eight-inch and ten-inch depths. The standard five-and-a-half-inch drum is still the most prevalent size but the deep tone and increased volume of the six-and-a-half-inch drum makes it a good solid rock drum.

Snare drums always have metal rims on the top and bottom. The top rim is used to produce the distinctive "rim shot", where the drummer hits the rim and head at the same time.

Snare construction is constantly under review. There are many styles on the market at any one time, but these fall into two distinct categories: straight throw-off and parallel action. The straight throw-off is a single lever which releases the snares in one movement to give a tom tom sound. This system is very simple, well-tested and, provided the snares are not tensioned too tightly, can produce an exceptionally clean, tight, punchy sound. All major drum companies make snare drums with this type of action; a notable example is the legendary Ludwig 400 series.

The parallel action system holds the snares parallel to the drum head, giving a cleaner sound. This type of snare comes in many shapes and sizes; early examples include the Rogers Dynasonic, Ludwig Supersensitive and Premier 2000. Carefully adjusted, this type of drum is capable of extremely fine, responsive snare sounds but, because of the mechanism's complexity and delicacy, and possibly because rock music does not require such a degree of sensitivity, the parallel action snare still has only a limited popularity.

Tom Toms

The basic kit includes two different-sized tom toms, but up to a dozen have sometimes been used. The different sizes give different tones. The standard and popular tom tom sizes have always been (diameter and depth) 12 by eight inches, 13 by nine inches, 14 by 14 inches and 16 by 16 inches. Nowadays it is quite common to see a setup ranging from six inches in diameter through eight, ten, 12, 13, 14, 15, 16, 18 and even 20 inches. This trend stems from the American manufacturer, Ludwig's concert tom range which was picked up and developed largely by the Japanese companies, Tama and Pearl. More recently, bottom heads have been added to these drums (concert toms are traditionally single-headed) giving a livelier sound.

Tom toms can be attached to the top of bass drums by special fittings or can be supported by stands similar to cymbal stands. The larger tom toms (floor tom toms) usually have adjustable legs and stand on the floor.

Roto-toms, manufactured by the Remo Drum Company, are shelless drums. The unique feature of roto-toms is that they can be tuned rapidly by rotation.

Cymbals

In the early days of rock music, cymbals played a minor role compared to their use in jazz where the ride cymbal carried the pulse. Rock cymbal setups were similar to those of jazz and usually included a pair of hihat cymbals (usually 14 inches in diameter and operated by a foot pedal) to the drummer's left; a ride cymbal (20 to 24 inches in diameter with a fairly pingy sound) to the right; and a thinner crash cymbal (16 to 22 inches in diameter with a lower, washy sound) to the left. Individual drummers augmented their setups with extra crash and ride cymbals but this lineup remained much the same well into the 1960s. The major manufacturer at this time was Avedis Zildjian, with K. Zildjian taking a smaller portion of the market and a few other companies competing for the cheaper end.

Right Charles Botterill, who played in Mantovani's orchestra, is shown here with an early drumkit, absurdly small by today's standards, featuring a bass drum, "side" drum and cymbals.

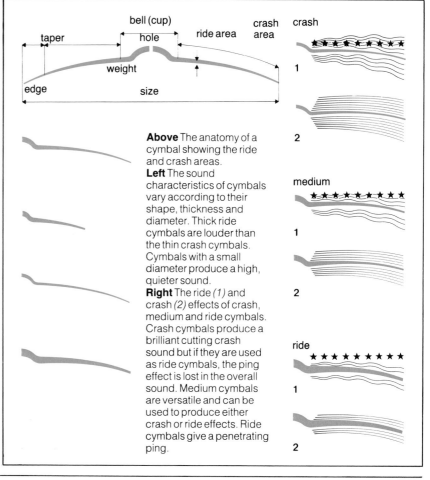

Above The anatomy of a cymbal showing the ride and crash areas.
Left The sound characteristics of cymbals vary according to their shape, thickness and diameter. Thick ride cymbals are louder than the thin crash cymbals. Cymbals with a small diameter produce a high, quieter sound.
Right The ride (1) and crash (2) effects of crash, medium and ride cymbals. Crash cymbals produce a brilliant cutting crash sound but if they are used as ride cymbals, the ping effect is lost in the overall sound. Medium cymbals are versatile and can be used to produce either crash or ride effects. Ride cymbals give a penetrating ping.

Left Blind Faith (Steve Winwood, Eric Clapton, Ric Grech, Ginger Baker) made their debut in June 1969 at a festival in London's Hyde Park and broke up not long after. The band included two former members of Cream, arguably the first "supergroup". Ginger Baker was one of the first drummers to put two drumkits together, and popularized the use of two bass drums. Always influenced by African drum sounds, he went on to study those patterns more closely and incorporate them more into his music.

Below Two innovative drummers of the early 1970s were Bill Bruford (a founder member of Yes) and the brilliant percussionist Jamie Muir, seen here in the studio with Robert Fripp (guitar) and David Cross (violin) in one of the later lineups of the influential "progressive" group, King Crimson.

At the beginning of the 1970s, a Swiss company called Paiste brought out a revolutionary range of new cymbals designed specifically for the rock drummer. These comprised flat ride cymbals producing a very pingy sound with few overtones; heavy ride cymbals where the sound died away quickly; very bright-sounding thin crash cymbals and, perhaps the most innovatory development of all, a pair of extremely bright-sounding hihat cymbals known as Soundedge. These hihats were designed so that the bottom cymbal had a corrugated edge which allowed a rush of air to escape when the cymbals were closed. The resulting sound was particularly clean, ideal for rock and recording.

This initial 602 range did have some disadvantages: the cymbals were delicate and had a tendency to crack if played carelessly. After more development, Paiste claimed to have counteracted these deficiencies and also brought out

the stronger and heavier 2002 range, designed specifically for heavy drumming.

The net result of this onslaught of high quality cymbals was to improve the market generally. Avedis Zildjian produced new designs which included the Flat Top, improved swish and pang cymbals and Chinese-type cymbals. Billy Cobham renewed interest in the Chinese cymbal and it has since become almost an essential piece of equipment.

Today, many brands of cymbal are available. The top end of the market is still dominated by Avedis Zildjian, K. Zildjian and Paiste but such makers as Tosco, Zilco and Camber produce acceptable cymbals at young drummer's prices.

Materials and Construction

Up to the beginning of this century, drums were tensioned by rope. The shells were wooden and reasonably consistent in size and thickness. The animal skins used for heads were carefully chosen for uniformity in weight and thickness, but the sound produced by these drums was still relatively dull. Machine technology led, naturally enough, to nut boxes and screw tensioning, cast or rolled steel tension hoops, and wire, instead of gut, snares. These developments meant that drums could be tensioned tighter and the sound began to brighten up.

The next major advance, and perhaps the most significant for rock music, was the invention of the plastic head by George Remo in 1957. Drummers were freed from the irritation of hearing their drums gradually detune in a steamy nightclub atmosphere. More importantly, the sound of a drum fitted with plastic heads was sharper and capable of cutting through the dense electric textures of rock.

Shells

The favorite shell material is maple wood. Maple shells are the loudest of all the wooden shell drums, but still have a warm, responsive tonal quality. Most manufacturers have a range of maple shell drums.

The drum shells of the 1950s were usually five ply, laminated and lapped in construction. (Each layer of laminate is always joined at a different point to make sure the shell is round and strong.) Up to the mid-1960s, most manufacturers strengthened the shell by fitting a counterhoop around the inside of the top and bottom lip but it was widely held that the counterhoops affected the tonal quality of the drum by impeding the flow of air. The American company, Gretsch, has always used straight five ply shells without counterhoops, and over the past fifteen years, this has become standard.

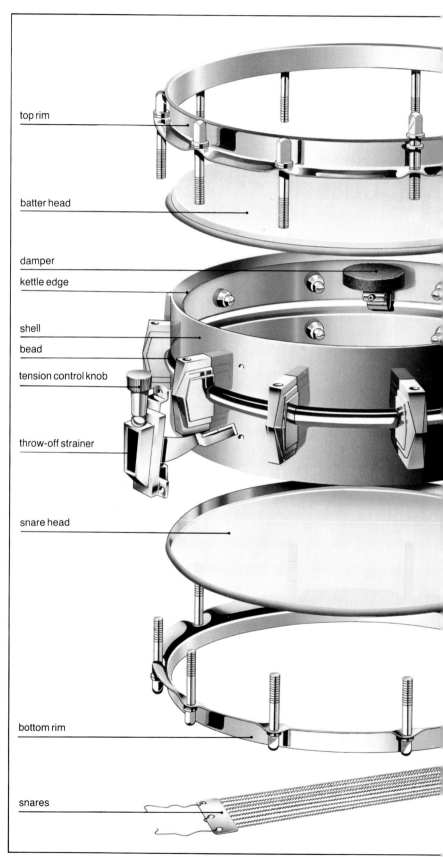

top rim

batter head

damper

kettle edge

shell

bead

tension control knob

throw-off strainer

snare head

bottom rim

snares

Some manufacturers, such as Sonor, have built heavier shells, up to 12 ply. This extra thickness and weight shortens the decay time of the drum's sound and gives a deeper and less boomy tone. The move to thicker shells has never gained mass acceptance, however, and the innovation of the 1970s, the synthetic drum, uses even thinner shells.

The first synthetic drums were made of acrylic or perspex-type materials and were transparent, although sometimes tinted grey or blue. Their flamboyant appearance instantly attracted rock drummers and, as a bonus, the sound was brighter and louder.

Although the drums worked well on stage, they were not immediately popular in the studio. It took the great stylist, Billy Cobham, to bring these drums to wider attention. His extremely bright, hard sound, featured on the early Mahavishnu Orchestra albums, *The Inner Mounting Flame* (1972) and *Birds of Fire* (1973), typified the sound of synthetics and led many young drummers to use drums made with the new materials. Ironically, the drumkit used by Cobham on *The Inner Mounting Flame* was wooden, but sounds made in the studio have often prompted manufacturers to give their instruments a new live sound.

Over the past ten years a variety of materials have been used in the manufacture of shells: phenolic resin (resin-impregnated masonite), which is not much harder than wood; steel, which makes very loud, heavy and impractical drums; fiberglass and perspex (acrylic or plexiglass), probably the hardest sounding material; and, more recently, plastic. For cheaper drums, even heavy grade industrial cardboard has been used.

Left The anatomy of a snare drum, showing an enlarged view of the tension rod and nut box design. Tension rods are used for tensioning the hoops. This snare drum is the legendary Ludwig Supra-Sonic (400 series), one of the most popular snare drums used in rock.

Above Every manufacturer has its own distinctive fittings design and most offer a wide range of finishes and materials, from plain, metallic or pearlized colors to laqueured wood or transparent perspex.

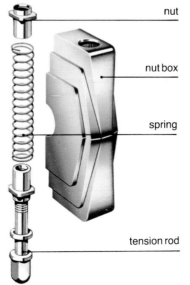

nut

nut box

spring

tension rod

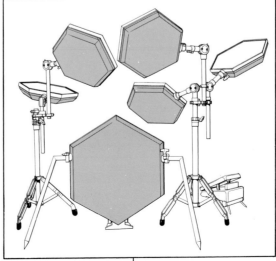

Left The Simmons SDS V electronic drumkit represents the first significant departure from the traditional acoustic kit. Each drum is two inches thick and has a perspex playing surface. The touch- and force-sensitive drums can be made to any shape; the hexagonal variety shown here make it easy to fit the kit together. The drums can be set up conventionally on stands; the bass drum is free standing and is played with an ordinary pedal. The electronics consist of seven modules, each of which contains four memories: in a six drum setup, 24 drum sounds can be created.

Heads

If the plastic head revolutionized drumming, this area of development has not been content to remain at a standstill. Many advances and new designs have appeared since the mid-1960s.

The first plastic heads were made of a simple film .005mm to .012mm thick fixed to an aluminum hoop and painted with a rough coat to simulate calfskin and aid brush response. This coat was found to wear off fairly quickly, and, since brushes are rarely used in rock music anyway, shiny surfaced heads were soon brought out. See-through heads, particularly necessary for see-through drums, followed.

At this point, George Remo, who supplies most major drum companies with heads, developed the C.S. head (controlled sound or black spot). The C.S. head is an ordinary head with another layer of plastic film, about half the dia-

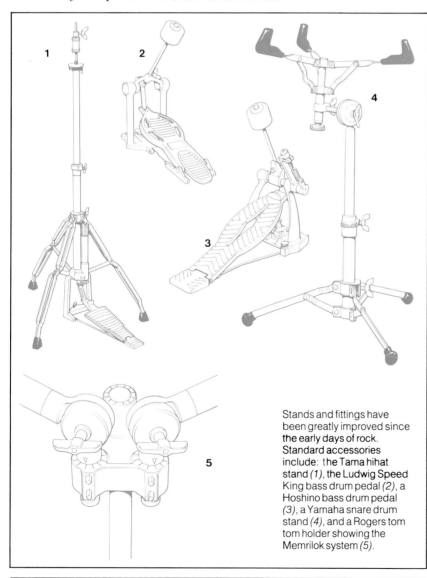

Stands and fittings have been greatly improved since the early days of rock. Standard accessories include: the Tama hihat stand *(1)*, the Ludwig Speed King bass drum pedal *(2)*, a Hoshino bass drum pedal *(3)*, a Yamaha snare drum stand *(4)*, and a Rogers tom tom holder showing the Memrilok system *(5)*.

meter of the head, fixed to its center. Because of the increased mass, the head as a whole will vibrate more slowly, even though the thinner part of the head which passes over the rim of the shell still vibrates freely. This results in a lower-pitched but "live" sounding note.

Another development was the hydraulic head, brought out by the American company, Evans in the late 1970s. This is a thuddy sounding head which consists of two plastic films separated by an extremely thin layer of oil. The heads are available in several colors but can be recognized by their distinctive rainbow appearance (similar to the effect of oil on water).

In response to this design, Remo developed his Pinstripe head which also employed a twin film, but like the C.S. head left a margin of thinner plastic around the edge to allow the head to vibrate freely. This resulted in a sound somewhere between the C.S. and hydraulic heads, quite deep in tone but with a respectably long decay time.

Left An unusual, multi-drum setup featuring an array of different-sized tom toms and two hihats, one foot-operated and one mounted for stick work.

Below Carmine Appice amid a jungle of microphone and cymbal stands. The drummer with Vanilla Fudge in the late 1960s, Appice was one of the most influential "heavy rock" drummers. Note the angle of the tom tom at the right of the picture.

Many different types of head are now available. These range from the Fiberskyn and Banana Skin to the Poke-a-dot which has stickon black dots. Joe Pollard of Syndrum fame has recently come up with a fiberglass head which is reputed to be made of bulletproof vest material. It has a totally dead sound but has become very popular in studio work, particularly on the snare drum.

Stands and Fittings

Stands and fittings are the bane of the drummer's existence. The equipment needed to support drums and cymbals is heavy, often unstable and prone to collapse, usually, it seems, just before a solo. Before the advent of heavy rock, stands and fittings were not designed for constant, punishing use, but since then design improvements have been made and stands are much less likely to wobble and are generally much sturdier.

Perhaps the biggest improvement in stand technology has been the Memrilok system introduced by Rogers in the early 1970s. It has since been adopted by many different companies under a variety of trademarks and in slightly different forms. Every drummer knows and dreads the occasions when, for some reason, the kit does not feel just right. Before this system was developed, some drummers used to mark the position of their drums on the stands with hose clamps to make sure that the kit was set up by the road crew in exactly the same way each time. The Memrilok system is based on this same general idea. Once the kit is set up satisfactorily, the drummer tightens a Memrilok ring on each pipe. Every time the kit is reassembled, the male Memrilok ring fits into the equivalent female fitting on the drum or cymbal stand and the drum or stand will be in its original position.

General improvements to drum stands have meant that snare drum stands wobble much less than they used to and tom tom holders are now fully adjustable. The modern tom tom fitting can be moved to any position: up, down, sideways, forward or backward.

Cymbal stands have also been greatly improved. In the 1960s, stands were quite unstable and were fitted with stiff wing nuts that often sheered off at a crucial moment. Today's stands have a very wide spread on their tripod legs and sturdy wing nuts.

With the trend towards bigger kits, drummers often found it difficult to reach their cymbals, as conventional cymbal stands could not be positioned close enough to them. The answer to this problem was the boom stand. This stand is similar to a microphone stand and has a boom

1

3

Drum manufacture The Premier Drum Company of Leicester, England produces more than 4,000 types of drums and percussion instruments. In the manufacture of wooden shelled drums and tambourines, the wood (usually beech or maple) is cut to length, shaped into a hoop and glued. The wooden hoops are clamped into position in metal rings and allowed to set. When they are removed from the clamps, they are perfectly circular and formed to the correct diameter *(1)*. To make tambourine shells, one large wooden shell is cut into smaller widths on a circular saw *(2)*. When the wooden shells have been covered with the finishes, fittings are attached by hand *(3)*. Metal drums are made by applying copper, nickel and then chrome plating to a basic metal alloy shell. The illustration shows snare drum shells being take from the chroming vat *(4)*. Fittings are attached by hand with the aid of a compressed air tool *(5)*. In the final stages of manufacturing a plastic head, the head is sealed into its support ring *(6)*. Drums and accessories are stored ready for shipping *(7)*. Each instrument is tuned and checked individually for sound quality *(8)*.

2

4

5

6

7

8

with a counterbalance and wide spreading tripod legs. Quality varies but Japanese manufacturers have done well with this product, making stands that not only remain upright under duress but are reasonably priced as well.

The hihat stand, the means by which the hihat cymbals are opened and closed, is an essential part of the drummer's equipment. In its most basic form it consists of a foot pedal, which, when pressed, will bring the two cymbals into contact. There is either a compression or tension spring which returns the cymbals to the open position when pressure is taken off the foot plate.

The hihat of the 1950s was usually set up either level with the snare drum, or, at best, two or three inches from it. When rock got louder, this arrangement caused problems. Drummers needed to lay the back beat down hard, but also had to keep up the eighth notes on the hihat with their right hand. In the early to mid-1960s, it was not common to see a drummer playing the hihat with his left hand.

The answer to this problem was to extend the pipe and rod of the hihat so that it could be set, say, a foot above the top of the snare drum and allow the left hand a good swing at the snare. Nowadays, most hihat rods and pipes are so long they often have to be shortened, but the choice of length is at least open to the individual drummer. Some players have solved the same problem by attacking the hihat with the left hand and leaving the right free to play the other drums and cymbals without any crossing over. Generally, hihats come in a wide variety of designs but only the simpler ones survive. The more complicated they are, the more likely they are to break and the less appeal they have for drummers.

Probably the most personal piece of equipment in the trap case is the bass drum pedal. The first pedals were thrown together from sewing machine parts but designs developed fairly quickly and the most reliable on the market today have been in existence for some decades.

The most famous bass drum pedal is the Ludwig Speed King. It has a sturdy metal foot plate which can be altered from an all-in-one pedal to a separate heel plate type. The linkage between the foot plate and the beater cam is metal and can take quite a pounding, although it is probably the weakest part of the pedal. The twin return springs are compression types, hidden inside the posts of the pedal, and there is a tension screw at the bottom of each post. To get the maximum speed and power from this pedal, it is essential to set the spring tension evenly.

The two other main styles of pedal are based on the Gretsch floating action pedal and the Rogers' Swivomatic, both of which have been

around for some time. The Gretsch is a very simple piece of machinery, similar in basic operation to the Speed King, but utilizing a single tension-return spring to pull the beater ball back from the head. This pedal is very fast and light but is somewhat flimsy in construction and it is not ideally suited for rock music. However, there are other makes of pedal based on this principle made by companies such as Premier, Pearl, Tama and Yamaha; these are sturdier.

The Rogers' Swivomatic, although very different in appearance from the Gretsch, works in much the same way. The tension spring is positioned so that it operates in the direction of the beater action. The amount of beater action (in other words, where its resting position is) can be adjusted independently of the spring tension so that the pedal can be set up according to each drummer's preference. Several other manufacturers have adopted this versatile style of pedal.

Below Perhaps the most influential drummer of the 1970s, the brilliant jazz-rock percussionist Billy Cobham played with Miles Davis before joining John McLaughlin's Mahavishnu Orchestra, and has since worked as a session player with numerous people, including soul artists James Brown and Sam And Dave, as well as recording his own solo work. Cobham is shown here playing a double kit; he helped to popularize various additions to the standard drum setup including Chinese cymbals.

Playing Styles

If it were not for the talent and dedication of individual players, a great deal of the hardware and equipment associated with drums would never have been developed. Out of the distinctive playing styles of the top professionals come unique sounds which young players are keen to imitate. Drum companies are increasingly quick to respond to this type of demand and often supply equipment designed by and for leading players as part of their standard range. When Ginger Baker first came to international prominence playing with Cream, the sales of double bass drums must have boomed around the world. A great many players have made permanent contributions to rock drumming and, in recognition of this, most companies now sponsor or employ top professionals to advertise their products and to act as advisers, developing new lines and improving existing instruments.

Playing styles have varied widely over the years. The definitive heavy rock drummers, Carmine Appice of Vanilla Fudge and Led Zeppelin's John Bonham, sealed the fate of small, flimsy drumkits with their vigorous approach. Appice's style can be heard to good effect on *Vanilla Fudge* (1967), especially on the track *You Keep Me Hangin' On*. Keith Moon of The Who probably destroyed more drums in a single month on the road than other drummers could get through in a lifetime. His wild, abandoned style, a feature of all of The Who's albums from

Above Two drumkits and two drummers feature prominently in the "ant music" of Adam And The Ants, whose popular tribal sound reflects the recent trend for bringing drums to the forefront.
Below The late Keith Moon of The Who with a Premier double kit . Moon's manic abandoned playing style brought flamboyance to rock drumming.

My Generation (1965) right through to *Who Are You*, was highly influential in the mid-1960s and preceded the freeform playing of Hendrix's drummer, Mitch Mitchell, by several years.

Flamboyance, however, is not directly proportional to influence. The Beatles' Ringo Starr and Charlie Watts of the Rolling Stones are both solid, economical drummers. Between the two of them, they probably influenced the playing and aspirations of more young drummers than anyone else. Almost any track from early Beatles or Stones albums demonstrates their abilities.

The early 1970s was the time of the intelligent drummer. Billy Cobham is one musician who has managed to combine flamboyance and intelligence with a brilliant technical talent. An entire style of jazz-rock drumming is based on his early work with the Mahavishnu Orchestra. Other noted players of the 1970s include Bill Bruford of Yes and the great session men, Harvey Mason and Steve Gadd who have contributed sensitive and precise styles to the repertoire of rock drumming. Mason can be heard on Herbie Hancock's *Headhunters* and Gadd has worked with such musicians as Paul Simon *(Still Crazy After All These Years)*, Chick Corea *(Leprechaun)* and Quincy Jones *(Stuff Like That)*. The funk session drummer Bernard Purdie and Al Jackson Jnr (Booker T And The MGs) have also had a great influence on more mainstream rock styles.

Future developments in drumming, as in any other area of rock, are always difficult to predict, but improvements in amplification and the emergence of electronic drums have encouraged drumming to come to the forefront in the recent work of many new bands. A fascination with "jungle" rhythms (and the use of a double drumkit) is a feature of the music of Adam And The Ants; David Byrne and Brian Eno have explored African drum sounds and percussion in their 1981 collaboration, *My Life in the Bush of Ghosts*. On this album, the various rhythm tracks are overlaid with fragments of taped voices. The drumming style of The Sex Pistols was perhaps the most influential in punk or new wave music of the late 1970s. New wave drummers often went back to the basic kit of the early 1960s; the simple driving sound is at the heart of many new wave recordings. Today, there is a greater acceptance of electronic drums and drum machines, and a trend toward the electronic dance music which can be achieved with these instruments.

Percussion

Percussion did not play a very important part in rock music until the mid-1960s. Prior to that

Above Kenny Jones, formerly the drummer for the Small Faces and later with Rod Stewart's Faces, joined The Who after Keith Moon's death. This setup features a range of single-headed tom toms with microphones positioned right inside each shell.

Right Santana brought the sounds of Latin percussion into the sphere of rock music for the first time and elevated percussion instruments from their previous role as lightweight novelties to a more lasting place in both recording and live performance.

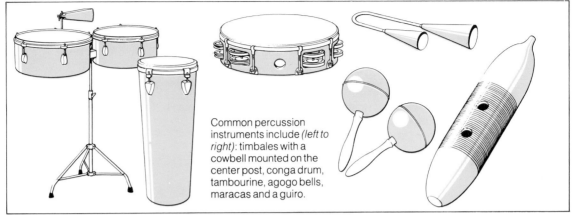

Common percussion instruments include (left to right): timbales with a cowbell mounted on the center post, conga drum, tambourine, agogo bells, maracas and a guiro.

time, percussive interference was limited to the use of the occasional cowbell in Latin American-flavored numbers. The Rolling Stones helped to popularize maracas with their single, *Not Fade Away*, and transformed the cowbell from a light-weight Latin specialty to a simple but potent driving force in rock when it was used to play a solid four-to-the-bar in *Honky Tonk Women*. The tambourine was another percussive instrument given prominence by the Stones: the playing may not have been virtuoso, but that has never been a criterion in rock music.

Percussion maintained itself at this simple but effective level until late in the 1960s when Santana exploded onto the scene. Their 1970 album *Abraxas* (Chepito Areas on percussion) brought the carnival sounds of Brazil to the attention of every drummer, yet the music was quite definitely rock. The sales of timbales, cow-bells, mambo bells, agogo bells, guiros, congas, bongos, cuicas, shekere and cabasas soared. Santana defined Latin rock so well that no other group effectively followed in their footsteps.

The most interesting use of percussive instru-ments after Santana was in jazz-rock, jazz-funk and the country funk of groups like Little Feat. Players such as Bill Summers with Herbie Han-cock, Acuna with Weather Report and the versa-tile session player Airto Moreira exhibited awe-some techniques on Latin instruments and in-jected powerful excitement into their music.

Victor Feldman's percussive contribution to Steely Dan led percussion well beyond the limits of Latin-flavored rock music. His conga, shaker, cabasa and tambourine playing forms an integ-ral part of Steely Dan's popular sound and his tuned percussion playing (vibes and marimba) is unique in rock. The other great tuned percus-sion player of the 1970s was Ruth Underwood of Frank Zappa's Mothers Of Invention.

Today, these different influences combine to guarantee percussion a place in rock music for a long time to come. Bob Marley used timbales and other percussive instruments in a reggae context; the Talking Heads' 1980 album *Remain In Light* uses percussion to create a densely textured sound that combines new wave music with funk elements. These days, very few record-ing sessions would be complete without at least some small touches of percussion.

Instruments

Most of the hardware comes from either South America or the innovative Latin Percussion Company run by Martin Cohen. Cohen's instru-ments are modeled on original Brazilian pieces but are constructed in stronger, modern materials. As a result, they are generally louder and brighter sounding than the original items and lend themselves very well to recording.

Percussive instruments include special drums, bells, and hollow gourds filled with beads. Timbales are two metal-shell, single-headed drums used as a pair. Rhythms are play-ed between the outside edge of the shells and a cowbell mounted on a center post. Fills are played on the drums, often as rim shots. The cuica is a single-headed metal drum with a resined stick embedded in the center of the skin and at right angles to it. It is played by rubbing the stick with the fingers while varying the ten-sion of the skin with the other hand. Congas come in three sizes: quinto, tumba and tumba-dora and are played with the hands. These are single-headed drums made of wood or fiberglass and stand approximately three feet high. The heads are made of calfskin or muleskin. Bongos, the virtuoso Latin drums, are similar in con-struction to congas but are much smaller, usual-ly five and six inches in diameter. They are also played with the hands and fingers. Tambourines are very shallow (two-inch) single-headed drums with metal rattles set in the shell. They are shaken and struck, often with the palm.

The cowbell is a tuned steel or brass bell, played with a stick. It is either mounted on a stand or held in the hand. Agogo bells are two tuned bells.

The guiro is a corrugated gourd played by rubbing a thin stick across the corrugations to make a dry, rattling sound. Shekere and cabasas are hollow gourds covered with a mesh of beads.. They are played by shaking or by rotating the mesh around the gourd to make a scraping noise. Maracas are hollow gourds filled with dried beans: they are played by shaking.

Below Contemporaries of Bob Marley's Wailers, Toots And The Maytals were one of the first Jamaican bands to bring reggae to a wider audience outside their own country. The intricate rhythms make considerable use of such percussion instruments as congas and cowbells.

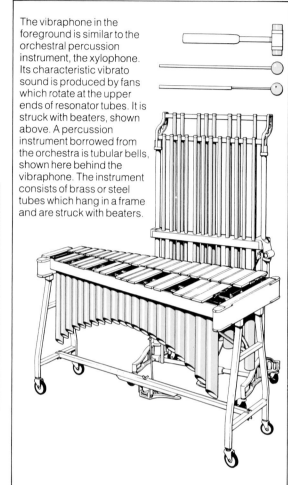

The vibraphone in the foreground is similar to the orchestral percussion instrument, the xylophone. Its characteristic vibrato sound is produced by fans which rotate at the upper ends of resonator tubes. It is struck with beaters, shown above. A percussion instrument borrowed from the orchestra is tubular bells, shown here behind the vibraphone. The instrument consists of brass or steel tubes which hang in a frame and are struck with beaters.

Right Earth, Wind And Fire are known for their enthusiastic live performances which have occasionally featured the group's drummer on a rotating platform. The band uses a wide range of percussion instruments to create their jazz-funk sound.

KEYBOARDS

The casual observer could be forgiven for thinking that all rock keyboards are synthesizers, such is their apparently key role in today's music. But the synthesizer is a relative newcomer to the keyboard arsenal, which includes much older instruments like the acoustic piano and the electric organ, along with more recent additions like electric and electronic pianos and electronic organs.

The acoustic piano is a rare sight in live rock due mainly to the sheer physical problems involved in taking a huge instrument like a concert grand around on tour. There are more technical problems, too: it is difficult to keep the piano in tune and to amplify it accurately and without feedback. All these problems result in the wide use of electric and electronic pianos – electric types use pickups to amplify mechanically-based instruments; electronic types produce their sounds by oscillators.

The Hammond organ suffers from similar physical problems to those of the acoustic piano and is rare in today's rock as a result. Other electric organs have also become less fashionable, although the Vox Continental sound achieved by Steve Naive of Elvis Costello's Attractions caused a minor revival for this instrument. From the obscure Mellotron to the omnipresent Fender Rhodes, keyboards provide a diversity of sound in all types of rock music.

The Acoustic Piano

Although there is no definite date which marks the piano's "invention", the early eighteenth century can be considered its developmental period. The creation of the piano owes much to the dissatisfaction with the performance of its immediate predecessors, the harpsichord and the clavichord.

The clavichord had hammers which struck the strings but its crude construction did not allow for the notes to be sustained without constant depression of the keys. The harpsichord had quills which plucked the strings, making use of a simple escapement mechanism which disengaged the quills from the strings after plucking, allowing them to vibrate freely. The piano was a curious marriage of designs that made use of the clavichord's hammer system – without its inflexibilities, and the harpsichord's escapement mechanism.

An Italian, Bartolommeo Cristofori (1655-1731), is widely accepted as the piano's earliest creator. In 1709, Cristofori, originally a harpsichord-maker, utilized his knowledge of other keyboard instruments to perfect an "action" (the instrument's mechanical part) that allowed the hammer to fall back from the strings once hit. This action formed the basis on which successive improvements were made. Sébastien Érard (1752-1831), born in Strasbourg, was the first to expand significantly upon Cristofori's original design to produce what is now known as the "double escapement". This allows notes to be repeated quickly.

Cristofori also invented the shifting soft pedal arrangement, the *una corda*, and gave the new instrument its name, an abbreviation of the name of one of his earliest pianos, the *gravecembalo col piano e forte*, literally "harpsichord soft and loud".

Design improvements in other areas soon followed. Érard was responsible for extending the compass of the instrument to five and a half octaves, inventing pedals for the soft/loud function (formerly knee-operated) and using iron braces to strengthen the frame and accommodate greater string tensions. Cross-stringing (arranging strings in two different planes) was originally devised to economize space within the instrument. By the mid-nineteenth century, these, along with numerous other improvements, formed the basis for the design of the modern piano.

Basic Anatomy

The piano is a weighty and fairly cumbersome instrument consisting of some 12,000 parts, most of which go to make up the action. Con-

Left This sixteenth century Flemish painting shows a young woman playing a clavichord. This popular predecessor of the piano acquires its distinctive tone from the addition of a small piece of metal to the hammer, which strikes the string.

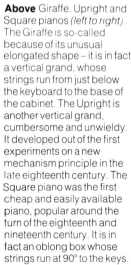

Above Giraffe, Upright and Square pianos *(left to right)*. The Giraffe is so-called because of its unusual elongated shape – it is in fact a vertical grand, whose strings run from just below the keyboard to the base of the cabinet. The Upright is another vertical grand, cumbersome and unwieldy. It developed out of the first experiments on a new mechanism principle in the late eighteenth century. The Square piano was the first cheap and easily available piano, popular around the turn of the eighteenth and nineteenth century. It is in fact an oblong box whose strings run at 90° to the keys.

struction can take anything up to 15 months for some large grands. A modern production grand can be loosely divided into six component parts: the casework, the pinblock, the soundboard, the plate, the strings and the action.

The casework is generally made of solid or veneered wood. It has little or no effect on the instrument's final tone but provides a sturdy base upon which the action, plate and soundboard rest.

The pinblock accommodates the tuning pins which secure one end of the strings to enable them to be tuned. To stop the tuning pins slipping due to the enormous tension of the strings, the pinblock is usually laminated maple.

The final tone depends on how well the soundboard performs. The soundboard is installed in the frame under tension by gluing "ribs" to its underside. This gives it a slight curvature known as the crown. On top are affixed the two bridges across which the strings lie.

The plate, a one-piece casting in iron, is the frame which has to take the tension of the strings. Thorough checking of the plate for defects is vital as it will have to withstand string tensions of between 18 and 20 tons.

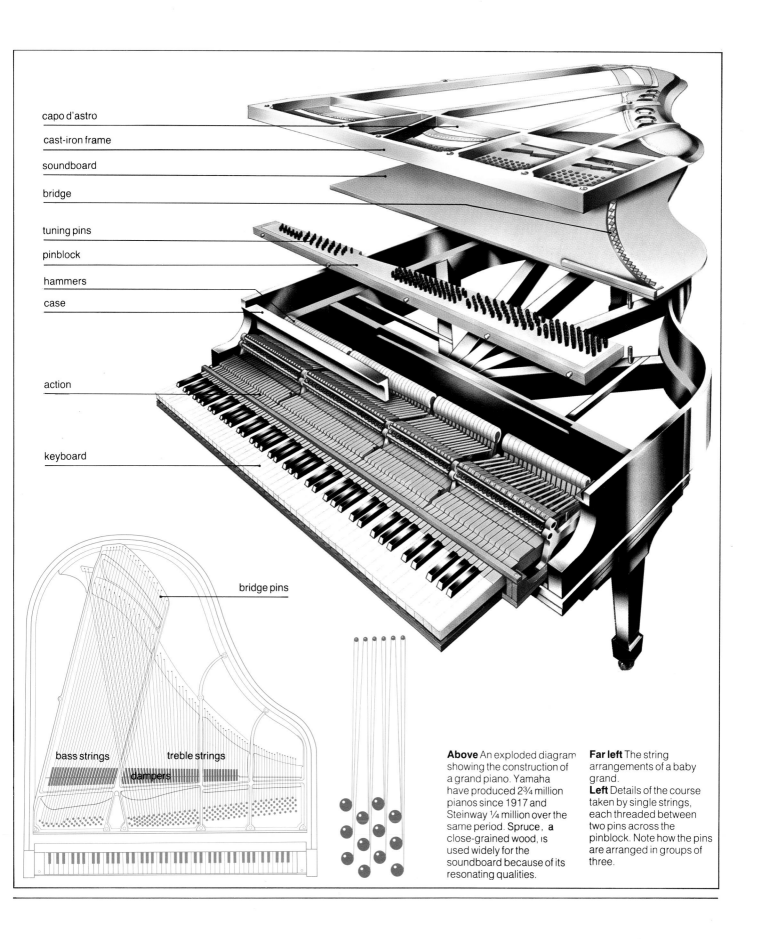

capo d'astro

cast-iron frame

soundboard

bridge

tuning pins

pinblock

hammers

case

action

keyboard

bridge pins

bass strings   treble strings

dampers

Above An exploded diagram showing the construction of a grand piano. Yamaha have produced 2¾ million pianos since 1917 and Steinway ¼ million over the same period. Spruce, **a** close-grained wood, is used widely for the soundboard because of its resonating qualities.

Far left The string arrangements of a baby grand.
Left Details of the course taken by single strings, each threaded between two pins across the pinblock. Note how the pins are arranged in groups of three.

About 14 gauges of cold drawn steel wire are used for the strings. All the bass and some of the tenor strings are wound to reduce the length of wire needed to achieve the desired note. If the smallest gauge wire were used throughout, the piano would be over 40 feet/12m long.

The piano's action is a precise piece of engineering. All the bearings are lined with felt ("bushed") to permit a smooth, almost noiseless operation. Constructionally the action is complex but its function relatively simple. Its main purpose is to provide a key-to-hammer linkage which will allow the hammer to fall back after striking the string (first escapement) and permit the rapid repetition of notes (second escapement).

Right It is difficult to mike up the piano to get an acceptable sound. Uprights, by virtue of their construction are almost impossible to amplify accurately. The grand piano with its exposed soundboard and strings is easier to mike up and for studio work either one or two mikes are usually used, placed directly above the strings at a distance of about one foot to avoid a "boomy" sound.

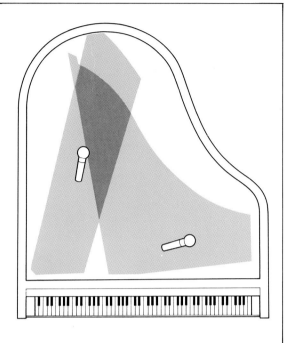

Below The piano player is Brian Wilson, the creative genius behind the Beach Boys, a California group who gave rock a new sound in the early 1960s, the sound of surf music. According to Nik Cohn, Wilson "invented California". Songs like *Fun, Fun, Fun* and *California Girls* were early hits; *Good Vibrations* (1966) is one of the all-time classic records. Later albums showed a greater diversification of styles and a break away from the surfing image.

Manufacturers

Just as no two pianists are alike in musical style, the same can be said of the pianos they use. Even successive production pianos from the same manufacturer can be somewhat different in character. The piano market is dominated by no one manufacturer, not because there is little to choose between them, but simply because prices, quality and the uses to which pianos are put differ so much. The market can comfortably accommodate many firms catering for a wide range of specialist needs.

Popular makes of piano for studio use can be narrowed down to a handful. Yamaha is a well known manufacturer and its phenomenally high piano production rate (30,000 a year) owes much to the extent to which instrument construction has been computerized. Steinway, with its almost mystical prestige, is arguably the best known piano manufacturer in the world. Other names such as Bosendörfer, Bechstein, Baldwin and Chappell are also widely known and used.

On Stage and in the Studio

Most of the major recording studios use grand pianos in preference to uprights, simply because grand pianos sound better. The strings and soundboard are exposed making it easy to place microphones; the bass strings are long, giving a rich deep tone. The upright by comparison is much harder to mike up due to its construction and the recorded sound is generally inferior to that of a grand.

As the piano is basically a mono instrument many studio engineers treat it as such, using only one mike placed directly above the strings. For solo work, sometimes two or even more mikes are used to create a stereo image. Since the piano has a tonal range which is very wide, greater even than a full symphony orchestra, mikes with a wide and flat frequency response are necessary to catch the characteristically subtle harmonics.

On stage, the piano can be amplified either by straight miking up using the studio technique or by using a pickup placed in the instrument a few inches from the strings. While acoustic piano is often heard on recordings, its use in live performance is relatively rare. It suffers from the usual problems associated with acoustic instruments adapted for electric rock – they are difficult to amplify accurately and powerfully. In addition to this, the acoustic piano – particularly the full-size grand piano – presents all manner of practical and physical problems. Attempts have been made to provide specially made pick-

Above The great Little Richard dominated the charts in the 1950s. His piano playing features on later albums by Canned Heat.
Right One of the most gifted pianists in popular music, Ray Charles' unique blend of gospel and blues had a great influence on soul and rock.
Below Jerry Lee Lewis was one of the first players to attack his instrument on stage, antics which included throwing his piano bench across the floor.

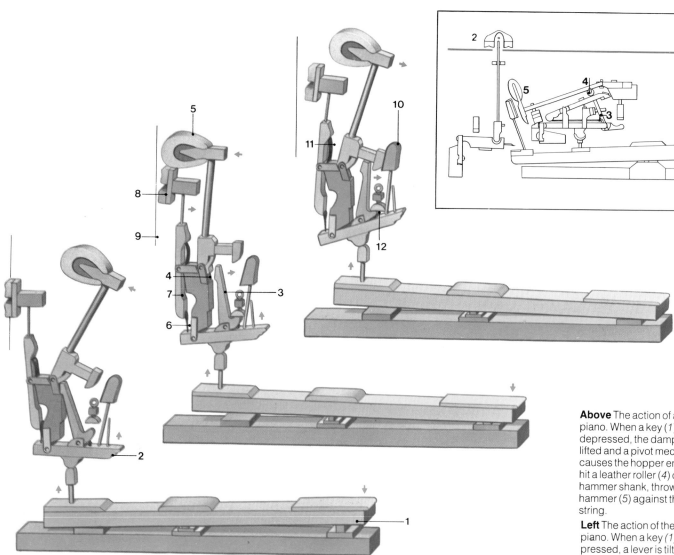

Above The action of a grand piano. When a key (1) is depressed, the damper (2) is lifted and a pivot mechanism causes the hopper end (3) to hit a leather roller (4) on the hammer shank, throwing the hammer (5) against the string.

Left The action of the upright piano. When a key (1) is pressed, a lever is tilted (2) which moves on a pivot. The right end of the lever moves up, pushing the jack (3) out of the notch (4) and against the hammer (5) which is propelled toward the string. The left end of the lever moves down, pushing the damper spoon (6) against the damper lever (7). This swings on a pivot to release the damper (8) from the string (9).
As the key is fully depressed, the hammer hits and rebounds from the string, producing a note. The check (10) prevents it springing back against the string. When the key is released, the damper spring (11) returns the damper against the string and the jack spring (12) returns the jacks into the notch.

ups for the piano, and the Helpinstill is probably the best and most common, being a long pickup which attaches to the soundboard at right angles to the strings, thus picking up the full piano sound and attempting to capture faithfully the extreme dynamic range of the instrument.

Use in Rock

The piano's range and creative resourcefulness are irresistible to the talented keyboard player. Singer-songwriters can often be seen perched behind a gleaming black Steinway, pounding out the accompaniment to their heartfelt compositions. But some players in this field demonstrate interesting musical abilities too – Randy Newman's acoustic piano cavortings are well worth a critical ear, and Elton John has been known to turn in a complex piano line.

Elton used a Steinway on his "solo piano" tour of 1979, accompanied only by Ray Cooper's percussion. His favourite piano is the Bosendörfer Imperial grand that he used on the 1970 album, *Tumbleweed Connection*. Live, his piano is usually amplified using a combination of a Helpinstill pickup and three microphones.

Heavier rock bands generally have less time for acoustic piano. Allen Lanier, keyboard player of the Blue Oyster Cult, does not think there is much room for the piano as a solo instrument in an electric band, but nonetheless uses a Helpinstill-equipped acoustic piano on many of the band's recordings.

Christine McVie of Fleetwood Mac uses a Yamaha C3 grand and a smaller Yamaha "console" piano on stage. On a recent tour the console piano was fitted with a metal bar which was switched down onto the strings to create a honky-tonk effect on the song *Sara*.

Jazz pianists have been continually absorbed into rock, ever since Chick Corea appeared (electrically and acoustically) on Miles Davis' influential album *Bitches Brew* in 1970 and Joe Sample's group The Crusaders changed their name from the Jazz Crusaders and toured with the Rolling Stones in 1975. Sample says, "You shouldn't attempt to play the acoustic piano in the same manner as a Fender Rhodes, and vice versa … the acoustic piano is a solo vehicle; it takes up all the space," underlining many rock players' frustration with the sheer range of the acoustic piano.

Even Frank Zappa, who often uses the instrument when composing, does not really consider himself a player, and says he thinks of the acoustic piano as "an elaborate percussion instrument". With many rock keyboard players finding the answers to their sound problems in synthesizers, there is still only one answer for a high quality acoustic piano sound: the acoustic piano.

Right Randy Newman's subtle ironic songs have often been recorded by other people and made hits. His unique style comes out of the combination of his lyrics, throaty soul voice and melodic piano playing
Below Elton John's exuberant stage antics follow in the tradition of Jerry Lee Lewis, although his early work demonstrated a less showy approach. Increasingly successful throughout the 1970s, Elton John is one of the few rock superstars to base his music and his act around the piano.

The Hammond Organ

Laurens Hammond (1895-1973) was a brilliant mechanical engineer who developed an automatic transmission system in 1909, a clock that did not tick in 1920, a three-dimensional film system in 1922 and a sugar refining process. It was his endeavors with clocks and time that led to his most famous invention, the tone wheel electric organ.

During 1933 and 1934, Hammond enlisted the services of an old colleague, John Hanert, a research engineer. Between them, they developed a product that used the synchronous motor Hammond developed for his clock for a completely different purpose. A synchronous motor is powered by an alternating current, similar to our domestic mains supply; this current can be considered to change direction (polarity) at a certain frequency: in Britain, the frequency is 50 times a second, in the United States, it is 60. The synchronous motor runs at a speed that is directly proportional to the frequency of the alternating current, so, as the mains electrical supply is stabilized to an exact frequency, a synchronous motor, run off the mains, will operate at a fixed number of rotations per minute.

The fruit of Hammond's and Hanert's labors was the Hammond tone wheel organ, which received its U.S. patent on April 24, 1934. In the original instrument, the synchronous motor was used to turn 95 tone wheels the size of large coins. Each wheel was cut or indented differently. Pointing towards the edge of each wheel was a

A new wonderland of music for him and the children

FITS IN A FOUR-FOOT SQUARE

Electrical impulses, instead of air-pressure, produce the exquisite tones of the Hammond Organ. It requires no pipes, no reeds—fits into any living room. The console and bench occupy only a four-foot square and can be easily moved by two men. The Hammond is installed by merely connecting it with an electric outlet.

A superb concert organ at the price of a fine piano

ANYONE WHO HAS ever played the piano, can, almost immediately, produce satisfying music on the Hammond Organ. It offers a rich, new musical experience—a whole new realm of self-expression.

At the keyboard of the Hammond, all the beautiful and varied voices of the organ are at your command—fascinating tone colors that give new depth, new charm to favorite compositions.

To children taking their first lessons these exquisite tones, so easily created on the Hammond, are a constant inspiration and encouragement.

This remarkable instrument provides the full, lovely tone range of the concert organ. Yet it

costs no more than a fine piano, fits any living room.

The enthusiasm which the Hammond Organ has aroused among famous musicians is impressive. Noted artists were among the first to buy it.

Give yourself the pleasure of hearing an organist play the Hammond—and the enjoyment of trying it yourself. Stop in soon at the showrooms of any of our dealers. Each one is the leading music merchant of his community. Consult your classified directory or write The Hammond Organ, 2907 N. Western Ave., Chicago.

Over 1000 churches use the Hammond...it is an appropriate donation for your church

$1250
and up f. o. b. Chicago—slightly higher for large installations

THE HAMMOND ORGAN

THE HAMMOND IS THE LARGEST-SELLING ORGAN IN THE WORLD

Above left Laurens Hammond; inventor of the tone wheel electric organ which bears his name.
Above An early advertisement for the Hammond organ. It was originally marketed and produced for use at home.
Right The Leslie Organ Speaker, designed originally to give Hammonds a livelier and deeper tone. The vented enclosure houses a rotating drum which directs the speaker's output around a circle at two rates to give either a tremelo or chorus effect. In more recent models as shown, there is also a rotating high frequency horn so the speaker can be used with other keyboard instruments.

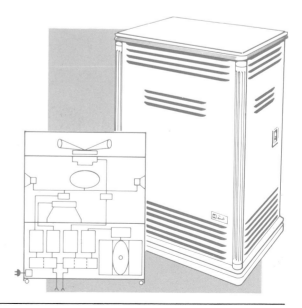

small chisel-shaped magnetic pickup, in which a tiny electrical signal was induced. The wheels spun at a fixed number of revolutions per minute, but their shape was such that the signals induced covered almost the entire audio spectrum; this shape determined both the pitch and shape of the waveform induced in the pickup. Hammond designed the tone wheels to produce fundamental pitches (sine waves with no overtones or harmonics) and developed a system of drawbars (control mechanisms) which would enable the player to blend harmonics with fundamentals at varying volumes. The nine drawbars, each with nine possible settings, made it possible, so the manufacturers claimed, to create 253 million different musical tones.

The original organ, designated Model A, had its public debut in April, 1939 at the Industrial Arts Exposition in New York's Radio City RCA building and received a surprisingly favorable reception. Inevitably, a comparison was drawn between the Hammond and the traditional pipe organ. Hammond made some greatly exaggerated claims regarding the performance of his new instrument and ran into trouble with the Federal Trade Commission. As a result, a bizarre "dark room test" was held pitting the $75,000 (£37,500) Skinner Pipe Organ in Chicago Uni-

versity's Rockefeller Chapel against the $2,600 (£1,300) Hammond Model A. The Hammond's loudspeakers were hidden among the Skinner's pipes, then classical organ passages were played to a panel of experts and students, who were asked to identify the organ being played. One-third of the experts' answers were incorrect and so were half the students' – this result was the same as it would have been if they all had guessed. The Hammond was vindicated: the age of the commercially available electric music instrument had begun.

Many different types of Hammond tone wheel organs were built but, for the rock musician, the Hammond B-3 became the prime instrument. The B-3, RT-3, D-152, C-3 and A-105 were all essentially the same except for varying styles of console and different pedalboards. The B-3 and its European equivalent, the C-3, were the smallest in this group.

The musician who really promoted the Hammond organ as a rock keyboard was undoubtedly Keith Emerson (The Nice and Emerson, Lake And Palmer). With The Nice, Emerson normally used two organs, a C-3 and an A-100, the latter taking the brunt of his unconventional stage act. He hurled knives at the instrument, threw it around like a guitar, smashed it on the stage and rode it bronco fashion. However, these antics were far more than mindless effects. Sticking knives into the organ held down certain keys and wheeling it across the stage took full advantage of the feedback produced at high amplification levels. In addition, the reverb spring could be "played" by plucking it with the notes held down. Emerson, and several other Hammond users, modified their instruments so that the synchronous motor could be slowed down or

Below left The Small Faces pose with a Hammond organ. Keyboard player Ian McLagan joined the group in 1965; like the rest of the band, he was heavily influenced by Booker T And The MGs. McLagan has since played with The Faces, Rod Stewart and the Rolling Stones.

Below The drawbar harmonic relations in a Hammond organ. The system of drawbars is based on the footage system in pipe organs where different lengths of pipe create different pitches. Drawbars can be pulled out singly or in combination. The numbers on the drawbars refer to the lengths in feet of the pipes to which they correspond; the pitch of each drawbar is given on the scale.

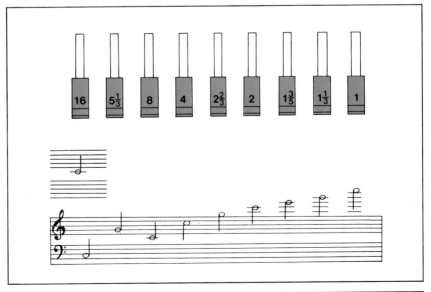

speeded up. This gave the effect of slewing the pitch of the entire instrument, resulting in a sound somewhat like a record player with a lot of wow.

Although Hammond intended the organs to be portable, the fact of the matter was that it normally took at least three people to move one. Although this was an improvement on the pipe organ, it was still impractical for the average rock band. To overcome this difficulty, the "split" Hammond was developed: the instrument was divided so that it could be carried in two sections. The split was made between the main keyboard housing and the legs, pedal and pedalboard assembly. Even then, the upper part was quite a heavy piece of hardware to man-handle.

High production costs and the advent of large scale integrated circuitry eventually resulted in the demise of the tone wheel organs. The Hammond Organ Company, part of which is still located in the original clock company's headquarters on Western Avenue, Chicago, now concentrates on the home organ market. The Model B3000, styled along the same lines as the B-3, with all its original features, is a recent development. However, its clean electronic simulation cannot recreate that warm, dirty, overdriven, mechanically generated sound of the old tone wheel Hammond, a sound which is a feature of many recordings, notably *Hold Your Head Up* by Argent and the track *America* from the last album by The Nice, *Elegy* (1971).

Electronic Organs

Until recently, the popularity of the electric organ seemed to be declining, faced with competition from the synthesizer, especially the polyphonic synthesizer. The organ had been the rock keyboard of the 1960s, with the Hammond tone wheel instruments taking pride of place, but a couple of other instruments were also important at the lower end of the market. The Vox Continental, used by The Animals on *House Of The Rising Sun*, and the Farfisa Compact Duo were the two main dual manual (two keyboards) organs; the Vox having a limited drawbar system, and the Farfisa basically employing preset voices. Pink Floyd used a Farfisa on *Set The Controls For The Heart Of The Sun*. The Vox Jaguar was a single manual organ that also received a lot of attention and was prominently featured by such bands as The Dave Clark Five.

During the early 1970s, the Hammond was the only survivor in this group. The lower-priced electronic organs (basically similar to electric organs but with electronic circuitry) fell by the wayside. There was one notable exception,

Above The Hammond organ contains 95 tone wheels, each cut or indented in a different way and made out of bakelite to eliminate noise. A drive gear turns the wheels and the changing magnetic field induces a signal in the small pickups which point towards the edge of each wheel. The wheels spin at a fixed rate, but the different shapes mean that the signals induced cover almost the entire audio spectrum.

Left Keith Emerson, keyboard player with The Nice and later Emerson, Lake And Palmer, is closely associated with the Hammond organ. His wild stage antics first drew attention when he was playing with The Nice – he stabbed, hit and threw his Hammond around the stage, partly to exploit the different effects and feedback which these acrobatics produced. ELP made their debut at the Isle of Wight Festival in 1970, displaying the technical virtuosity which put them at the forefront of British "technorock".

Above Steve Naive of Elvis Costello's Attractions caused a revival in popularity for the Vox Continental's reedy vibrato sound in the late 1970s.

however, the Crumar Organizer, a single manual, five-octave organ that employed the nine drawbar voicings found on the Hammond organs. The Crumar was a budget-priced instrument that captured some of the Hammond sound.

Not until the end of the 1970s did manufacturers realize that there was a demand for a quality single manual organ that sounded like a Hammond to take over from the original Crumar Organizer. The Japanese companies Korg and Roland brought out two such instruments at this time, the CX-3 and VK-1. Both have the nine drawbar arrangement, five-octave keyboards, rotating speaker simulations and harmonic percussion; the Korg CX-3 is even styled along the same lines as a Hammond and has an overdrive control to create the typical Hammond distortion. Its development and use shows there is still room for electric/electronic organs in today's synthetic rock music.

The Mellotron/Novatron

The Mellotron was born in the most unlikely of surroundings, in a small wartime engineering factory just outside Birmingham, England run by three brothers, Norman, Frank and Leslie Bradley. In 1962, the company, then known as Bradmatic Ltd., was approached by an American to supply 70 matched tape replay heads. The heads were intended for a keyboard instrument in which each note was produced by running a strip of recording tape across a replay head. The new instrument was known as the

92

Chamberlain, and although it was at a primitive stage of development it had tremendous potential.

The Bradleys, with their engineering background, were approached by the American entrepreneur to redesign the instrument. Such personalities as Eric Robinson, the bandleader, and David Nixon, a well-known magician, were among several keen financial backers of the project. In 1964, the Mark I Mellotron first appeared, the instrument taking its name from *Melo*(dy) and (Elec)*tron*(ics). Unfortunately, the Mark I was inherently unstable. At the beginning of 1965, the redesigned Mellotron Mk II became available.

The Mellotron Mk II was a dual manual instrument. Each keyboard comprised 35 notes and was divided into three sections. The left-hand keyboard was split in two; one half was the rhythm section and the other half was the accompaniment which gave a fullness to the melody played on the righthand keyboard.

The Eric Robinson Organization, as well as partly financing the project and handling the sales, was responsible for recording the master tapes from which the ⅜-inch tapes for the instrument were copied. For every key on the Mellotron, there was a tape, and each one contained 18 different passages (six lengths of three parallel tracks). Each tape was 42 feet long, and,

Left Mike Smith, keyboard player with The Dave Clark Five, popularized the use of the Vox Jaguar and Vox Continental.

Below Captain Sensible of the punk group The Damned is a more unconventional keyboard player. He has often played with his Vox Continental wearing gloves or using his fists.

as only an ⅛-inch stretch would affect the output, great difficulty was encountered in setting up these instruments.

These initial tapes included recordings of single notes from acoustic instruments together with entire passages played by brass bands, skiffle bands, jazz outfits and string quartets, amongst others. Each note played the specific passage (or a variation) in the relevant key. A nice touch was the bottom note, which always rounded off the rhythm at the end of a piece. Unknown to the owners of these early machines (for contractual reasons), many of the tapes feature musicians who were (and still are) household names. When all the three sections – melody, accompaniment and rhythm – were played together, it sounded uncannily like a real band.

The B.B.C. (British Broadcasting Corporation) decided that the Mellotron was an ideal instrument for their sound effects department and commissioned Streetly Electronics (the new name for the company), to supply a Mellotron Mk II with 1,260 special effects. This figure represented the total number of sounds that the Mk II could achieve (70 notes by 3 channels by 6 banks). One of the best Beatles' singles ever released, *Strawberry Fields Forever* (1967), featured a Mellotron as did the acclaimed debut album by King Crimson, *In the Court Of The Crimson King* (1969). Mike Pinder worked for Streetly Electronics for eighteen months before leaving to join the Moody Blues full time; the Mellotron was almost entirely responsible for the group's powerful sound. The Mellotron is also featured on Julie Driscoll's *This Wheel's On Fire* (1968) where it was played by Brian Auger.

The Model 400 Mellotron, a single manual with a 35-note keyboard which first appeared in 1970, became the most popular version of the instrument. However, as the popularity of the instrument increased, so did Streetly's problems. The Musicians' Union decided to black the instrument, preventing media performances of the Mellotron; simultaneously, a financial wrangle with the distributions of the instrument, Dallas Music, led to the collapse of Mellotronics (the part of the company run by The Eric Robinson Organization). This resulted in one of the most ludicrous anomolies of the musical instrument market: the manufacturers, Streetly Electronics, were still financially viable, and continued to build the instruments, but the official receiver, brought in to wind up the affairs of Mellotronics, sold the name, Mellotron, to an American firm which specializes in reconstructing existing instruments but not manufacturing them. So, although Streetly's new instruments

are almost exactly the same as the originals (with a few minor modifications), they cannot be called Mellotrons. Streetly now market them under the name of Novatron, and, not surprisingly, people are confused.

The Novatron 400 is much simpler in design than the Mellotron Mk II. As with the Model 400 Mellotron, it has a single 35-note keyboard with one set of tapes offering three voice selections. The motor rotates a long spindle/roller that runs under the entire length of the keyboard. When a key is pressed, a pinch roller presses the tape against the drive spindle and pulls the tape across the replay head. As soon as the key is released, a spring returns the tape to its initial position. The duration of any note is limited, therefore, to around seven seconds. The beauty of this system lies in the way that the tape returns to its initial position once the key is released. When using tapes of various instruments, the attack of every note (normally the most complex part) is faithfully and accurately recorded, making it possible to record, for example, four bars of a jazz band, and have the sound come in exactly as the note is pressed.

The tapes are housed in a tape frame, which can be exchanged very easily. The manufacturers will convert any master tape to $\frac{3}{8}$-inch tape and fit up a tape rack, or, alternatively, a tape conversion kit is available so that the Novatron can be adapted to use domestic $\frac{1}{4}$-inch tape, which can be fitted easily into the instrument. Streetly have a comprehensive tape library of effects and voices for sale. The most popular are string, brass and flute recordings but with the increasing popularity and capabilities of polyphonic synthesizers, the demand for these voices from the relatively large and cumbersome Mellotron/Novatron is slackening considerably.

There are, however, two main areas where the Mellotron still excels. No other instrument can produce a choir voicing like the Mellotron/Novatron because the instrument's tapes include recordings of real choirs. The instrument can also be used live to provide a closer approximation of an album track. Special effects used in the studio are recorded on the instrument's tapes for replay on stage: Patrick Moraz (Yes) uses the Mellotron in this way.

Other Replay Keyboards
The Mellotron was not the only instrument to use recordings of original sounds and replay them via a keyboard. The Orchestron, developed in the mid-1970s by an American company, Vako, was also based on the same principle. Unlike the Mellotron, the Orchestron used an

Above Rick Wakeman built up a reputation as a keyboard virtuoso with The Strawbs even before he joined Yes in 1971. Trained as a classical pianist, he was in demand while still at college as a session player for such artists as David Bowie. He left Yes in 1973 to pursue a solo career but later rejoined. He is noted for grand scale orchestral arrangements and for such "concept" albums as the successful *The Six Wives Of Henry VIII* (1973). Here he is shown surrounded by a variety of keyboards and synthesizers: on the right, a Fender Rhodes; on the left, a Mellotron/Novatron; in the background, a number of Minimoogs.

optical disc, rather like a gramophone record, but containing information in circles (one for each note) rather than a continuous spiral. This information contained the waveform for a certain voice so that, when a key was held, a light-sensing resistor picked up the information for that note and produced an electrical waveform which was, in turn, amplified. The Orchestron had two major drawbacks. First, as the disc revolved continuously, recording or replaying changes in amplitude and timbre during the course of the note was impossible—all that could be reconstructed was a continuous tone with basically the same waveshape as the original instrument. Secondly, the discs were very sensitive to dust and scratches and the sound was therefore not very clear.

Rick Wakeman, unhappy with the Mellotron's size and unreliability, helped to finance the production of an instrument known as the Birotron, which used an eight-track cartridge as the recording/replay medium. Unfortunately, although the idea seemed promising, the venture never really took off commercially, and only a few such instruments can be found now.

With the advent of bubble memories, electronic devices that store vast quantities of information, the future looks set for the appearance of a digital Mellotron-type instrument, where all the sounds can be stored in tiny integrated packages, and the information read electronically.

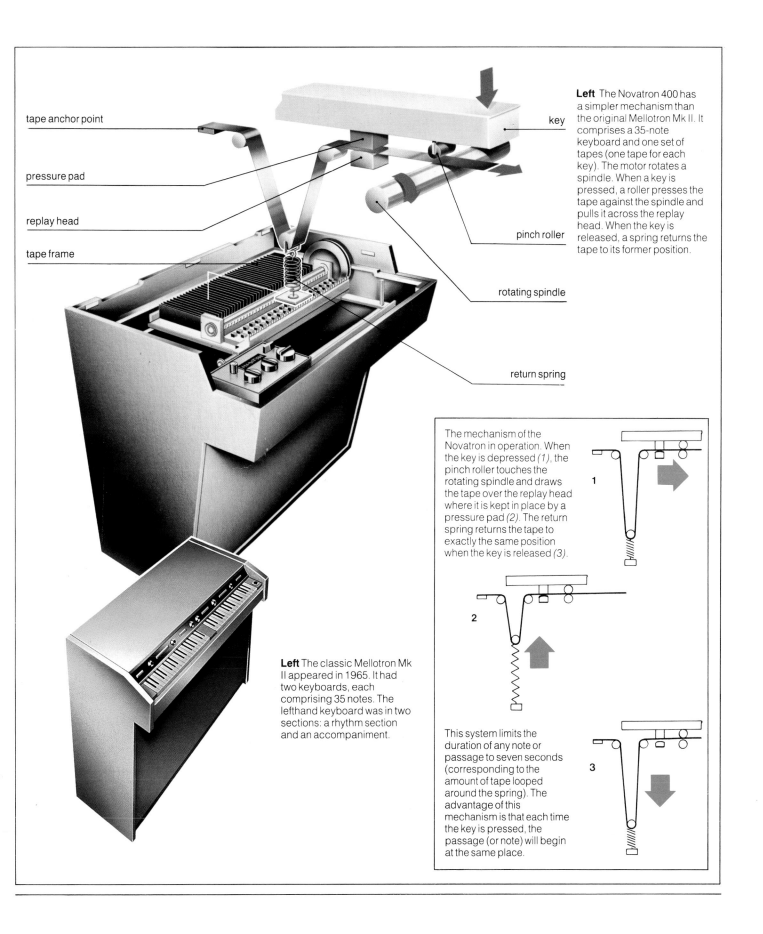

tape anchor point

pressure pad

replay head

tape frame

key

pinch roller

rotating spindle

return spring

Left The Novatron 400 has a simpler mechanism than the original Mellotron Mk II. It comprises a 35-note keyboard and one set of tapes (one tape for each key). The motor rotates a spindle. When a key is pressed, a roller presses the tape against the spindle and pulls it across the replay head. When the key is released, a spring returns the tape to its former position.

Left The classic Mellotron Mk II appeared in 1965. It had two keyboards, each comprising 35 notes. The lefthand keyboard was in two sections: a rhythm section and an accompaniment.

The mechanism of the Novatron in operation. When the key is depressed (1), the pinch roller touches the rotating spindle and draws the tape over the replay head where it is kept in place by a pressure pad (2). The return spring returns the tape to exactly the same position when the key is released (3).

1

2

This system limits the duration of any note or passage to seven seconds (corresponding to the amount of tape looped around the spring). The advantage of this mechanism is that each time the key is pressed, the passage (or note) will begin at the same place.

3

Electric and Electronic Pianos

Originally, the term "electric piano" referred to any acoustic piano that was played automatically. This category included player pianos that used rolls of paper to determine the music played. When B.F. Miessner produced an instrument that was, in essence, an acoustic piano without a soundboard, but with a series of pickups, one for each string, he was credited as the inventor of the "electronic" piano.

Nowadays, the definitions have changed somewhat: Miessner's instrument is known as an electromechanical, or an electric piano, while the term electronic is reserved for pianos that produce the basic signal purely by electronic means (using oscillators).

Miessner leased patents to the Everett Piano Company who went on to produce the Everett Orgatron, an electric organ whose sound was created by blowing air over metal reeds to make them vibrate and then transforming the movement into an electrical signal with electrostatic pickups. Wurlitzer, the American organ company famous for their ubiquitous cinema organs, took up this principle from the Everett Piano Company (now, incidentally, owned by the Hammond Organ Company) and eventually turned this "piano-to-organ" evolution full circle when they came up with a new design of electric piano using the reed system.

The Wurlitzer EP 200

The classic Wurlitzer EP 200 was originally designed in the early 1960s for use at home but its rich sound soon made it popular for rock performers, too. *Dreamer* by Supertramp and Queen's single, *You're My Best Friend,* are well-known recordings which feature the Wurlitzer sound.

Unlike its organ ancestors, the Wurlitzer electric piano uses a simplified piano action to strike the metal reeds, causing them to vibrate. These vibrations are transduced into an electrical signal, amplified, and then fed either to the instrument's own power amp and speakers, or to an external amplification system.

Tuning the Wurlitzer piano is quite complicated. Each metal reed is different in length and has a lump of solder on the end. By adding to the solder, the mass of the reed is increased and the pitch is lowered; conversely, by filing the reed down, the pitch can be raised. It is important, however, that the lump of solder remains roughly the same shape, otherwise the timbre of the signal produced will be altered.

Each note that can be produced by the Wurlitzer EP200 has its own corresponding reed.

Top Georg Csapo of the British group Bethnal, playing an RMI Electra-Piano, one of the earliest electronic pianos. **Above** Peter Hammill of Van Der Graaf Generator, shown here playing a Clavinet, is an exponent of Hohner's other electric piano, the Pianet. The Pianet gives a mellow tone, while the Clavinet is more percussive, making it admirably suited to funkier styles of playing.

The Rhodes Electric Piano

An American serviceman in the Army Air Corps, Harold Rhodes, developed the piano that bears his name during the Second World War when he was asked to teach hospital patients to play the piano to boost their morale. Using spare parts from aircraft, he built a small (two-and-a-half-octave) instrument with aluminum rods for tone bars. These rods were hit by bare wooden keys. The success of this "piano" led to hundreds of similar instruments being built and distributed among the forces. From this basic design, the keyboard was lengthened, pickups added, and various improvements made, until the instrument was more or less as it stands today – the Fender Rhodes.

The Fender Rhodes now comes in four basic models: the Stage 73, the Suitcase 73, the Stage 88, and the Suitcase 88. The "73" and "88" refer to the number of notes that make up the keyboards. The Stage models consist basically of a keyboard, tone generation assemblies and

Above The Crumar Roadrunner is a relatively lightweight electronic piano, worn here by Billy Preston. A session player with many of rock's top groups, including The Beatles, Preston has also toured frequently with the Rolling Stones.

Left Stevie Wonder, one of rock's greatest musicians, was already a star at the age of 13. With the maturing of his talent, evidenced on *Music Of My Mind* (1972), he became known and respected worldwide. Tracks such as *Superstition* and *Higher Ground* demonstrate his use of the percussive qualities of the Clavinet.

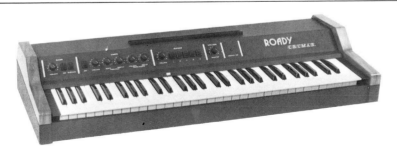

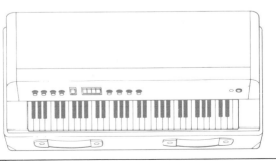

Above The portable Crumar Roady RP 29 is one of the latest electronic pianos.

Left Another portable electronic piano is the attractively designed Yamaha CP 20. It has a touch-sensitive keyboard.

pickups, and require external amplifiers and speakers. The Suitcase models come complete with their own stereo amplifier and speaker system, together with a stereo vibrato unit.

The mechanics of the Rhodes are very simple. The key activates a hammer by means of a cam system; as the key is depressed, the dampers are lifted from the metal rod (known as the tine), which is then struck by the hammer. The tine vibrates, inducing a signal in the pickup which is then combined with the signals emanating from the pickups of all the other keys and fed to the output. The Stage models require no power supply (no mains or batteries), but work in a similar fashion to an electric guitar, the signal induced being strong enough to drive an external amplifier.

The Suitcase models are mains-powered to drive the amplification section and also to power the stereo vibrato circuitry. This unit takes the mono signal emanating from the pickups, and pans it across the stereo picture, producing a vibrato-type effect, the speed of which can be varied. The Suitcase version is also equipped with a more comprehensive set of tone controls.

Tuning a Rhodes piano is a relatively simple procedure. Each tine has a small spring attached to it and by sliding this spring towards the fulcrum point, the pitch is raised; conversely, by moving it away, the pitch can be lowered.

The Fender Rhodes has a characteristically bell-like tone which lends itself to jazz-rock styles, particularly the music of Chick Corea, Joe Sample and Herbie Hancock. However, the timbre of the instrument can be altered quite dramatically by adjusting the position of the pickup to the tine, and by moving the point at which the hammer strikes the tine to produce a richer, harsher tone.

The Rhodes has changed little over the past ten years, and its unique qualities will probably justify its existence for a fair while longer. Bill Payne of Little Feat is a noted player of this instrument but there is a place for the Fender Rhodes in the keyboard setups of most major groups.

Other Electric Pianos

The Hohner Pianet and Clavinet are two unique instruments that fall into the general category of electric pianos. The Pianet has led more keyboard players into the realm of electric instruments than probably almost any other machine, primarily because of its low price; Peter Hammill of Van Der Graaf Generator is a noted exponent.

The Pianet, originally designated Model N

Left Harold Rhodes with the Stage 88 model of his invention, the Fender Rhodes electric piano.

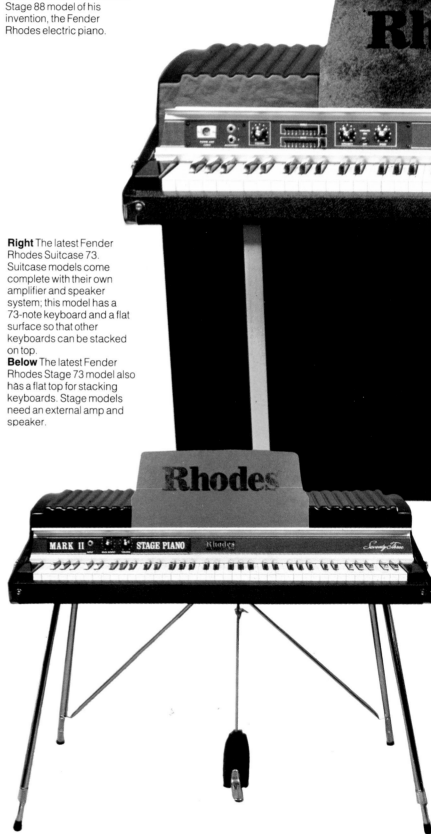

(and mains-powered), has been updated as the Model T, which, like the Stage Rhodes, requires no power supply. The principle on which the Pianet works is simple, yet clever. At the end of each key is a plastic sticky pad, which rests on a metal reed. When the key is played, the pad pulls on the reed, which bends until the resistance of the reed overcomes the sticking force of the pad. The reed then springs back and oscillates; a pickup located next to the key transforms this signal into an electrical signal, which is subsequently amplified.

The Clavinet (notably, the Model D6) is a stringed instrument that has a mechanism whose workings can be compared to the action of hitting the strings of an electric guitar against the fretboard. A string is located under each note, which when played, impinges the string on a metal anvil, causing the string to vibrate. This vibration is then picked up by a series of bar pickups located under the strings, then filtered and amplified. Tuning is achieved by a simple screw adjustment that alters the tensioning of that string.

The Pianet has a warm, smooth, mellow sound, while the Clavinet has a percussive, funky quality – its role in a band is often equivalent to that of rhythm guitar. This rhythmic sound is exploited to the full by the Clavinet's most famous player, Stevie Wonder, especially on such tracks as *Superstition (Talking Book)* and *Higher Ground (Innervisions)*.

The last major instrument in the world of the electric piano is a relatively new development: the portable electric grand. Yamaha have produced two such models: the CP 70B, and the larger, 88-note CP 80. An American company, famous for its piano pickups, Helpinstill, also manufacture a portable electric grand. The strings are used as the generation medium and pickups are attached in much the same way as they are in Miessner's original instrument. To get a good piano sound, strings must be as long

Right The latest Fender Rhodes Suitcase 73. Suitcase models come complete with their own amplifier and speaker system; this model has a 73-note keyboard and a flat surface so that other keyboards can be stacked on top.
Below The latest Fender Rhodes Stage 73 model also has a flat top for stacking keyboards. Stage models need an external amp and speaker.

as possible. Various cross-stringing techniques have been evolved to accommodate the extra length. To make the instruments portable, the keyboard and hammer sections split away from the harp containing the strings. The result is an instrument that can be easily moved by two people but which also gives a fairly good amplified grand piano sound. Understandably, these pianos are becoming increasingly popular with the touring musician.

Electronic Pianos

Over the years, the electronic piano has evolved (parallel to the electronic organ) from the one oscillator per key type (*e.g.* the RMI Electra-Piano) to instruments using the 12-oscillator top octave system. (A series of oscillators generate all the tones required for the top octave, and all the other pitches are derived by dividing these frequencies successively by two – if the frequency is halved, the pitch drops an octave.) More recently, with the advent of microelectronics, the electronic piano has relied on a single high frequency oscillator, running at around two mil-

Right Electric piano mechanisms. The Wurlitzer (1) uses a simplified piano action. A hammer strikes a metal reed and the resulting vibrations induce signals in the pickup plates. Each reed is different in length; the pitch is dependent on the reed's length and on the size of the lump of solder on its tip. In the Fender Rhodes (2) the key makes a hammer strike a metal tine which vibrates, inducing a signal in the pickup. The pitch depends on the length of the tine and position of the tuning spring. In the Clavinet (3), a string is located under each note. When the key is played, the string hits a metal anvil and vibrates, inducing signals in a bar pickup underneath. The Pianet (4) has sticky pads at the end of each key. The pads rest on metal reeds; when the key is played, the reed pulls back from the pad and oscillates, inducing a signal in the pickup.

Left Rick Wright, keyboard player of Pink Floyd, made extensive use of the Fender Rhodes on his solo album

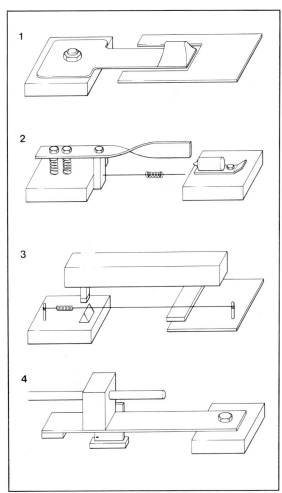

lion vibrations a second, from which all the pitches in the chromatic audio spectrum can be obtained. Examples include the Crumar Road-runner and Yamaha CP 20. At present, work is being carried out on several microprocessor-based pianos, where the computer will not only create the pitches, and the relative partials, but also shape the amplitude and timbre of each note. ARP already have a simplified piano using microprocessors, as do HH Electronics with their P73, an instrument used by Duncan McKay, sometime keyboard player for Cockney Rebel and 10cc.

The majority of present electronic pianos use the master high frequency oscillator system for reasons of cost, reliability, and ease of manufacture. However, electronic pianos of this kind cannot approach the complex sound and feel of a conventional acoustic piano. There are many problems involved in simulating a piano voicing: the timbre changes continuously with the amplitude; the strings (three per note on most acoustic instruments) are not phase-related in any way, so the acoustic instrument sounds much livelier than its electronic equivalent; and

Above The portable electric grand, the Yamaha CP 70B has been a popular recent development. The keyboard and hammers split away from the harp. There are pickups on each string and no soundboard. The development of this instrument has meant that for the first time, a good grand piano sound can be achieved on stage without the attendant difficulties of transporting a full-size acoustic instrument.

the complex action and touch sensitivity are impossible to simulate.

Electronic piano manufacturers try to avoid these problems in many ways. The older single-oscillator-per-key instruments did have the advantage in that each note was not phase-related to the others so, to get a fuller, livelier sound, manufacturers either include a chorus or phasing device, or build the instrument with two independent sets of tone generators to simulate two strings per key. These notes can be detuned against one another to give a honky-tonk effect, or tuned in unison. This fills the sound out considerably and creates a more natural tone. The Yamaha CP 30 is a prime example of this type of system and is used by Rick Wakeman.

As the acoustic piano is so expressive thanks to its touch characteristics, many electronic pianos are equipped with circuitry to provide a similar, although less dynamic, facility. The electronic piano is now accepted as an instrument in its own right. These keyboards can create a wide variety of acoustic simulations, as well as their own characteristic voicings.

SYNTHESIZERS

The synthesizer is one of the most revolutionary musical developments of this century. Critics have branded the instrument mechanical, clinical and non-musical, but Dr. Robert Moog, who developed the first electronic synthesizer in 1964, had an answer for these adverse comments: "There is nothing more contrived than a box with holes in it the shape of an 'f', with maple on one side, spruce on the other ... electronics is as natural as wood or metal working. There's no reason why an electronic instrument cannot be every bit as expressive and appealing as a traditional acoustic instrument."

For many people, the mention of a synthesizer still calls to mind a room full of complicated circuitry resembling a telephone switchboard, but today's models can be compact and portable enough to fit into a small briefcase. The synthesizer is equally at home on stage as in a studio and is being used increasingly in a variety of rock idioms. A musical instrument in its own right, the synthesizer is capable of being used creatively to produce a wide range of new sounds and can also imitate the sounds of conventional instruments.

The Principles of Sound

Sound is vibration in air. This vibration (caused by a vibrating source) disturbs the particles of air, creating alternate areas of compression and rarefaction – or sound waves. A sound wave is somewhat like the ripples that occur when a stone is dropped into a pool of water; the wavelength or cycle is the distance between one wave crest and the next.

Sound travels at approximately 1,100 feet/ 370 m per second, a rate that varies according to the density and temperature of the medium through which the sound is traveling. The frequency of a sound is the velocity divided by the wavelength; it is expressed in Hertz (Hz) per second.

Any sound can be considered to have three basic components – pitch, timbre (tonal quality) and loudness. In simplest terms, a synthesizer is a machine that will build up a sound from scratch, using electronic circuitry to determine each of these three parameters. The term pitch is normally used when referring to the number of vibrations made each second when a note is sounding. In a synthesizer, these vibrations take the form of electrical currents moving backward and forward in a circuit. However, when these currents are transduced (converted into a different form of energy) by means of an amplifier and loudspeaker into an audible sound, the vibrations are set up in the air, but there will still be the same number of vibrations per second (that is to say, the frequency will be the same). The human ear can detect frequencies from around 40 Hz up to 14,000 Hz.

A pure frequency with no overtones or harmonics is known as a fundamental. Sound is a complex mixture of the fundamental tones and series of harmonics or overtones. The sound produced by most musical instruments has harmonics and overtones related to the fundamental. Synthesizers construct the sound in one of two ways: either the sound is built up from a series of sine waves of varying frequency and amplitude, which is known as additive synthesis; or a tone rich in harmonics is produced and the unwanted frequencies then filtered out, which is know as subtractive synthesis. An acoustic piano produces sounds with continuously changing harmonics that make its accurate synthesis almost impossible.

The loudness of a note from a musical instrument can also be a complex parameter. In the case of the acoustic piano, the volume level peaks almost as soon as a note is played; the amplitude then starts to die away as the strings' vibrations are damped by the air; then, as the piano key is released, the dampers act to deaden

Above Sound waves are somewhat similar to the waves created when a stone is dropped into a pool of water. A vibrating source disturbs particles of air creating alternate areas of compression and rarefaction.
Right The Japanese synthesist, Isao Tomita, famous for his synthesized versions of classical music, in front of his Moog modular system in his studio.

the strings completely, though there is still a small amount of sound audible until the strings are firmly damped. A synthesizer has, therefore, to be able to determine this continuous relationship between the amplitude of the note and its duration. The amplitude of the various harmonics is also varying during the period the note is heard, and, therefore, some form of extra control has to be taken over these signals.

The History of the Synthesizer

It was not until 1954 that the electronic music synthesizer emerged as an instrument in its own right; up to that point, the devices produced had either had severe limitations in terms of size, performance, or accessibility, or had been experimental development machines, used to assist the design of more conventional instruments, such as electronic organs. The RCA Music Synthesizer was to change this. Developed by Dr. Harry Olsen and later to be redesigned and installed at the Columbia and Princetown Universities as the RCA Mk II, this instrument was the forerunner of today's synthesizers. It employed two keyboards, and the instructions for the synthesizer were programmed via punched-paper rolls, which were synchronized to two master disc recorders, each with six recording channels, enabling complex synthesizer recordings to be realized.

In the summer of 1964, Robert Moog, who had been selling Theremin kits until then, announced that he had developed a prototype electronic music synthesizer using the principle of voltage control. By 1966, several major re-

cording composers and producers had been sold production versions of this instrument. Meanwhile, Buchla, in California, was working on much the same lines, producing a device known as the Electrocomp.

It was in 1968, however, that the synthesizer achieved worldwide recognition. Walter Carlos produced an album that was to become the greatest-selling classical record of all time. It was called *Switched On Bach*, and featured many of Bach's best-known works realized entirely on one of Moog's synthesizers. Stimulated by the intense interest generated by that album, the synthesizer's popularity has kept growing.

How Synthesizers Work

The synthesizer uses electrical currents moving in a circuit to simulate the vibrations which form sound. Musical sounds, particularly those produced by acoustic instruments, are composed of complex waveforms. The synthesizer is designed to reconstruct these particular voicings by adding or subtracting areas of sound.

Because the synthesizer is an electronic instrument, it cannot be triggered by vibration alone; some means must be employed to transform pitch into voltage. Although guitar, wind, percussion and voice synthesizers are all available, the keyboard synthesizer has emerged as the most popular type. The keyboard is a logical choice for a control medium; when a key is played, a switch contact is made which produces a control voltage.

The synthesizer is based on the principle of voltage control. Each note played on the keyboard produces a different voltage; these voltages are used to control various parameters related to the final output signal.

Three basic modules are the building blocks with which the synthesizer creates a specific sound; they determine the pitch, tone and volume. The voltage controlled oscillator (VCO) sets the pitch of the note produced; the voltage controlled filter (VCF) gives the note its tonal characteristics; and the voltage controlled amplifier (VCA) shapes the note. In most synthesizers, the control voltage is routed from the keyboard to the oscillator, then as a signal to the filter, and finally to the amplifier. All synthesizers also include at least one envelope shaper, the voltage signal from which varies the amplitude over the duration of the sound. Attack, delay, sustain and release are the usual envelope generator variables. Other features can also be included to modulate the sound even further. These range from low frequency oscillators, which can give a vibrato effect, to noise generators and audio mixers.

Above Walter Carlos was responsible for popularizing the synthesizer with his album, *Switched On Bach*. The picture shows a Moog 55 modular system set up with patchcords in Carlos' studio. **Inset** The prototype of the first Minimoog.

Synthesizers also usually include some form of performance controls. These allow the player to change various characteristics of the note which it is actually sounding. The performance controls make the synthesizer a truly creative instrument, one capable of being played and not merely programmed in a set way.

The Keyboard

The keyboard is the most usual control medium for producing the control voltage. Each key on the keyboard is designed to produce a different voltage. To raise the pitch of the sound one octave, the voltage is incremented by a fixed value.

The standard adopted by most manufacturers is that of one volt per octave. In this way, if a bottom C when played produces zero volts, the next C up will produce one volt, the next two

Below Dr. Robert Moog demonstrating one of his modular synthesizers at the International Audio and Music Fair at Olympia in London, 1970.

volts, and so on. Although the frequency doubles for each jump of an octave, the voltage increases by a fixed amount. Because there is this fixed ratio between each note, when the synthesizer is used to accompany a fretless instrument such as a violin, there may be a tuning discrepancy.

When a key is depressed, it is important to retain the voltage until another key is played. For this reason, the keyboard circuitry must include some form of voltage memory. In a monophonic synthesizer (where only one note can be sounded at a time), it is also necessary to have some sort of priority system in case two notes are played together. Several systems can be used: the lowest, highest or last note can have priority, or in some systems, a voltage can be generated between the two notes being held (if more than two are pressed, a mean voltage is produced).

As well as producing a voltage proportional to the pitch of the key being played, the keyboard's circuitry must also incorporate some means of letting the rest of the synthesizer's circuitry know when, and for how long, that key is held. Another set of keyboard switches, or contacts, produce a trigger and/or a gate pulse. A trigger pulse is a short duration voltage that occurs the instant the key is pressed signaling the beginning of a note; a gate pulse is a fixed voltage that is present for as long as the key is held. The gate pulse is more commonly used and its voltage is independent of the pitch of the key held. Both the trigger and gate pulse are designed to initiate and control the envelope generators, which shape the final note.

Voltage Controlled Oscillators

The control voltage passes from the keyboard to the oscillator, usually in a permanent direct link, and determines the frequency at which the VCO oscillates. The VCO's output can take the shape of various different waveforms which correspond to different types of sound, the most common of which are the sawtooth and square waves. (The name of a waveform refers to its shape when shown in a graph tracking the compression and rarefaction of air particles during the course of a particular sound.)

A continuous sawtooth wave, pitched in a middle register (around the central notes of a piano), has a somewhat brassy quality, while a square wave sounds rather hollow, like a clarinet. Other waveshapes include the triangle and the sine wave. The sine wave is a pure fundamental tonal element, sounding like a flute. It is very useful for simulation and generating effects but is quite difficult to construct electronically, and the triangle wave is often used as a substitute. The shape of these two waveforms is similar, although the triangle wave does have additional harmonic overtones which give it a slightly brighter quality. In addition to these basic waveforms, a sub-octave square wave is sometimes also found. This serves to "beef" up the sound, especially in synthesizers which incorporate only one oscillator.

Although only one oscillator is needed for the synthesizer to function, the range and capabilities of the instrument are greatly increased if a second oscillator is available. When there are two VCOs, the voltage is fed simultaneously to both so they track the keyboard exactly. Two oscillators give a much warmer sound, in the same way as a 12-string guitar, with six pairs of strings, each pair tuned in unison, produces a richer, livelier effect than a normal six-string guitar. With a dual oscillator synthesizer, the two oscillators can be set in different registers, or spaced at intervals (an octave or a fifth apart, for example) to create even more variety.

The oscillators must track the keyboard accurately and they are usually tuned to the keyboard rather than the other way around. Tuning is quite tricky, especially since a VCO has to cover something in the range of a 10-octave span. A variation of pitch caused by a discrepancy of three millivolts (3/1000 volt) can be detected by the human ear, so the adjustments are fine.

A VCO can also be modulated by voltages from other sources as well as the control voltage from the keyboard. It can accept modulation and pitchbend voltages from the performance control, tuning voltages and sometimes control voltages from other oscillators.

Voltage Controlled Filters

VCFs are electronic filters which operate rather like sophisticated tone controls. They act so as to remove certain bands of frequencies across the audio spectrum. There are four main types: high pass, which removes frequencies below a certain level; low pass, which removes frequencies above a specified level; band pass, which removes signals at all but a certain frequency; and band reject, or notch, which removes signals at a certain frequency. The frequency around which attenuation begins is known as the cut-off frequency.

Ideally, the filter should operate at an exact frequency and then cut the signal off completely either above or below this level. This is not the case; instead, attenuation takes place at a rate of so many decibels (dBs) per octave: most synthesizers use filters with a 24dB/octave response, so that a frequency an octave from the

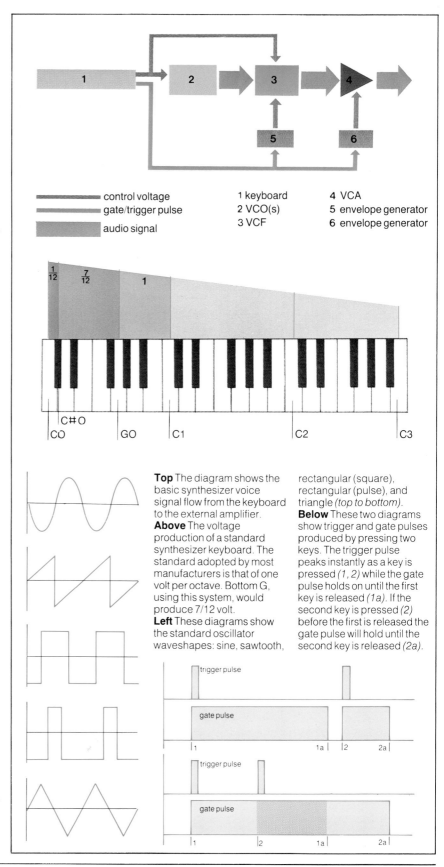

control voltage
gate/trigger pulse
audio signal

1 keyboard   4 VCA
2 VCO(s)   5 envelope generator
3 VCF   6 envelope generator

Top The diagram shows the basic synthesizer voice signal flow from the keyboard to the external amplifier.
Above The voltage production of a standard synthesizer keyboard. The standard adopted by most manufacturers is that of one volt per octave. Bottom G, using this system, would produce 7/12 volt.
Left These diagrams show the standard oscillator waveshapes: sine, sawtooth, rectangular (square), rectangular (pulse), and triangle (top to bottom).
Below These two diagrams show trigger and gate pulses produced by pressing two keys. The trigger pulse peaks instantly as a key is pressed (1, 2) while the gate pulse holds on until the first key is released (1a). If the second key is pressed (2) before the first is released the gate pulse will hold until the second key is released (2a).

Left The latest Moog synthesizer is the Source, Moog's first programmable. A monophonic instrument, the Source has new forms of control parameters. A touch panel allows the player to select functions which are displayed in the digital readouts on the left and are stored in the instrument's memory, which can store and recall 16 presets.
Below left The Roland SH2000 has preset tabs which give simulations of acoustic instruments at a flick.

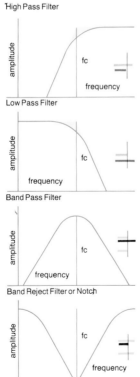

High Pass Filter

Low Pass Filter

Band Pass Filter

Band Reject Filter or Notch

Above The four types of voltage controlled filters: "fc" indicates filter cut-off frequency.

cut-off frequency would be 24dB quieter.

Filters vary from synthesizer to synthesizer but almost all synthesizers have a low pass filter, with a voltage controlled cut-off frequency. Some instruments have a state variable filter, a filter that can operate in any of the four main modes. Another variable is the resonance of the filter which will cause an increase in amplitude at the filter cut-off frequency. By increasing the filter's resonance, the increase in amplitude at the cut-off frequency can become so great that the filter oscillates, producing a pure sine wave. The VCFs found on most synthesizers receive the control voltage from the keyboard so that the filter's cut-off frequency follows the pitch of the oscillator. If this voltage is used when the reso-nance is causing oscillation, it is possible to actually "play" the filter.

Every manufacturer uses a slightly different filter design and consequently instruments vary in tonal quality. Japanese synthesizers sound more nasal than Western machines.

Low Frequency Oscillator
In addition to the signal generating oscillators (VCOs), a synthesizer has a low frequency mod-ulation oscillator, which usually is not voltage-controllable. Occasionally, as with the Mini-moog, one of the signal VCOs can be switched down to the sub-audio frequencies and can be used as a modulation oscillator. Generally these oscillators operate at a frequency below the threshold of hearing. The waveshapes produced by this oscillator can be used to modulate the frequencies of the VCO(s) and/or the filter and, in some cases, the shape of the pulse wave. These waveshapes are normally sine (or sometimes triangle), square, and occasionally a random signal for special "spacy" effects. A sine wave frequency modulation of the oscillators is better known as vibrato, and a square wave modula-tion produces a trill effect. If a sine wave is used for pulse width modulation, the sound becomes much fuller, as if the waveform were being fed through a chorus unit. Some less expensive units with a single VCO use pulse width modulation as a substitute for the second oscillator, but the

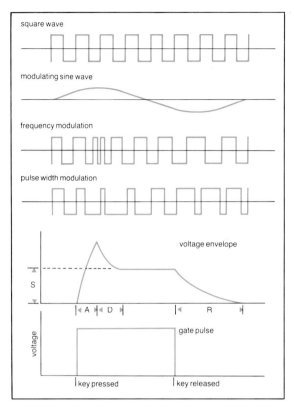

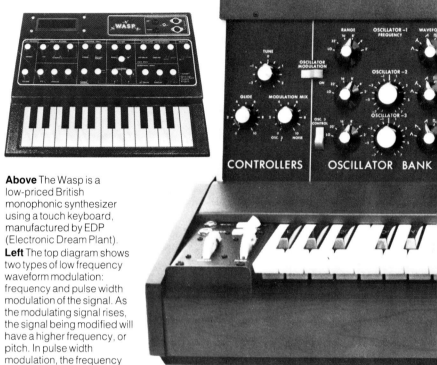

Above The Wasp is a low-priced British monophonic synthesizer using a touch keyboard, manufactured by EDP (Electronic Dream Plant).
Left The top diagram shows two types of low frequency waveform modulation: frequency and pulse width modulation of the signal. As the modulating signal rises, the signal being modified will have a higher frequency, or pitch. In pulse width modulation, the frequency remains the same, but the balance between the peaks and troughs in the signal is altered, creating a different tone similar to a chorus effect. The diagrams below show the ADSR envelope: attack time, decay time, sustain voltage level and release time.

effect is not quite the same. Modulation is often introduced by means of a performance control.

The Noise Generator

An additional sound generator can be found on most synthesizers: the noise source. White and pink noise are the two types generally encountered. White noise is considered to be a random mixture of frequencies right across the audio spectrum, sounding like radio static with a continuous hissing quality to it. Pink noise is white noise with the bass frequencies boosted.

Audio Mixer

The signals from the tone and noise generators are mixed together before being processed further. This is usually achieved by either a separate volume control for every waveshape and noise source output, or by means of a separate level control for each oscillator, and one for the noise source. In some cases there is just a switch for each oscillator.

The Envelope Shaper or Generator

The function of the envelope shaper is to shape the amplitude of the note (when used in conjunction with the voltage controlled amplifier) and to vary the filtering (if necessary) during the course of a note. A synthesizer must have at least one envelope generator, in which case this is shared with the filter and voltage controlled amplifier; otherwise, there are two separate circuits. The envelope generator is fired by the trigger or gate pulse produced by the keyboard.

There are several different types of envelope generator, but the most common are the ADS (attack, decay, sustain) and ADSR (attack, decay, sustain, release) configurations. The ADS generator produces a rising waveshape, whose rise time depends on the attack control setting. When this reaches a maximum level, the voltage drops back to a rate dependent on the decay control, until it reaches the set sustain level, where the voltage remains until the key is released. It then dies away at the decay rate. The ADSR envelope performs in almost the same way except the release time can be different from the decay time.

When used with the filter, the envelope generator produces a control voltage that changes the cut-off frequency. This results in that characteristic *wah* sound that seems to have become synonymous with the synthesizer. However, this facility can be used to much wider effect to create harmonic percussion simulations for organ voices or brass sounds; by sweeping a ringing (that is, oscillating) filter, it is possible to simulate a drum sound. This percussion simulation provides the well-known disco drum sound that is a feature of so many disco records.

The Voltage Controlled Amplifier
The VCA is purely an electronic element that varies the amplitude of the signal from the filter in proportion to the voltage derived from the envelope generator. It controls the loudness of the sound. The greater the control voltage the greater the amplitude of the signal output, which is subsequently fed to an external amplifier and speaker.

Performance Controls
Performance controls are really the most important feature of any electronic music synthesizer, especially for traditional players, yet they are often overlooked or treated as a luxury. A performance control makes it easy to change the characteristics of a note while it is actually sounding. This allows the player to inject expression and feeling into the music. Most synthesizers have a series of controls to allow changes to be made quickly and accurately.

These controls are mainly used for pitchbend and low frequency modulation of the oscillators. (Pitchbend alters the pitch of the note.) It is also important to be able to control the release time of the envelope shapers easily. This function often takes the form of a switch that sets the release time to almost zero, killing the amplitude of a note as soon as it is released. Other controls can include a glide rate control, which

Above Probably the most popular monophonic synthesizer ever produced, the classic Minimoog was in production from 1971 to 1981.

introduces an element of slew between notes (instead of the control voltage from the keyboard jumping to the level of the next key played, it will glide or sweep at a set rate), and a control for the output volume.

Manufacturers have developed many different performance control mechanisms, but the most popular ones are wheels, the lever, the joystick, the strip, touch-sensitive keyboards and pressure pads. Where wheels are used there are normally two, one for pitchbend and one for modulation. Examples are the Minimoog and Sequential Circuits Prophet 5. The Roland Jupiter 4 and most other Roland products have a single lever for pitchbend. The joystick is a single control for both pitchbend and modulation; it can be found on the Korg PS 3200. A more musical control is the strip which is used primarily for pitchbend. This raises or lowers the pitch depending on the point where it is touched. Rocking one's finger on the strip gives a vibrato effect. Examples include the Yamaha CS 80 and the Micromoog.

Many instruments have a keyboard that can produce a control voltage which varies according to how the key is placed. There are two main types of touch-sensitive keyboards: pressure-sensitive (or force-sensitive) and velocity-sensitive. The former produces a control voltage that varies according to how hard the key is pressed. Velocity-sensitive keyboards include circuitry which actually times how fast the key is depressed and produces a control voltage proportional to this period. These voltages can then perform the functions of pitchbend, modulation and even amplitude control. Examples include the Yamaha CS 80 and the Multimoog. Pressure pads are similar to touch-sensitive keyboards. They produce a control voltage proportional to the force applied to them. There are normally three pads: two for pitchbend and one for modulation. The ARP Odyssey incorporates pressure pads.

Keyboard Synthesizers
Monophonic
Monophonic instruments generate only one set of control and trigger voltages which are used to drive a single "voice". In other words, only one note can be played at a time. There are several different types of monophonic synthesizers.

Fully variables are instruments that have the basic VCO-VCF-VCA signal flow already connected internally, but the player still has access to all the controls so a sound can be built up from scratch. These instruments are most useful for recording, where quick sound changes are not required. Examples include the Minimoog,

A selection of synthesizers:
the Korg Micro preset (1);
the ARP Odyssey (2); the
Roland modular system (3).
Right Captain (Brian) Eno in
1973, using a VCS3 fully
variable modular system,
manufactured by the British
company EMS.

Above The control panel of the Prophet 5, the first programmable polyphonic voice assignable synthesizer, which was introduced in 1977 and is very popular for stage use. The controls are *(left to right)* the modulation section, routing and low frequency oscillator; the voltage controlled oscillators; audio mixer; voltage controlled filters and filter envelope; the voltage controlled amplifier and loudness envelope. The programmer section runs along the bottom.

Yamaha CS 30, Roland SH 2, ARP Odyssey, and Sequential Circuits Pro-One.

Used almost exclusively in the studio, modular instruments are the most versatile monophonics and consist of interchangeable units (VCOs, VCFs and so on) each performing a certain function. These modules have to be linked together, normally by "patch cords", and it is time consuming to set up a particular sound. However, this is compensated by the extreme versatility of the instrument. The original synthesizers from Moog and the first ARP (the 2500) were of modular design; others include the Moog Series 55 and the Roland 100 M System. Modular synthesizers normally either include, or are used with, an analog sequencer.

The preset synthesizer is primarily used as an imitative device. The voicing is preprogrammed and there are very few front panel controls, except a series of buttons or switches that are used to select a certain sound. These models do employ the traditional circuitry, but in most cases this is not apparent externally. The Kawai 100P and Korg Sigma are presets.

The programmable synthesizer combines the versatility of the fully variable with the ease of use of the preset. A series of different voicings can be recorded in a digital memory, normally designed so that the voicings are retained when the power is turned off. Examples include the Oberheim OB-1A and Roland Promars.

Voice Assignable Polyphonic
Polyphonic instruments can sound several notes simultaneously. In most cases the controls on the front panel are common to all voices, that is, all the notes, although pitched differently, will have the same timbre and envelopes. There are exceptions – the Oberheim four- and eight-voice synthesizers have separate, programmable controls for each voice. Several duophonic (two voices) instruments exist (for example, Yamaha CS 40M), but most polyphonic instruments offer four-, five-, six-, seven-, eight-, ten- or 16-voice complements.

There are only two main types of homogeneous voice assignable polyphonic instruments – programmable and preset. Because it is quite a complex business decoding which voice should be assigned to which key, most of the multiphonic instruments use a microprocessor (a small computer) system which gives the designer the ability to include, at little extra cost, programmability, or preset features. Duophonic instruments take advantage of two of the priority systems used with monophonics to assign the two voices. One voice takes a low note priority, the other a high.

Polyphonic programmable synthesizers have become some of the most popular instruments of the past few years. They are particularly sought after because they provide a manageable alternative to playing many different keyboards. The Sequential Circuits Prophet 5, which appeared at the end of 1977 did more to popularize the synthesizer in live performance than any other instrument, and with the recent emergence of the dual manual Prophet 10, the multiphonic synthesizer has really come of age.

At the lower end of the market notable developments include the Casiotone range of preset polyphonics. Casio's range of products use a "consonance/vowel" system – for simulating existing instruments the voicing is constructed in two parts: the attack, or consonance, and the body, or vowel.

Fully Polyphonic

The fully polyphonic synthesizers rely considerably on electronic organ technology. They employ either one or two master tone generators, which are divided to provide pitches for every note. The Korg PS range of polyphonic synthesizers have two sets of 12 voltage controlled top octave generators which are further divided to produce the pitches for the lower octaves. The advantage of this system is that pitches in the same octave are not phase-related; the sound is livelier, and acoustically more authentic.

An instrument with two independent pitches per note (voice), provides a fuller, warmer sound, and a far greater range of capabilities. Consequently, many fully polyphonic instruments are designed with two channels of tone generators that can be varied independently. Once the pitches have been produced, they have to be filtered and shaped.

Moog, in their Polymoog, provided the first custom integrated circuits to be used in a synthesizer. Each of these chips the size of a thumbnail contained the bulk of the circuitry needed to filter and shape the sound produced by each note. Under each key sat a small circuit card containing a chip and its associated circuitry. Without such a development the Polymoog would probably have been twice the size (and the price). The output from the chips were then mixed together, and fed to a master filter and on to the output.

Because they require considerable circuit repetition, fully polyphonics find it difficult to compete with the polyphonic voice assignables in terms of cost and features. But the fact that many musicians need to have more notes at their disposal than the polyphonics can offer – particularly for long sustained runs – ensures a future for the fully polyphonic instrument.

Digitals and Computer-based Instruments

These are the boom instruments of the 1980s but they are still very expensive. There are two types of computer-based instrument: those producing actual voltage waveforms from digital codes – direct synthesis; and those using the computer to produce the various control signals that are used to construct a signal from series of pure sine waves – additive synthesis. Many polyphonic voice assignable instruments use forms of computer control, but they are limited by the design of the computer software (the instructions that

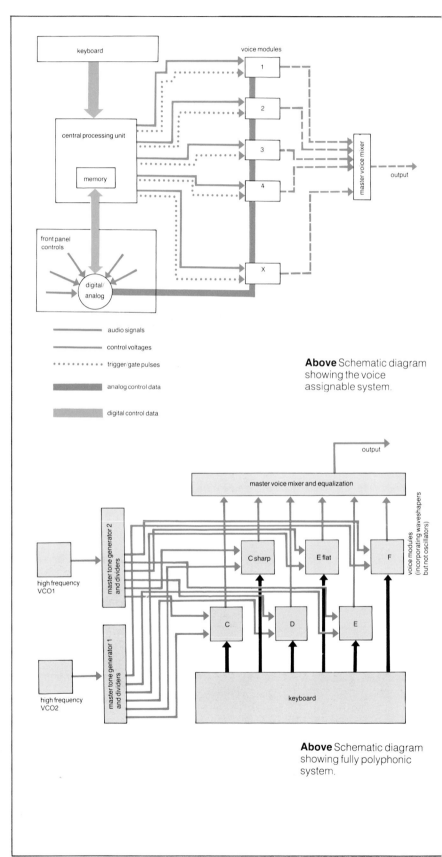

Above Schematic diagram showing the voice assignable system.

Above Schematic diagram showing fully polyphonic system.

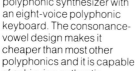

Left The Casio CT 401 is a polyphonic synthesizer with an eight-voice polyphonic keyboard. The consonance-vowel design makes it cheaper than most other polyphonics and it is capable of achieving authentic sounds.
Below The Polymoog is fully polyphonic and has the first custom integrated circuits to be used in a synthesizer. The pedal unit provides performance controls.
Bottom The Korg PS 3300 is a polyphonic synthesizer with a detachable keyboard: it has been used by Keith Emerson.

tell the computer what to do). More advanced systems give the musician almost complete freedom to construct a piece of music.

A typical computer system has a standard keyboard with the contacts arranged to produce a digital code, a keyboard like a typewriter for talking to the computer (sometimes replaced by a bank of control knobs and switches), a VDU (visual display unit) for programming, and some form of data storage system, normally a floppy disc unit. Examples of these instruments include the Fairlight CMI, Synclavier from New England Digital Inc. and the GDS (General Development System) from Crumar.

String Synthesizers and Pseudo Polyphonics
Electronic instrument designers have made countless attempts over the years to simulate a string section. Many of these attempts were very successful but it was not until the late 1960s that a good commercial string simulator became available. This was the Freeman String Synthesizer, an instrument that produced some of the most refreshing electronic renditions of string sections ever heard. Unfortunately, this instrument did not stay in production for long but it did open the way for many new models.

A string synthesizer is normally a fully polyphonic keyboard instrument producing either one or two channels of sawtooth waveforms. These are usually filtered passively (without a voltage controlled filter) and then the amplitude is shaped. The instrument is less complicated than the fully polyphonic and is designed to do just one main task – produce a good faithful string sound.

The Solina is probably the most popular string machine. It was originally manufactured by MCH in Holland, then the design was licensed to ARP and the machine appeared in the United States as the ARP String Ensemble. Today, however, the polyphonic synthesizer has taken over from the string machine and can, in most cases, produce just as faithful a simulation.

The trend today is moving toward the pseudo polyphonic synthesizer which can produce a range of orchestral sounds at a reasonable cost. This is usually achieved by having a single master filter rather than a separate VCF for each note. The major limitation with this system is that the filter can only be modulated by one waveform, so every note has to share the same filter contour. To alleviate this problem, a system of multiple or single triggering is employed. Multiple triggering causes the envelope of the filter to be fired every time a key is pressed, while single triggering requires all notes to be released before a trigger can be generated by any newly

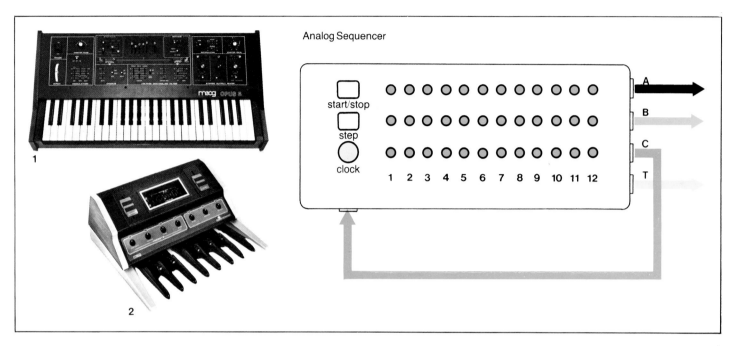

Analog Sequencer

depressed key. In addition to orchestral voicings, some pseudo polyphonics have a fully variable synthesizer section using the pitches generated for the other voicings. Although this section offers a full polyphonic complement of notes, it is necessary, for reasons of cost, to assign these pitches to only one VCF (rather than one for each note). The ARP Omni II, Roland RS 505, Moog Opus 3 and Yamaha SK 20 are examples of pseudo polyphonics.

Sequencers

A sequencer provides control voltages and gate pulses for driving a synthesizer voice module, and can be used as an alternative to, or in conjunction with, the instrument's keyboard. A series of notes are programmed into the unit, which can then be replayed at varying speeds, in different ways or with different voicings. This makes the sequencer ideal for live performance. The sequencer is normally used for bass patterns, rhythmic backing, or for a melody line. There are two types: analog and digital.

The analog sequencer consists of several rows of control knobs, usually arranged in columns of three, and rows of 12 or 16. Each row represents a step or musical note. The sequencer looks at the three control knobs in turn and feeds the voltage levels set, into the synthesizer. The pitch is usually controlled with one channel; the cutoff frequency or amplitude with the second; and the third channel is fed back into the sequencer's voltage controllable step pulse generator, to set the duration of each note. Each make of sequencer varies in capacity and facilities but they

Above left The recent Moog Opus 3 *(1)* is a pseudo polyphonic which includes string, organ and brass sections and can produce a reasonably full sound. The Moog Taurus *(2)* is one of the few pedal synthesizers. It was originally part of the Constellation polyphonic programmable synthesizer.
Above right Schematic diagram of an analog sequencer. Channel A goes to the VCOs; B to the VCFs and C to the sequencer's voltage controlled clock. T is the trigger pulse.

all fulfil the same basic task. The Korg SQ 10 and the ARP Sequencer are both analog sequencers.

Instead of programming each note step by step, the digital sequencer operates somewhat like a tape recorder. A sequence is played on the keyboard of the synthesizer and fed into the sequencer's memory; this sequence can then be played back at different rates and transposed into different keys. Polyphonic digital sequencers are just starting to come onto the market but these are only compatible with certain polyphonic instruments. The Microcomposer (MC 8) manufactured by Roland, employs techniques used by both the analog and digital sequencers. It is a polyphonic digital machine programmed by a series of buttons. Voltages and gate pulses are recorded digitally, step-by-step, to give a complex, but accurate sound. This unit is designed to be used in conjunction with a modular synthesizer.

The analog sequencer has several advantages over the digital. Parameters other than pitch can be programmed, it is easier to edit a sequence and overall the instrument is more versatile. However, the digital sequencer can store a far greater number of notes, and can be programmed very quickly.

Other Synthesizer Controllers

Although the keyboard is the main control medium used for the synthesizer, there are other devices that produce (or can be made to produce) the necessary control voltage and trigger pulses for driving the conventional synthesizer module. There are also several hybrid instru-

(the ARP Avatar and 360 Systems Spectre) which produce a single control signal for driving a synthesizer module, to hexaphonic devices with six separate voice modules, one for each string. Some guitar synthesizers require a special custom guitar, others use a special pickup that can be attached to an existing instrument, but with the possible exceptions of the Roland GR 300 and the more recent GR 100, no single type of guitar synthesizer has captured the market's attention. Because the guitar is such an expressive instrument, it seems unlikely that the guitar synthesizer is ever going to amount to much more than an upmarket effects unit.

Pedal Synthesizers
The only major difference between pedal synthesizers and monophonic keyboard synthesizers is that pedal synthesizers sit on the floor and are played with the foot. The pedalboard is normally a 13-note C-to-C type, either preset or preset/programmable. These instruments are used as often by guitarists as keyboard players, and can provide an extremely powerful bass backing. The Moog Taurus, the most popular synthesizer pedal unit, is used extensively by Genesis and The Police.

Drum Synthesizers
Drummers are often wary of venturing into non-acoustic areas. The drum synthesizer, however, has generated an interest in electric drums, even though the persistent use of a certain sound on almost all disco records (a sine wave swept down) betrays this innate conservatism. Drum synthesizers can achieve much more than this particular sound but the fact that they require some form of amplification tends to dissuade some drummers from using them. A typical drum synthesizer produces a control voltage proportional to the force with which the drum is struck, together with a trigger pulse, to drive a synthesizer module. Any drum synthesizer must have an adequate dynamic range – it is important for a drummer to be able to vary the device's output from a tap to a good thump. The appearance of such models as the Simmons SDS V electronic drumkit brings closer the day when electronic kits can replace acoustic instruments, especially since cymbals as well as drums can now be simulated.

Wind Synthesizers
The wind synthesizer is one of the more workable alternatives to the keyboard as a control medium. Not only can a monophonic control voltage be produced easily by switches located in the conventional fingerhole positions, but by

Above Chris Franke, synthesist with the German group Tangerine Dream is shown here surrounded by various synthesizers, including a Prophet 5, Elka 6, Korg polyphonic ensemble, a Minimoog and a customized modular system. **Left** The Yellow Magic Orchestra, a Japanese synthesizer band formed in 1978, are now Japan's top album sellers. The group uses a Roland MC8 computer on stage and play a variety of synthesizers including a Prophet 5, a Polymoog, an ARP Odyssey and Oberheim eight-voice synthesizers.

ments that use unique forms of voice generation that fall under the general heading of synthesizer.

Guitar Synthesizers
More time and money has been spent trying to produce a synthesizer that will appeal to guitarists, than has been spent on any other form of alternative controller. Designing a guitar synthesizer presents complex technical problems. It is necessary to produce a control signal that will track subtle effects achieved by bending the strings and damping the action, and which will also follow fast runs.

Guitar synthesizers range from monophonics

lar compositions played entirely on one of Moog's first modular synthesizers. Carlos' success spawned many imitators but none, with the possible exception of Tomita, approached the same degree of success. Isao Tomita, the Japanese synthesist, is famed for his version of classical pieces realized on the synthesizer, but these works are far more loosely based on the original scores; this is particularly noticeable on the album *Snowflakes Are Dancing*, where Tomita creates some beautiful versions of Debussy's tone poems.

The keyboard player Keith Emerson pioneered the live use of the synthesizer. His modular system was specially built for him by Moog. With the help of his friend Mike Vickers, who crouched down beside the instrument and reprogrammed and retuned it during the show, Emerson managed to incorporate the synthesizer into his live act.

The early synthesizers had terrible tuning problems. At that time, one of these machines caused enough worries and the notion of an all-synthesizer live band was out of the question. As technology advanced, the instruments became more stable and reliable. Tangerine Dream took advantage of these innovations and became the best-known of the German synthesizer bands. Tangerine Dream's album *Phaedra* is the most popular example of their music. Kraftwerk, also from Germany, utilize synthesizers in a somewhat more mechanical manner to capture the industrial mood of the twentieth century. This is reflected in such compositions as *Autobahn* and *Pocket Calculator*.

Nearly all the better known rock and jazz-rock keyboard players have used the synthesizer, some more successfully than others. George Duke is well-respected for his technique and precise use of the performance controls.

The early and rather unmusical exploits of Captain Eno of Roxy Music, with his VCS 3 synthesizer, have evolved into some of the most interesting forms of electronic music of the past few years. Brian Eno, as he is now known, has grown up with the synthesizer, and has become one of the first true synthesists, as opposed to a keyboard player using a synthesizer.

Over the past three or four years, the synthesizer has been taking over from the guitar as the frontline instrument of many bands. The success of bands such as Ultravox, Gary Numan, Yellow Magic Orchestra, Devo, The Human League and Orchestral Manoeuvres In The Dark, show that the synthesizer has become an essential instrument in a rock band, rather than the keyboard player's answer to the guitarist's foot pedal.

using a wind sensor, the performance control parameters, such as pitchbend, amplitude and modulation, can be controlled by the way in which the instrument is blown. Although the wind synthesizer makes no acoustic sound, the sensing devices in the mouthpiece make the instrument most expressive. The best known wind synthesizer is the Lyricon.

Above Keith Emerson switched allegiance from Moog to Korg and is now a Korg endorsee. Emerson was one of the first players to use a Moog modular system on stage as a member of The Nice in the late 1960s.

Mobile Synthesizers
Keyboard players have always wanted to move around on stage. Many players, including Jan Hammer, have removed the keyboard from their synthesizers and strapped it round their necks. George Duke even had built a specially designed keyboard controller (the Clavitar) so that he could play his ARP Odyssey and Minimoog by remote control. More recently, several manufacturers have developed special mobile synthesizers. Moog have introduced an instrument known as the Liberation which weighs just 14 pounds, yet consists of a keyboard and all the controls found on a conventional synthesizer; the performance controls are conveniently positioned on the neck of the instrument, giving it the appearance of a guitar with a keyboard. Other keyboard controllers that can be worn include the Keytar and the Syntar.

Use in Rock
The one person who did most to promote the synthesizer as a musical instrument was Walter Carlos. His 1968 album *Switched On Bach* consisted of renditions of some of Bach's most popu-

EFFECTS UNITS

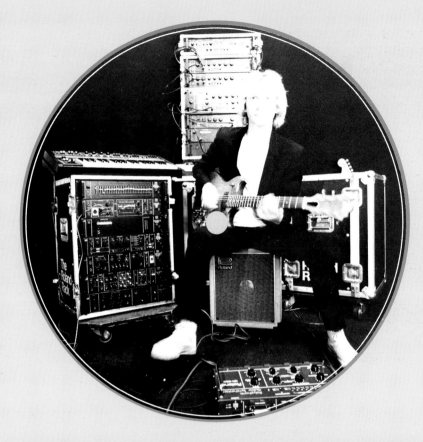

Effects units both widen the range of sounds which can be obtained from instruments and amplifiers and give musicians additional control over the type of sound they wish to produce. Basically, they work by degrading or enhancing the original sound, either mechanically, or, more usually, electronically.

On stage, effects can be seen spread across the floor at the feet of guitarists and keyboard players, small boxes or boards operated by footswitches, pedals or a combination of these. For live performances, effects can either be directly controlled by the musicians or linked to the mixing desk and operated by the sound engineer. In the second case, they usually will be the rack-mounted type found in studios.

Stage effects have many creative and original uses. Most importantly, they enable players to produce distinctive, individual sounds. They can also add interest and variety to live performances and help to recreate the type of sounds that can be obtained in the recording studio: indeed, many effects units have evolved directly from studio techniques. No doubt effects also come in handy to disguise bad playing; strategic use of phasing, for example, can give an inexperienced guitarist extra time to hunt for the next chord. But although this type of use has given effects a bad reputation in some circles, and purists may dismiss them as gimmicky toys, effects do provide the opportunity to experiment with many different types of sound.

Technology has been responsible for many changes in effects unit design since the days of the battery-powered tin box which could be noisier to operate than the effect it created. Today, most units are fairly sophisticated and can incorporate the latest in electronic gadgetry. It is worth bearing in mind that manufacturers often give their effects units misleading names; this is not helped by the fact that such effects as echo and reverberation are very similar and often confused.

Echo and Delay

Echo has been used for centuries as a form of voice enhancement both by Alpine yodelers and church-going hymn singers, and naturally enough musicians wanted to recreate that sound on stage. Various methods were found to produce reverberation effects (a continuous indistinct repeat sound), including the spring and plate devices still in use today, but for distinct echo sounds, tape recorders were found to be most effective. Using a tape loop passing the record and playback heads it was possible to create very clear and accurate repeats of the original signal and purpose-built devices soon became available for live performances.

To create an echo a live signal is recorded on one track of a multitrack tape recorder and then fed back from the playback head onto the second track and recorded there. Each time the signal passes playback it diminishes, so the echo dies away gradually. The delay is the distance between the two heads.

The best early machines were the WEM Copicat and the Maestro Echoplex, both of which are still in use today, the latter continuing to find favor with professionals like Ry Cooder and Gary Moore. The main advantage of tape machines is that the quality of the delayed signal is good, while disadvantages include the need for regular head cleaning and tape replacement,

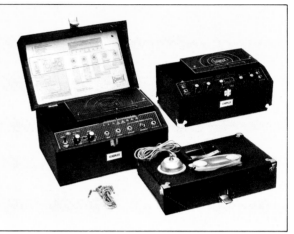

Right The Maestro Echoplex is a good quality echo chamber still in use today despite competition from modern analog and digital echo units. The models shown are the EP3 *(left)* and EP4 *(right)*.

and the possibility of the loop breaking in mid-gig. However this good quality prompts many top professionals to stay with tape machines rather than switch to the modern analog or digital versions. Japanese companies like Roland and Korg now produce tape machines which incorporate many up-to-date facilities. The Roland Space Echo RE-201 has become very much the standard professional tape echo chamber while Korg's machine, called the Stage Echo, is used live by bands like Wishbone Ash.

As well as repeat echoes, tape machines also give that close, single, "slap-back" effect which

Above The first WEM Copicat echo unit appeared in 1954; subsequent models have been in popular use since the early 1960s. The Copicat is a tape machine using a continuous loop of tape.

Right The American manufacturer MXR make a range of effects units including footswitch types for phasing, flanging, delay, chorus and distortion.

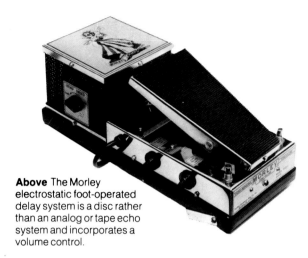

Above The Morley electrostatic foot-operated delay system is a disc rather than an analog or tape echo system and incorporates a volume control.

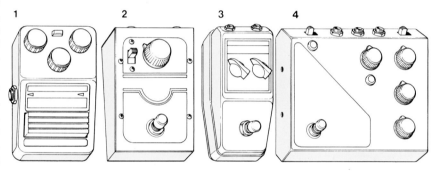

can be heard on many early rock and roll numbers, for example Elvis Presley's *Heartbreak Hotel*. Tape machines can even tackle reverb, but because of their mechanical limitations (the distance between heads) they cannot achieve the short delay times that are available on analog and digital machines.

Analog machines use electronic circuitry to store the signal for the prescribed delay time and then release it to produce repeat echo, delay, and reverb effects. Unfortunately, the longer the delay, the lower the quality of the delayed signal. At the other end of the scale, however, analogs can produce short delay times. These short delays can give a double-voice, or automatic double tracking (ADT) effect; that is, the effect of two people playing or singing in unison. Some devices, like the Bell Electolabs Automatic Double Tracker or the Yamaha E1005 can add pitch modulation to the double-voice effect to give the sound more body. This is known as "true" ADT. Analog delays come in two distinct varieties: footswitch pedals such as the MXR or the Carlsbro Echo, and box-type units produced mainly in Japan by Roland, Ibanez and Evans, amongst others.

Digital delay lines use computer technology to convert the input signal into digital "words", which allows for longer storage time without a drastic drop in quality. Because the cost of all this sophistication is high, units such as the MXR Digital Delay tend to be used mainly on PA rigs and by top players. Stuart Copeland of The Police uses a couple of DDLs on stage to achieve complex drum rhythms and repeat hold effects.

Fuzz

While those early rock singers were echoing their way to fame and fortune, guitarists were cranking up their old tube amps in an attempt to be heard at the back of the hall. Overdriving

Top Spencer Davis formed the original Spencer Davis Group in 1963 and the band rose to fame in the mid-1960s with hits like *Keep On Running* and *Gimme Some Lovin'* featuring the vocals and fuzz-laden keyboard playing of the young Stevie Winwood. Winwood left in 1967 to form Traffic and Davis *(center)* went on to reform the group several times.
Above 1. Guyatone analog echo unit.
2. Used by Hendrix and Carlos Santana, the Little Big Muff is a sustain unit with harmonic distortion control.
3. A standard foot-operated fuzz unit, the Jen Fuzz.
4. The Electro-Harmonix Memory Man is an electronic echo unit which can produce slap-back echo, repeat arpeggios and delayed split stereo.

the amp caused tube distortion which in turn produced a warm, gritty sound rich in harmonic overtones. This distinctive effect became very popular and musicians soon wanted to achieve the same distortion at lower volumes or with a transistorized amp.

In the early 1960s Gary Hurst of Sola Sound designed and built the Tone Bender fuzz box which was used by Jeff Beck for the first time on the 1965 Yardbirds' single, *Heart Full of Soul*. Sola Sound claim that this was the first-ever footswitch-type effects box. Later, Jimi Hendrix made considerable use of the Electro-Harmonix Big Muff distortion pedal for fuzz and sustain (holding the note) effects, but it was Eric Clapton's guitar work on such Cream recordings as *Sunshine Of Your Love* and *Politician* that did most to popularize the sound.

Early fuzz boxes broke up the signal and produced an extremely coarse sound but most modern units can be adjusted to emulate more closely the effect of an overdriven tube amp. Boss make separate fuzz and overdrive pedals for these two effects. Most other manufacturers produce footswitch distortion boxes but Boss and Morley also make treadle-operated types, called Rocker Distortion and Power Wah Fuzz.

Although fuzz is sometimes used with electric organs to achieve the type of rough sound Stevie Winwood produced on the Spencer Davis Group's *Gimme Some Lovin'*, fuzz is predominantly a guitarist's effect that is still used extensively today by exponents of heavy metal rock.

Wah-Wah

Wah-wah is also very much a guitarist's tool, and came to the fore at much the same time as fuzz, but it is hardly ever used nowadays. These treadle-operated pedals simply change the tone of the guitar's sound from muted (heel down), to a crisp bright treble (toe down) and can be used in rhythm to accentuate the beat, or as a means of making the guitar "sing".

Jimi Hendrix was almost single-handedly responsible for popularizing the wah-wah, and the album *Electric Ladyland* is full of prime examples, especially such tracks as *Burning Of The Midnight Lamp*, *Voodoo Chile* and *Still Raining Still Dreaming*. The wah-wah can also create that unique sound featured on the theme music to the film *Shaft*, when damped guitar strings are struck percussively as the pedal is rocked rapidly back and forth.

The most popular wah-wah is undoubtedly the Jen Cry Baby but others are available from Morley, Ibanez, Boss and Colorsound. Other manufacturers like MXR, Vox and Hohner have utilized the envelope filter circuitry used in synthesizers to create automatic wah footswitch pedals, the wah being triggered by the plucking of the string and the length of the effect being dependent on the force used. Names for these devices include Envelope Filter, Wah, and Instant Funk.

Voice Boxes

The talking sounds that Jeff Beck's guitar makes on *She's A Woman* or Pete Frampton produces on the album *Frampton Comes Alive* are the product of exotic pieces of equipment such as the Electro-Harmonix Golden Throat or the Ibanez VOC Talking Machine, known collectively as voice boxes or voice tubes. The guitar is plugged into the box which then sends the signal up a flexible tube attached to the microphone stand. With the end of the tube in his mouth the guitarist can modulate the sound vocally and the effect is picked up by the microphone. Again, manufacturers have used electronics to produce neat footswitch or treadle-operated pedals known as vowel sound boxes. The Electro-Harmonix Talking Pedal and the Colorsound Vocalizer create A-E-I-O-U noises from the guitar when the treadle is set at different positions.

Above Steve Hackett joined influential group Genesis in 1971 and was their guitarist for some time until leaving to pursue a solo career. He is shown here on stage using a variety of effects and an original Roland GR 500 guitar synthesizer.

Phasing and Flanging

In the late 1950s, during the recording of the theme music for the film *The Big Hurt*, another strange effect was stumbled upon. This discovery was not made use of until much later in 1967, when the recording engineers at Olympic studios set up the effect using two tape machines. The subsequent recording caused something of a stir. The record was The Small Faces' *Itchycoo Park* and "phasing" entered rock's vocabulary.

Those sweeping sounds are the product of phase cancellation, a phenomenon that occurs when two identical signals recorded on two separate tapes are mixed. When one of these signals is delayed by varying amounts (tradition has it that this was originally achieved by slowing one tape recorder by hand pressure on the tape spool "flange"), a more exaggerated sweep is obtained, which has come to be known as flanging. (John Lennon supposedly referred to *all* George Martin's studio effects as "flanging".)

Progress in electronics has given rise to devices that comprise a collection of notch filters which, when swept up and down the audio frequencies, give automatic and easily repeatable phasing effects. These devices generally offer a variety of sounds from slow convoluting sweeps through to fast vibratos. In the mid-1970s, when the Electro-Harmonix Smallstone Phase Shifter was the bestselling device of its kind, phasing was very popular with guitarists and keyboard players alike. Brands like MXR, Boss, Dod and Ross are available today in footswitch pedal designs while Morley and Maestro offer phasers

Below British guitarist John Martyn is best known for his unique acoustic guitar playing. His jazz-influenced style was first apparent on *Bless The Weather* and later developed more fully on *Solid Air* and *Inside Out*. His style is based on his use of the acoustic guitar with an Echoplex to achieve repeat patterns and melodies. He is shown here playing a Martin acoustic and operating a pedalboard of effects built into a flight case.

with total foot control. A rack type called the 12 Stage Phaser is also available from Moog.

The basic difference between phaser and flanger devices is that the latter incorporate time delay circuitry to achieve the filtering effect. Hendrix numbers like *House Burning Down* and *Bold As Love* offer typical examples of that whooshing flanging sound and although the effect has been used for weird percussion and vocal sounds, it remains a guitarist's unit.

Morley make a treadle-operated flanger pedal; ordinary footswitch flangers are available from most other manufacturers, including Electro-Harmonix's exotically named Electric Mistress.

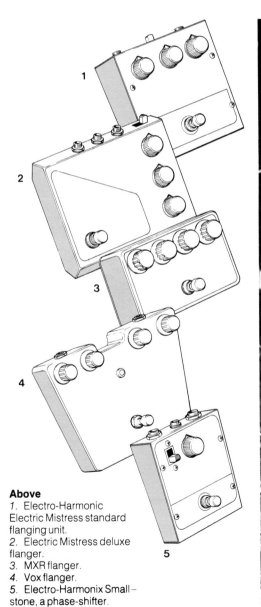

Above
1. Electro-Harmonic Electric Mistress standard flanging unit.
2. Electric Mistress deluxe flanger.
3. MXR flanger.
4. Vox flanger.
5. Electro-Harmonix Smallstone, a phase-shifter.

Chorus

The time delay circuitry on flangers will also produce vibrato and chorus effects. Chorus is used on a number of different instruments and has proved by far the most popular effect of recent years. The Police, The Pretenders and Roxy Music have all used chorus on record to give their six-string guitars that warm, jangly 12-string effect, while an electric bass can be encouraged to emulate the fluid sound of Jaco Pastorius' fretless playing that can be heard on Joni Mitchell and Weather Report recordings. Supertramp used chorus to give their Wurlitzer electric piano the special warmth it displays on *Breakfast In America* and this effect makes most other keyboards sound rich and full-bodied, too.

Most chorus pedals are footswitch types like the Boss Chorus CE1 (stereo) and CE2 (mono), the MXR Stereo Chorus, and the Ibanez CS-505, though Morley produce a switchable chorus/flanger treadle-operated unit.

Drum Machines

The drum machine or rhythm box has a mixed reputation; early models certainly did sound inhuman and mechanical and were not always used to satisfactory effect. However, in recent years, their precise rhythm patterns have formed integral parts of many recordings: Blondie's *Heart Of Glass, Delius* from Kate Bush's *Never For Ever* and *Same Old Song* from Roxy Music's *Flesh And Blood* album are good examples. Genesis not only used a drum machine on *Duke* but also took it on tour, while other bands such as Orchestral Manoeuvres In The Dark, The Human League and Ultravox have used them quite extensively live. The Police have used rhythm boxes as a guide for recording, then removed the sound from the final mix when the drum track has been laid down.

Drum machines are now extremely complex instruments and, with the addition of optional accents and fills, they sound much less clinical. The budget-priced Boss Dr. Rhythm even has its own microcomputer which can be programmed with different rhythm patterns for instant recall. At the other end of the market, the highly sophisticated Roland 808 and the Linn drum machine find favor with many top professionals. These machines are constantly changing and developing in complexity. There are many

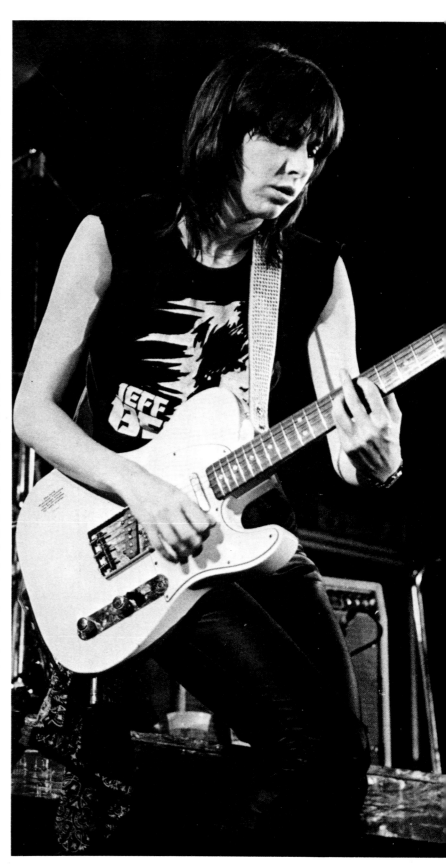

Right Chrissie Hynde of The Pretenders. The group have used chorus on their recordings to add warmth to the guitar sound.

Left Roxy Music's early albums were an interesting blend of Brian Ferry's witty, literate vocals, the avant-garde electronics of Eno's synthesizer work, the sax and oboe playing of Andy Mackay *(right)* and Phil Manzanera's *(left)* textured guitar sound. After Eno's departure, the band opted for a more straightforward commercial approach.

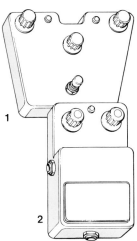

Left The Vox chorus pedal *(1)* is wedge-shaped so that it will fit into a semicircle when used with other Vox pedals. The Boss chorus pedal *(2)* is sturdily made and is fitted with non-mechanical switching which cuts out the thud when the unit is switched on.

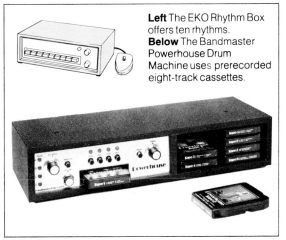

Left The EKO Rhythm Box offers ten rhythms.
Below The Bandmaster Powerhouse Drum Machine uses prerecorded eight-track cassettes.

keyboard-top models available from Roland and Korg. Less complex pedal units come from Electro-Harmonix and Colorsound. The Musicaid Clap Trap can simulate clapping and other percussive sounds; these effects can be triggered in a number of ways. Ultravox, 10cc, The Police and Status Quo are just a few of the bands who use the Clap Trap live.

Other Effects

The most basic effects unit is the volume or swell pedal, a simple treadle-operated volume control unit available from DeArmond, Morley and Colorsound, amongst others. In the toe-down position the volume can be adjusted to give a louder solo sound; the heel-down position reduces the level or fades the sound out completely. Other noise control pedals include the Noise Gate, which has no effect on actual playing, but cuts out background hiss and hum when you stop.

There are also a number of devices on the market for altering tone. Pedals like the Electro-Harmonix Hogs Foot and Screaming Tree are simply bass and treble boosters, while others like graphic and parametric equalizers are a little more complex. Graphic equalizers use slider controls to vary the intensity of frequency bands, while the relatively expensive parametric equalizers are more precise, allowing selection of the exact frequency and the most suitable bandwidth. Equalizers are basically more accurate forms of tone control; adjustment can be made to the sound at specific points. Carlsbro

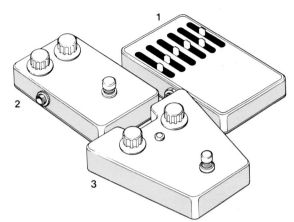

Left The MXR Graphic Equalizer (1) comes in six- and ten-band versions. The MXR Dyna-Comp (2) is used to smooth out instrument sounds. The Vox Compressor (3) is used for both evening out the signal and for sustain effects.
Below Lol Creme playing a Fender Stratocaster fitted with a Gizmotron, invented by Creme and fellow member of 10cc, Kevin Godley. The Gizmo works by bowing the strings of the guitar with six small wheels.

pert Pete Cornish has built pedalboards for Pink Floyd, Steve Hackett, and Andy Summers of The Police. Each board contains the favorite effects of the individual customer, without the drawbacks that separate units can create. Some musicians have even tried their hand at designing their own effects. The most notable attempt of recent years was Lol Creme and Kevin Godley's Gizmotron, a mechanical device that bows the strings of the guitar when a pushbutton selector is pressed. Used extensively on their album *Consequences*, the Gizmo can produce sustained violin sounds and many other effects, but it has yet to take the music world by storm.

makes footswitch pedal versions of both types, while Moog's graphic and parametric equalizers are both rack-mounting. Graphics are available from most other effects companies in either footswitch or rack design.

Compressor pedals are designed to even out the peaks and troughs in the signal, variations which are often caused by uneven guitar picking or varying output response on electric keyboards; they also add "punch". Some, like the MXR Dyna Comp and the Boss Compression Sustainer, can be adjusted to add distortion-free sustain, while others like the Vox Compressor or the Colorsound Supa Sustain offer these compression and sustain effects in separate packages.

Octave dividers are available from Colorsound (the Octivider) and Electro-Harmonix (the Octive Multiplexer) and can switch to a signal one octave below the one being played or sung. These units are very effective for guitar and bass duets. Electro-Harmonix also make a ring modulator pedal called the Frequency Analyser which splits the input signal into a triad of notes spaced at equal intervals; at the other end of the price scale, companies like MXR and Eventide produce rack-mounting pitch modulators and harmonizers that allow for all sorts of sophisticated harmony effects.

Hohner, Bell Electrolabs and Eurotec have all produced modular effects systems that have dispensed with the need for interconnecting leads. All the effects are powered by one mains unit. Many other companies produce pedals that contain up to three effects in one unit, for example the Colorsound Wah Fuzz Swell, while Ibanez make two rack-mounting units, the UE-400 and UE-700, that contain four or five effects and can be controlled by a footswitch.

Many musicians are now using rack systems that would be as much at home in the studio as on the road; others prefer to have custom pedalboards made for them. British electronics ex-

Left Manufacturers now produce effects pedals that can be clamped together to form a comprehensive pedalboard.

Below Guitarist Dave Gilmour of Pink Floyd has his own pedalboard custom-built by Pete Cornish which includes a variety of different effects from different manufacturers.

WOODWIND, BRASS AND STRINGS

The basic rock instruments are the electric guitar and bass, the drumkit and the electronic or electric keyboard, but this foundation has been built upon and decorated with various levels of instrumentation adapted from "non-rock" areas. These acoustic instruments adapted for rock are largely borrowed from the orchestra, and fall into two distinct categories – woodwind and brass, or strings.

The popular picture of rock would encourage the view that instruments like the saxophone, the flute and the violin are alien and even abhorrent to the average rock musician. In reality, rock is concerned about exploring different sounds, and in the recording studio the creative rock musician has often turned to these ostensibly "classical" instruments for a fresh-sounding flourish or a decorative solo.

In rock music, perhaps the most commonly used among these acoustic orchestral instruments are the saxophone and the violin. Other acoustic instruments adapted for rock include the harmonica which has seen wide use in rock and related music forms.

The Flute

The modern flute derives from various early one-note whistles which primitive people made from bones or pieces of wood. Today's instruments have developed from these, through recorders, pan pipes and fifes. Most earlier flutes were played vertically, held downward from the mouth, but the "sideways" flute began to gain popularity because of its greater volume and its corresponding application to more dynamic use.

The six- and eight-keyed wooden flutes of the eighteenth century led to the invention of the modern-style flute in 1847 by Theobald Boehm, a flute player and inventor from Munich. In 1832, Boehm had introduced a conical-bore flute with a new arrangement of holes and an original key and ring layout which required different fingering. His later design of 1847 is virtually the same as the flute used today, with a cylindrical bore and a parabolic head shape.

Although most modern flutes are made of metal (silver is claimed to sound better than the more expensive gold or the cheaper plated metals), Boehm's designs were initially found to

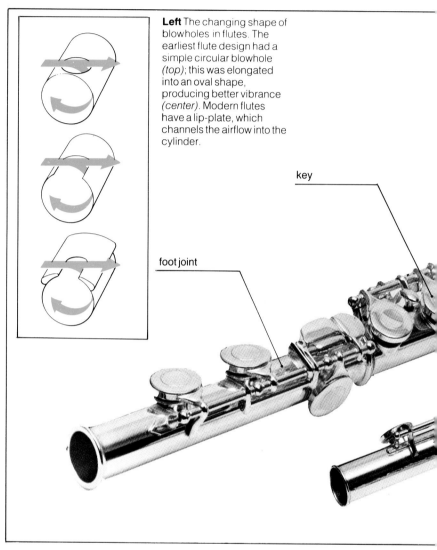

Left The changing shape of blowholes in flutes. The earliest flute design had a simple circular blowhole *(top)*; this was elongated into an oval shape, producing better vibrance *(center)*. Modern flutes have a lip-plate, which channels the airflow into the cylinder.

key

foot joint

Left Ian Anderson has been central to the English "progressive" rock group Jethro Tull, founded in 1968 Anderson's contribution as flute player is unusual, as this instrument is rarely seen outside studio sessions in rock music. Anderson's inspiration came initially from Roland Kirk, but his one-legged impish posturings and "rural" attire are more in keeping with the group's eighteenth century namesake.

be more acceptable in wood. Cocus wood was most popular, along with blackwood and boxwood.

Basic Anatomy

The modern metal flute consists of three sections: the head (which is closed just above the blowing hole by a stopper); the body, or middle joint (the tube with most of the keys on it); and the foot, or foot joint (a short extension tube with few keys). The flute is tuned by varying the distance which the head is pushed into the body. There is no key for activating the higher octaves as there is on most other woodwinds – this is done by playing technique, the player having to control positioning of the jaw and breath pressure to get the full three-octave range from the instrument.

The most common size of flute is the concert, or "C" flute, which is pitched in G, and larger

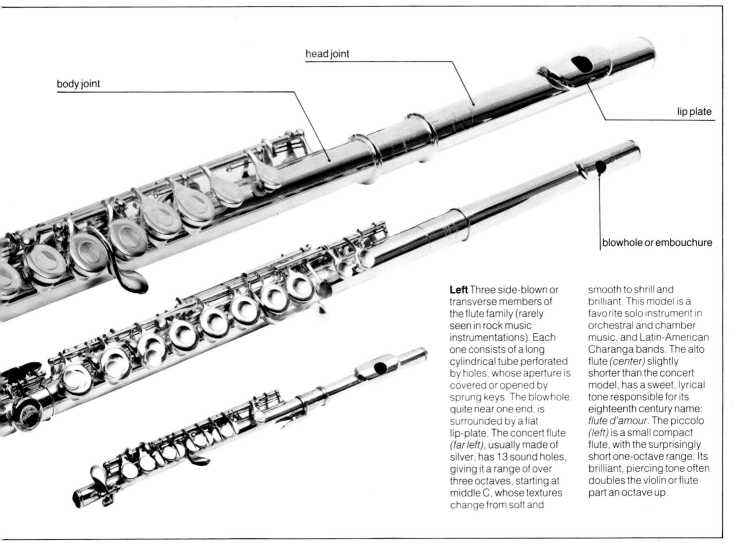

body joint

head joint

lip plate

blowhole or embouchure

Left Three side-blown or transverse members of the flute family (rarely seen in rock music instrumentations). Each one consists of a long cylindrical tube perforated by holes, whose aperture is covered or opened by sprung keys. The blowhole. quite near one end, is surrounded by a flat lip-plate. The concert flute *(far left)*, usually made of silver, has 13 sound holes, giving it a range of over three octaves, starting at middle C, whose textures change from soft and smooth to shrill and brilliant. This model is a favorite solo instrument in orchestral and chamber music, and Latin-American Charanga bands. The alto flute *(center)* slightly shorter than the concert model, has a sweet, lyrical tone responsible for its eighteenth century name: *flute d'amour.* The piccolo *(left)* is a small compact flute, with the surprisingly short one-octave range. Its brilliant, piercing tone often doubles the violin or flute part an octave up.

still (and even more uncommon) is the bass flute which has a sort of U-bend in it, and which, like the concert flute, is pitched in C.

The actual sound of a flute is made by blowing a small jet of air across the hole in the instrument's head. This jet breaks up on the opposite rim and vibrates above and below it, vibrating the air within the flute in turn. The tone of the instrument is a function both of the strength and direction of the jet of air and the construction and materials used.

Use in Rock

Amplification of the flute for live rock is necessary, but miking up is difficult to achieve. The Barcus Berry flute transducer gives a fair sound and is quite adaptable, although feedback can be a problem. The flute's normal stopper is removed and the transducer (or "bug"), integrated into a replacement stopper, is fitted,

working from the column of air in the flute's head against which it rests.

The flute has had limited use in rock music, although the best-known player is undoubtedly Ian Anderson of Jethro Tull. His breathy, stuttering style owes much to jazz players like Roland Kirk – indeed, the group made some of its earliest performances at British jazz festivals. Anderson's one-legged posture and strange stage antics have diverted attention from his instrument, but the flute remains at the heart of the group's sound. The earlier Tull albums, *This Was* or *Stand Up* provide rare examples of the flute in rock. Another European exponent of the flute in rock is Thijs van Leer of the Dutch group Focus, and he can be heard in fine form on the group's early 1970s recording, *House Of The King,* and on many other Focus compositions. More recently, some players have preferred to obtain a flute sound from a wind synthesizer.

The Saxophone

The saxophone was invented in the early 1840s by a Belgian, Aldophe Sax, who patented it in Paris in June, 1846. Sax had started to build some instruments in about 1842 which he called saxhorns (essentially valved bugles) and it is thought that the saxophone came from his experiments with reed mouthpieces on brass instruments.

The saxophone quickly became popular with military bands. It was adopted by the French army and its use spread from there. The instrument owed some of its early popularity to Sousa's marching bands in the United States toward the end of the nineteenth century, and it was also taken up by many of the dance bands of the earlier part of the twentieth century.

Although the saxophone has never become a proper part of the orchestra – it is one of the few new instruments invented in the past two centuries – it has been widely used in popular music of all forms, particularly jazz.

Basic Anatomy

The saxophone is basically a conical tube with around 23 openings, stopped by pads rather than the fingers of the player. The modern sax has a wider bore, metal reflector pads and a narrower mouthpiece than the older instruments and consequently produces a brighter, more penetrating sound. Most saxes come with plastic mouthpieces but professional players

Above left Lene Lovich has a very distinctive image with her auburn braids entwined into elegant displays with Spanish lace and combs and her layers of sombre, frilly clothes. Her vocal style is well-controlled, lyrical wailing, undoubtedly derived from the Eastern European folk music of her Czech ancestors. Lene's saxophone playing is forceful but fairly minimal.

Above right Roxy Music's Andy Mackay has contributed oboe and saxophone playing to the group's many facetted sound since the band's early days. His training in electronic music is sometimes hidden behind his standard rock riffs.

replace these with ebonite (a hard resin) or metal versions. There are four main sizes of saxophone: the E-flat soprano; the B-flat soprano; the E-flat alto; and the B-flat tenor, the last two being the most widely used. Selmer and Buescher are the two most noted manufacturers.

The single reed in the saxophone, made from specially cut and shaped cane, vibrates when blown and beats against the resonator in the mouthpiece. The reed's action, and therefore the overall sound, is also affected by the size of the tip opening (the gap between the tip of the reed and the mouthpiece rim); the lay (the aperture between the reed over its length and the mouthpiece); and the shape and size of the interior chamber of the mouthpiece. Players must find the correct quality reed for their particular style and sound requirements. Reeds come in various grades of hardness; generally, soft reeds are easier to blow. A too-soft reed will vibrate too much, making higher notes slip down to lower ones; a too-hard reed will not vibrate enough, making lower notes ill-defined.

Use in Rock

As with any acoustic instrument adapted for rock use, amplification is a problem for saxes. There are two alternatives: most players seem to prefer the straightforward way, which is to use a normal microphone connected to a backline amp or direct to the PA; the other way is to use a

mouthpiece

crook

keys

bell

Above Five members of the 12-strong saxophone family, all made of metal, which is responsible for their distinctive sound: *(left to right)* baritone in E flat, tenor in B flat and C, alto in E flat, soprano in B flat, bass in B flat.

Below Ian Dury's band of Blockheads get their jazzy sax sounds from Davey Payne. He doesn't often play this many instruments at once – although having cut his playing teeth in the huge and anarchic free improvising group, The People Band, it wouldn't be surprising.

Above A saxophone mouthpiece is identical to that of a clarinet, so players of one instrument can easily switch to the other. A single reed (of cane, plastic or fiberglass) is bound to the mouthpiece by metal ligatures.

Left The tenor saxophone is identical in principle to the clarinet, except for its conical, upturned bell, which amplifies and resonates the notes to give the characteristic sound so central to jazz. Although the sax has always been *the* jazz instrument, it appears often in rock music, adding extra color and dimension to the conventional instrumentation.

bug, a transducer attached to the instrument.

The Barcus Berry transducer is probably the most commonly used bug; it sticks onto the reed just below where the player lips it. Some players find this placement interferes with their playing: if this is the case, it is possible to drill the mouthpiece and attach the transducer flush to the column of air inside.

The usual criticism of bugged saxes is that the sound produced is too hard and "electronic" in tone, and that it does not begin to reproduce the quality and range of the acoustic horn. However, the sax can be used effectively in an electronic mode. Elton Dean of the Soft Machine experimented with these sorts of sounds in the late 1960s and early 1970s, as did Lol Coxhill with Kevin Ayres and others.

Another method of amplifying the saxophone is to use a small mike, such as a Tootal-Bug, in the bell of the instrument. This system can pose feedback problems if used through a backline amp, but fares better when put directly through the PA. Clarence Clemens, Bruce Springsteen's sax player, has taken this all a step further by using a radio mike in the bell of his instrument.

Most rock players of the saxophone are rooted in jazz traditions and the players who influence them are mostly jazz players like John Coltrane, Dexter Gordon and Charlie Parker. The instrument turns up in a variety of rock idioms. Rudy Pompelli of Bill Haley's Comets set a style in the 1950s by playing the sax on his back. In the 1960s and 1970s, the sax was used in variations of soul, jazz-rock, funk and disco and has recently risen in popularity with the emergence of "Two-Tone" bands, such as Madness and The Beat.

Perhaps the easiest to play of all the woodwinds, the saxophone is an expressive and powerful instrument. Its versatility is evident in its different applications: its use in "progressive" rock (Mel Collins in King Crimson, Jim King in Family); its fluid solo quality in the session-player rock of the 1970s (Phil Kenzie's alto on Al Stewart's *Year Of The Cat* or Raphael Ravenscroft's alto on Gerry Rafferty's *Baker Street*); the manic presence of Davey Payne's Roland Kirk-like stereo horns on Ian Dury's *Hit Me With Your Rhythm Stick* or the jazzy stutterings of Saxa on The Beat's *Mirror In The Bathroom*.

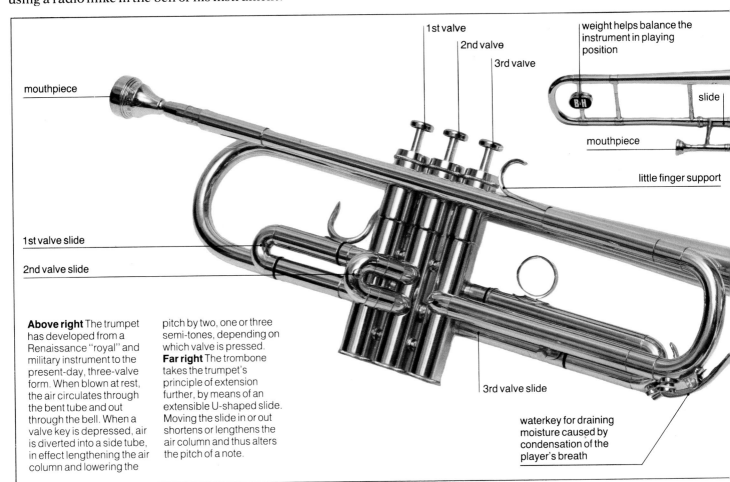

1st valve

2nd valve

3rd valve

weight helps balance the instrument in playing position

mouthpiece

slide

mouthpiece

little finger support

1st valve slide

2nd valve slide

3rd valve slide

waterkey for draining moisture caused by condensation of the player's breath

Above right The trumpet has developed from a Renaissance "royal" and military instrument to the present-day, three-valve form. When blown at rest, the air circulates through the bent tube and out through the bell. When a valve key is depressed, air is diverted into a side tube, in effect lengthening the air column and lowering the pitch by two, one or three semi-tones, depending on which valve is pressed. **Far right** The trombone takes the trumpet's principle of extension further, by means of an extensible U-shaped slide. Moving the slide in or out shortens or lengthens the air column and thus alters the pitch of a note.

Brass Instruments

Brass instruments are rarely used in rock as solo instruments but can be found quite often in that rock phenomenon, the brass section. The brass section is usually composed of two, three or four players who use a combination of brass instruments to augment a standard lineup. These sections originated in soul bands of the 1960s where their presence was an integral part of the arrangements and the music (examples include most Stax recordings and Otis Redding's *Live at Monterey*).Later the brass section was incorporated into straight rock bands; in some cases (Blood, Seat And Tears and Chicago) as part of the group proper; in others as a frill for live performances (Rolling Stones and Wings); occasionally as a semi-permanent addition (Graham Parker And The Rumour).

The trumpet and the trombone are the most common instruments to be found in the brass section, along with perhaps a couple of saxophones. The most widely used trumpet is the three-valved B-flat variety, while the medium bore is the most popular slide trombone. Barcus Berry-type transducers are used for amplifying.

Above Chicago is a seven-piece brass-rock band. Their music has been described by keyboard player Robert Lamm as "basically rock, but we can and do play jazz". For the first time in a rock group, three horn players (trombone, trumpet and saxophone) were integrated into the fulltime lineup, instead of the four-piece using studio session musicians for the brass sections. This extended instrumentation was matched by the New York group, Blood, Sweat And Tears.

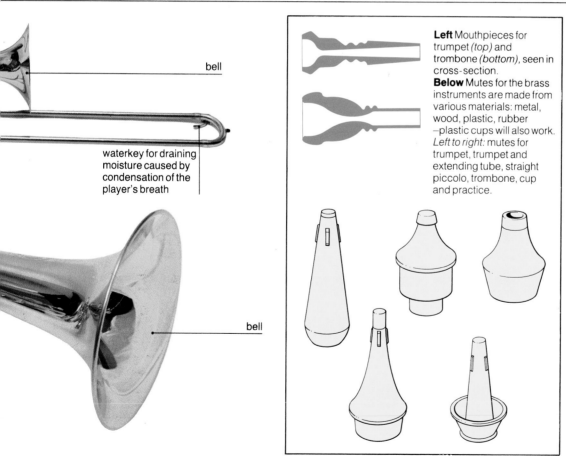

bell

waterkey for draining moisture caused by condensation of the player's breath

bell

Left Mouthpieces for trumpet *(top)* and trombone *(bottom)*, seen in cross-section.
Below Mutes for the brass instruments are made from various materials: metal, wood, plastic, rubber —plastic cups will also work. *Left to right:* mutes for trumpet, trumpet and extending tube, straight piccolo, trombone, cup and practice.

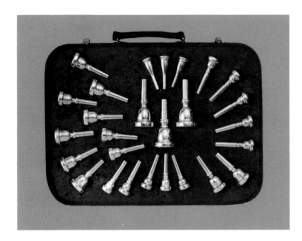

Left A selection of mouthpieces for use on brass instruments, contained in a purpose-built traveling case.

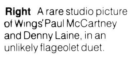

Right A rare studio picture of Wings' Paul McCartney and Denny Laine, in an unlikely flageolet duet.

Left Roy Wood has been the centerpiece of many Birmingham-based groups since the mid-1960s including The Move, Eddy And The Falcons, Wizzard and ELO, each with their own distinctive style. The Electric Light Orchestra was established by Wood to recreate live the complex multilayered sounds achieved by The Beatles in the studio on *Walrus* and *Strawberry Fields*. Wood brought in strings and brass but could play virtually any of the instruments in the lineup.

Above The Albion Band is a flexible grouping drawn from some of England's most competent folk players. The Albions' music harks back to the days of village dances (their first album was called *Morris On!*) and musical evenings around the village green.

Left Chicago seen here live on stage at the Hammersmith Odeon, London, in 1976. Note the drummers *and* percussion backline and the three horn players out front.

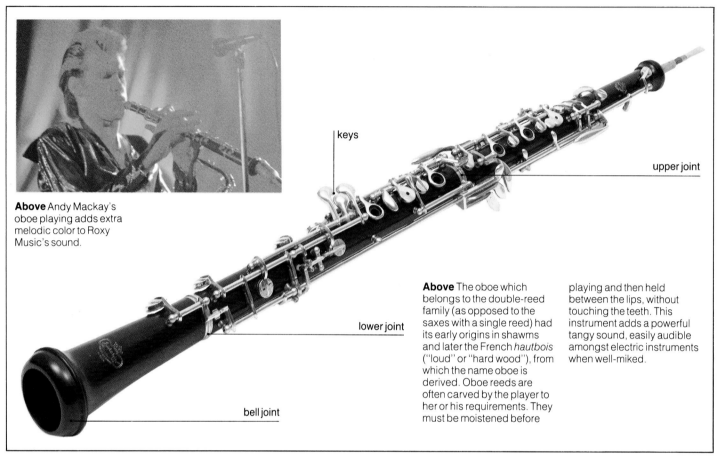

Above Andy Mackay's oboe playing adds extra melodic color to Roxy Music's sound.

keys

upper joint

lower joint

bell joint

Above The oboe which belongs to the double-reed family (as opposed to the saxes with a single reed) had its early origins in shawms and later the French *hautbois* ("loud" or "hard wood"), from which the name oboe is derived. Oboe reeds are often carved by the player to her or his requirements. They must be moistened before playing and then held between the lips, without touching the teeth. This instrument adds a powerful tangy sound, easily audible amongst electric instruments when well-miked.

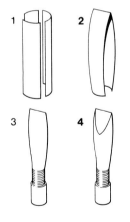

Above *Making an oboe reed* The cut reed *(1)* is folded *(2)* and shaped; its tip is cut off *(3)* with a sharp blade and the two edges are shaped *(4)* to give the appropriate and tailored sound. It is then bound tightly with nylon thread to a reed tube called a staple.

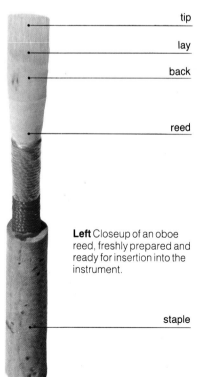

tip

lay

back

reed

staple

Left Closeup of an oboe reed, freshly prepared and ready for insertion into the instrument.

The Harmonica

The mouth organ has existed in various forms since about 1000 B.C., although the instrument as we know it today can probably be attributed to a German instrument designer called Buschmann who began to take out patents for experimental mouth organs in 1821.

The mouth organ, or harmonica, is a box full of reeds – the reeds are blown into or sucked on as the instrument is moved across the player's lips. Each small compartment seen at the edge of the standard "vamper" instrument contains two reeds of the same pitch – one works on pressure (blowing) and the other on suction. Chromatic harmonicas provide complete 12-note octaves as opposed to the vamper's single key, and each compartment contains two reeds each for the natural note and the chromatic note.

Little Walter Jacobs is credited as the first of the many blues players to amplify the harmonica, and the blues style has been adapted by some rock players notably Stevie Wonder and Mick Jagger. In folk areas, Bob Dylan's strapped-on harmonica set a trend in the early 1960s. More recently, the harmonica seems largely to be reserved for use in revivalist r'n'b bands.

Far right John Mayall has never deviated from his passion for the blues and is a proficient harmonica player. His "train blues" style of playing owes much to the Chicago blues players who are his greatest source of inspiration.
Right Bob Dylan's early one-man act consisted of wailing his plaintive poetry accompanied by acoustic guitar and harmonica. The mouth organ was suspended in front of his mouth by a metal frame. In recent years, Dylan has forsaken this folk method for a more conventional playing style.

Right Harmonicas or mouth organs have developed from traditional Asian instruments. They consist of a two-tiered series of chambers (equivalent to the pipes in the Asian forms) covered by reeds fixed at one end and free at the other. Harmonicas are made in varying lengths, the length determining the pitch of the instrument.
Below The mechanism of a harmonica: blowing out vibrates the reeds fixed nearest to the soundholes; sucking in affects those fixed to the opposite side. The player's tongue covers the holes which are to remain unplayed and silent.

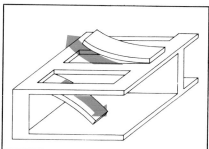

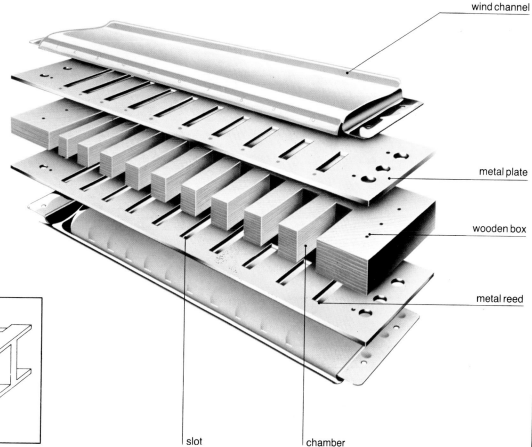

wind channel

metal plate

wooden box

metal reed

slot

chamber

The Violin

Although the very earliest violins were used primarily for contemporary popular music, the violin is now almost totally synonymous with classical music: solo violin playing is relatively rare in rock, probably due at least in part to the high technical demands made on players who wish to develop anything approaching mastery of the instrument.

The violin evolved in the late fifteenth and early sixteenth centuries from various bowed instruments of even earlier origins. The shape became standardized toward the end of the 1600s. The last major changes to the instrument were made in the nineteenth century, and included a heightening of the bridge, thickening of the sound post and bass bar, and a flattening of the body, all resulting in a more piercing, stronger tone.

Basic Anatomy

The pressure of the four strings holds the bridge down onto the top, or belly, of the violin, the bridge thus transmitting the strings' vibrations to the belly. The belly is made of a soft wood, usually pine, and vibrates relatively freely over the sound post, a small, thin rod of pine acting as a fulcrum between the belly and the instrument's back, which is made of harder wood, usually maple. The belly is also supported from beneath by the bass bar which runs the length of the body, contributing to the instrument's resonance and distributing pressure evenly over the whole body.

The chin rest was added in the early nineteenth century – formerly the instrument was held at the player's chest, shoulder, or against either side of the neck, and folk players can still be seen holding the violin against their upper arm.

Amplification

American musician and instrument designer Lloyd Loar obtained a patent for an electric viola with a single-coil pickup as early as 1935, but few manufacturers have produced purpose-built electric violins or violas since then, probably due as much as anything to the lack of demand from players. Amplification of the violin in rock is best effected by the use of transducers, or "bugs" – small sound pickups which attach either to the body or to the bridge of the violin. If the bug is attached to the bridge, it is usually placed near the bass side as this is the most active part of the violin and will therefore tend to give a reasonably balanced sound.

Transducer manufacturers such as Barcus Berry also supply replacement bridges with the

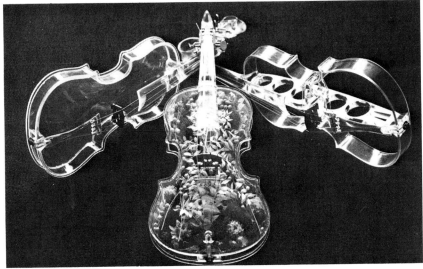

Opposite above The fresh sharp edge of a violin makes an occasional appearance in rock bands. One of the first to introduce this classical instrument to rock was the French player, Jean-Luc Ponty whose amplified electric explorations began in Frank Zappa's Mothers Of Invention in 1969.

Above left The folk roots of the violin have been a more usual source of inspiration. Lindisfarne, formed in Newcastle in the late 1960s, epitomised this style of folk-rock; their lineup also included harp and mandolin.

Left The late 1960s was a period when there was a vogue for violins in rock: Curved Air first featured Darryl Way.

Above right Bethnal's delicate violin details, evident in their late 1970s music, were quickly overshadowed by punk's simplicity.

Opposite below Disco brought new electronic sounds and Chic were the first to use these transparent violins in a string section.

bug built into them, along with kits to enable electric violinists to install a permanent volume control and jack-plug socket into the body of their instrument. FRAP (Flat Response Audio Pickup) make a transducer called the 3D which senses sound movement in three dimensions and has an extremely wide frequency range. The best position for the 3D on a violin is the back of the instrument, just over the sound post, and the pickup comes with its own special preamplifier to boost the signal for a backline amp or PA. Feedback can be a problem with electric violins, and players usually compensate by stuffing the body of the instrument with cotton wool, or by taping over the f-holes.

Use in Rock

Where the violin does occur in rock, the player often comes from a jazz or folk background. In Britain the folk tradition has produced some fine musicians. Perhaps the best-known player is Dave Swarbrick, who originally came to wider attention when he joined the folk-rock group Fairport Convention in July 1969 after many years of professional playing with the Ian Campbell Group, Martin Carthy, and others. Fairport's classic folk-rock album *Liege And Lief*, issued in December 1969, contains many excellent examples of Swarbrick's violin playing, especially *Matty Groves* and the medley of jigs and reels including *The Lark In The Morning*.

Right Dave Swarbrick's passionate involvement in English traditional music as evidenced by his electrified folk violin playing, had an instant effect on Fairport Convention's sound when he joined. Since the demise of that group, Swarbrick has made solo albums and been a regular session guest on others.

Below Chic's transparent plastic violins inject an unusual element into American disco music.

Left Chic created the paradox of the live disco group, with their elegant brand of dance music created by the bass player Bernard Edwards and guitarist Nile Rodgers. They have subsequently worked as producers, with many kinds of singers including Diana Ross and Deborah Harry.

From the jazz source, and France, comes successful virtuoso player Jean-Luc Ponty, who has been doing much to popularize the solo violin in recent "fusion rock" (solo albums include *Imaginary Voyage*, 1977 and *Cosmic Messenger*, 1980). Ponty's background includes time with the ever-innovative Frank Zappa, playing on *It Must Be a Camel* from the *Hot Rats* album (recorded summer 1969) and, more notably, on Zappa's *Music For Electric Violin And Low Budget Orchestra* (recorded October 1969) which goes some way to realizing Zappa's desire in the late 1960s to record a work mixing classical composition techniques with rock.

Other notable rock violinists include Jerry Goodman, at one time with the American group Flock; Ric Grech, who has played with Family and Blind Faith; George Csapo of Bethnal, one of the few British bands of the late 1970s to use violin; Papa John Creach, who played occasionally with the later lineups of Jefferson Airplane; Eddie Jobson, who has played with Frank Zappa, Curved Air, UK and Roxy Music; Darryl Way, a British violinist who played in a classical-rock mode with Curved Air, renowned for the track *Vivaldi;* Don "Sugarcane" Harris, who also played on Zappa's *Hot Rats;* Dave Arbus, who played with East of Eden and can be heard on The Who's *Baba O'Riley;* and David Cross, who played electric violin and viola with later incarnations of the seminal English "progressive" rock band, King Crimson.

The String Section
The importance of strings in rock – whether a quartet of violin, viola, cello and bass, or an orchestral string section – has diminished somewhat in recent years. This is due partially to the vast improvements in the quality of sound

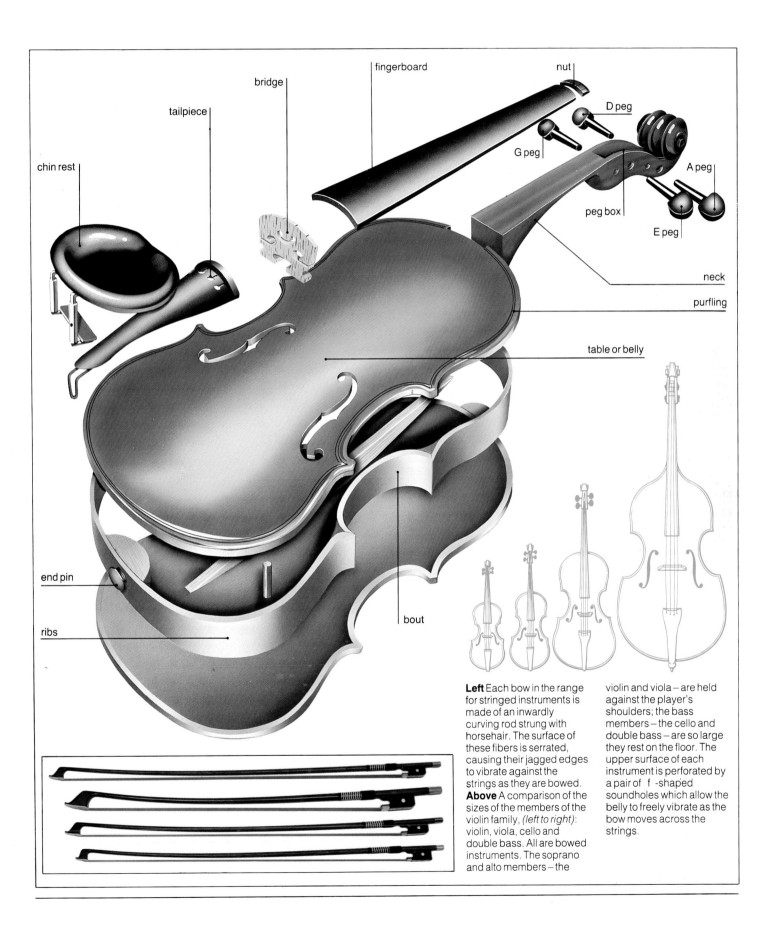

fingerboard

nut

bridge

D peg

tailpiece

G peg

A peg

chin rest

peg box

E peg

neck

purfling

table or belly

end pin

ribs

bout

Left Each bow in the range for stringed instruments is made of an inwardly curving rod strung with horsehair. The surface of these fibers is serrated, causing their jagged edges to vibrate against the strings as they are bowed.
Above A comparison of the sizes of the members of the violin family, *(left to right)*: violin, viola, cello and double bass. All are bowed instruments. The soprano and alto members – the

violin and viola – are held against the player's shoulders; the bass members – the cello and double bass – are so large they rest on the floor. The upper surface of each instrument is perforated by a pair of f -shaped soundholes which allow the belly to freely vibrate as the bow moves across the strings.

which can be obtained from the various electronic keyboard instruments, now capable of reproducing string and orchestral sounds. However, Van Morrison's superb *It's Too Late To Stop Now* double album, recorded live at London's Rainbow theatre in 1973, amply demonstrates how a string section can add to and improve upon basic rock sound and instrumentation.

Forever Changes, an album by West Coast American group Love, is generally cited as the first rock record to feature an orchestra as an integral part of the sound, and was recorded in 1967 with most of the orchestrations arranged by David Angel. The middle and late 1960s also saw The Beatles do much to popularize the use of large and small string sections in rock. Particularly important are the string quartet in *Yesterday* (recorded early 1965); *Eleanor Rigby,* with its four violins, two violas and two cellos (recorded mid-1966); Mike Leander's string arrangement on *She's Leaving Home* and the

41-piece orchestra on *Day In The Life* (both from *Sergeant Pepper's Lonely Hearts Club Band* recorded in the first half of 1967); and the thumping cellos of *Strawberry Fields Forever* (recorded December 1966) or *I Am The Walrus* (late 1967).

It was these thumping cellos which inspired the formation of the Electric Light Orchestra (ELO), originally the brainchild of Roy Wood. From its beginning, ELO have taken the cello-laden Beatles recordings as a stimulus for their music, relying heavily on amplified strings and particularly the cello, utilizing transducers in the same way as explained earlier for violins. ELO's first album, still with Wood, has strong string sounds on *Look At Me Now, First Movement,* and indeed most of the record. The amplified cello and electric strings generally have been at the centre of ELO's more recent commercial success, with Lynne at the helm assisted by regular cello players Melvyn Gale and Hugh McDowell, and violinist Mik Kaminski.

Below The Electric Light Orchestra, Roy Wood's brainchild, with its cellists and violin player, carries on where The Beatles' orchestral arrangements left off.

AMPLIFICATION

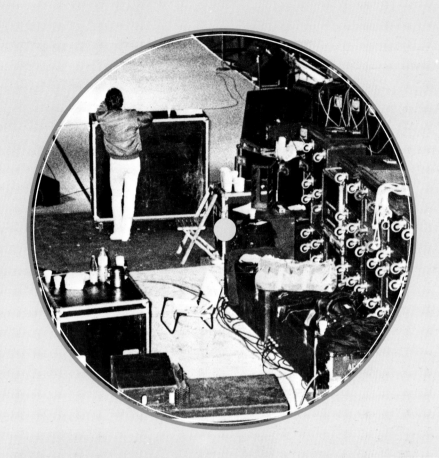

By any standards the amplifier is the unsung hero – or villain – of rock music and its struggle with its detractors. Back in the 1950s, when the electric guitar was harangued as a dangerous influence on young people, it was the amplifier that really should have been the target for invective.

In the 1960s rock got even louder and the protests continued. An obscure British politician claimed that rock music destroyed brain cells. Others tried to show that exposure to high sound pressure levels damaged hearing. In fact, at the normal rock concert levels, it is debatable whether sound can ever cause permanent hearing loss. Volume as much as stridency won rock its reputation: rock is a music of intense dynamic range. One minute there is silence, apart from gentle acoustic chords, the next minute the music sweeps up into a crescendo amplified a hundredfold – a dynamic range well beyond the reach of even the most powerful and skilled concert orchestra.

The idea that rock might even exist without being amplified is absurd, but amplification is about far more than merely boosting the weak signal of an electric guitar. The amplifier a musician chooses will add a great deal to the character of the sound he or she produces (more than the player usually realizes). Guitarists will sit and talk for hours about the relative merits of a '58 Gibson Les Paul guitar as opposed to those of a '63 Fender Strat, but only a handful of them acknowledge the contribution the right amplifier can make to overall sound and style. What constitutes the right amplifier is a matter of some considerable controversy amongst musicians and there is something of a rift between the designers and engineers who make modern instrument amplifiers and the musicians who use them. The roots of it lie in the development of the amplifier itself.

Early Amplifiers

The electric guitar basically was conceived to enable guitar players to be heard over the howling and tooting brass sections of the dance bands of the 1930s and 1940s. In those days few guitarists were soloists, but as soloists emerged, so did the need for increased volume. Engineers started experimenting with basic pickups that converted the vibrations of the guitar string into electrical energy. These weak signals were then amplified by what might be regarded as little more than tube radios without the receiver stage. The volume was relatively low – about five to ten watts, a far cry from the 100-watt amp of today.

The first type of amplifier was composed of one unit, that is to say, it contained both the electronic circuitry which boosted the signal from the guitar and the loudspeaker which reproduced that signal. Based on the standard radio circuitry of the time, it used the only available means of amplifying the guitar's output, the thermionic device – "tube" in the U.S.A, "valve" in Britain.

The tube and the integral (or "combo" for combination amplifier) features remained for quite a while. The technology was good enough for the demands being placed on dance band guitar players and there was no attempt to improve the amplifier as there was to springboard the guitar into an electrical and electronic age.

When rock music took off, more power was needed. The small combination amplifiers began to get bigger and bigger. In the United States, Leo Fender turned his considerable skills toward making amplifiers. As early as 1949 he and Donald Randall produced the Super Amp; by 1954, the range had grown and Fender offered at least eight models, including the original Fender Bassman, an amplifier to match the recently invented Fender bass guitar.

Power was beginning to emerge, too. The Bassman could deliver 50 watts, as could the Twin (so-called because it featured twin 12-inch speakers). This was real power to the American rock and rollers and enabled them to get their music across to larger audiences.

While Fender dominated the amplifier market in the United States, other manufacturers were busy copying him, both in his own country and in Britain. The two most successful British manufacturers were Selmer and Vox. In the late 1950s a Fender amp was a rare sight on an English stage; semi-professional and amateur guitar players tended to use Selmer combos like the Zodiac, the Thunderbird or the exotically named Treble 'n' Bass 50. The big bands used the king of British amps, the Vox AC30.

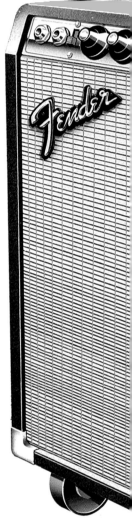

Above Part of the manufacturing process for amplifiers involves checking and testing. Here amplifier chassis are being run for 24 hours in a "quiet" room to listen for unwanted noises.
Below Pete Townshend, shown here playing a Les Paul, has always exploited the sound of distortion, achieved by overdriving the amplifier. An early user of the Marshall stack, he changed to Hiwatt and for some time has used Hiwatt 100-watt amps on stage.

Left The classic Fender Twin Reverb, in production since 1954. For a tube amp, it has a very "clean" sound; it is a 100-watt amp that peaks at 220. Some amps are rated on their peak output power rather than their average: this can cause misleading comparisons since amps rarely reach their peak. The

Twin Reverb has vibrato and reverb effects built in which can be controlled by footswitches. The vibrato can be varied in speed and intensity. This amplifier is closely associated with country players but has found favor with a number of rock performers including Eric Clapton.

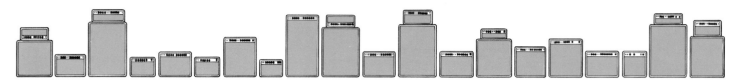

The AC30 is probably the most important amplifier ever made in Britain (along with the Marshall 100-watt amp). This amp, which drove The Shadows to fame, was a squat black box with a diamond-patterned speaker grille cloth; its appearance belied its unusual loudness. The Vox AC30 was a 30-watt tube amplifier fitted with two 12-inch Celestion speakers. It did not look impressive but it worked well, and over the years achieved a dedicated following. Despite a relatively low output power, the AC30 is still used today by such musicians as Queen's Brian May, who uses a stack of these amplifiers piled up high and linked together for extra volume. The AC30 was only one of the amplifiers that Tom Jennings' Vox company made. They produced AC15s and, later, AC50s, AC100s and a whole host of other products, but the AC30 remains the amplifier which players associate with the Vox name.

By 1963, at the height of the Beat boom, performing musicians were again faced with the need to make themselves heard. The AC30 and its Selmer equivalents were still the most popular items of equipment on British stages while the Fenders reigned supreme in the United States. None of them were loud enough for the job they were now being asked to do. The Beatles were playing venues such as Shea Stadium using 50-watt amps for bass guitar and 30-watt amps for guitar – power outputs which would be shunned by even the garage bands of today.

Some attempts had been made to improve existing models. Fender had split their amplifiers from their speaker cabinets in some cases; partly to help cut out the vibrational damage caused by having the speaker and tubes in the same box, partly to improve the acoustic qualities of the speaker section. Both Vox and Selmer had taken the same steps with their AC30 Piggyback and Treble 'n' Bass models. This was a particularly important development for the bass guitarist. With four strings tuned an octave below the bottom four strings of a guitar, the bassist was finding that low frequency notes not only did considerable damage to electrical components but also were much harder for the human ear to pick up than higher notes. Bass players needed more power than guitarists to be heard and bigger speakers to handle these low notes. For this reason, from the earliest days of rock Fender had offered 15-inch speakers with their Bassman.

Right The original Watkins (WEM) Dominator tube amplifier had an output of 17 watts and was first produced in 1959. It found widespread use with the British Beat bands of the early 1960s and was used to amplify bass, guitar and vocals. The angled cabinet was reputed to give a better sound dispersion.
Below The 1966 version of the WEM Dominator retained the 17-watt chassis but had a redesigned cabinet.

Below Many manufacturers produce a vast range of speakers (drive units) in different sizes and with the capacity to handle different frequencies. The range shown here is manufactured by Celestion. Rola Celestion speakers were fitted to some of the original Vox AC30 amps.

Vox and Selmer both tried to increase the volume with new 100-watt tube amplifiers which rode on top of separate speaker cabinets. Vox's AC30 was still popular for club gigs but the professional players on tour started to take the new amp with them. It was not a complete success, although its popularity benefited when George Harrison or John Lennon could be seen wired up to it. The AC100 was usually run into a sealed enclosure containing four 12-inch speakers and two Middax horns. Bass players used it on top of a smaller enclosure containing two 15-inch speakers. Many users complained that the new amplifier did not sound as good as the old AC30. Others claimed that it was not much louder, either. Newer American brands such as Ampeg were also not loud enough.

The Marshall Stack

The solution to the problem of volume came from Britain, although, ironically, the fact that British bands touring the United States were inaudible in the larger venues provided the initial stimulus. This solution brought another dimension with it: a new sound, the sound of overload and distortion.

Amplifiers had always overloaded. Players struggling to make themselves heard above their audiences (or their drummers) had turned their amps up until the sound pouring out of the speakers was fed back through their guitar pickups in a particularly painful circle of squealing and howling. To stop this horrible noise, the amp was soon turned down again. Another noise as bad as feedback occurred when the sound got so loud it strained the speakers or the tubes so that they ran into distortion.

Pete Townshend, Eric Clapton and Jeff Beck were attracted by this exaggerated sound. Townshend frequented a music shop in the London suburb of Ealing run by a drummer called Jim Marshall. Tentatively, in the early 1960s, Marshall produced his first amp and the "stack" was born.

Marshall rebuilt a fairly standard tube circuit and placed it on top of two cabinets with four 12-inch speakers in each. Technically, the amplifier was not that sophisticated but in the tiny clubs where The Who were playing at that time it was impressively loud and it was producing a sound that nobody had ever really heard *used* before, rather than merely endured – distortion.

Above The range of Fender amplifiers in production today. Most amplifiers are available fitted with either Fender or JBL speakers.

Below The Beatles were one of the famous groups who used Vox amplifiers. Here George Harrison's Gretsch Country Gent and John Lennon's Rickenbacker are both going through Vox AC30s (on chrome stands), while the Hofner Violin Bass played by Paul McCartney is amplified by a Vox AC50 Piggyback bass amplifier. The Jam are one of the more recent groups to continue to use Vox amps today.

Suddenly, exactly what electronics designers had been trying to avoid for years, an unnatural discoloration of the guitar's signal, was being actively sought by the customers. Engineers could not understand it; many still can't.

No one knows who first used feedback and distortion as an integral part of playing. It might have been Townshend, it might have been Jeff Beck playing with The Yardbirds. Certainly both were playing their amplifiers almost as much as they were playing their guitars. Beck would sometimes end a Yardbirds' gig by leaving his guitar howling on top of his pile of amps, or inducing a screech while holding a note. Townshend, too, was doing much the same thing. A whole new style of playing evolved where the amplifier was turned up so high that one note could scream and hold on for minutes, an effect which suited blues-based rock music perfectly. The player would bend the string he was holding down and a mournful, wailing sustained note poured out of the speakers. Definitive examples can be heard on tracks like *Beck's Bolero* or *The Supernatural* where Peter Green plays a blinding solo on John Mayall's *A Hard Road* album.

Jeff Beck, who typically prefers no particular make, and the late Jimi Hendrix are probably the best amplifier players. Beck's ability to control amp feedback and his use of a sweet distor-

tion are legendary. On his interpretation of *Goodby Pork Pie Hat* from the *Wired* album even the hum of his amp can be heard. Almost any Hendrix track demonstrates Hendrix's abilities but *Purple Haze* or *Voodoo Chile* are good examples.

Like an acoustic arms race, guitarists now let power run away with them. Townshend started using not just one Marshall 100-watt amp and two stacks but two or even three amplifiers. He could certainly be heard, but that was no longer the only object of the game.

Other companies tried to duplicate Marshall's success. Names like Hiwatt came and stayed, others like Vamp, Impact and Beck (no relation) soon disappeared. Most of these others producers simply opened up Marshall's amp and tried to copy it. In many cases their failures were merely commercial although some copy Marshalls were also poorly designed. Hiwatt did not copy Marshall, however, and have maintained their following down the years including, curiously, Pete Townshend himself, who, though epitomizing the Marshall user, switched to Hiwatt fairly early on and has more or less stayed that way ever since.

Transistor Amplifiers

By the early 1960s the basic tube amp was technically an electronic dinosaur. Radio and television manufacturers had found that tran-

Top Amplifiers set up on stage with two Strats and a Les Paul. The amplifiers are two Hiwatt Custom tube 100-watt amps and a Mesa Boogie top; also shown are a range of effects units and a MXR digital delay unit.
Above The Simms-Watts all-purpose AP100, a 100-watt transistor amp.
Right Marshall stacks were initially popularized by The Who, Jimi Hendrix and Led Zeppelin and are still widely used today by heavy metal bands. Hendrix actually used a doctored Marshall bass amp with extra circuitry to help achieve his distinctive guitar sound. Motorhead are shown here with their Marshall stacks; the company logo has been altered on two of them to read "Sasha" and "Marsha".

sistors were cheaper to produce, more reliable and less prone to distortion – features that many makers believed would appeal to the guitarist, too. Like many new ideas, early transistorized guitar amps were poor in practice. Vox produced the T60, supposedly a 60-watt lightweight transistor bass amp, and possibly one of the worst ever made. Burns also made transistor amps which were just as bad.

The transistor amp could not be wound up to sing in quite the same way as a tube amplifier. When run into distortion it tended to produce a foul, harsh tone full of grating odd-order harmonics as opposed to the tube's even-order harmonics. The early transistor amp was less reliable too, but it was so much easier to build than a tube amp that manufacturers were determined to get it right.

New names began to appear, products of people whose experience lay in fields where the

Below Mesa Boogie have become popular amplifiers since their introduction in 1972. As well as small combos, the company also make the "Mini-Stacks" shown here. Boogie amps have attracted something of a cult following and can be heard on *Some Girls* by the Rolling Stones, *Rumours* by Fleetwood Mac, The Who's *Who Are You* and Al DiMeola's *Elegant Gypsy*.

purpose of amplification was just to amplify, not change the character of the input signal. Their suggestion to rock players who wanted the discordant din of distortion was to use a fuzz box. However, not every guitar player wanted that "tube sound" and those who did not were quick to embrace the new products of new makers like HH and Carlsbro whose amplifiers were cheap, superbly reliable and pleasant.

After a while the transistor amplifier makers reluctantly accepted that some musicians really did want a tube sound and they started to put distortion circuits into their amps to simulate it. The first attempts were not good but they have been getting closer over the years. Carlsbro, and Norlin with their Robert Moog-assisted Lab Series range, are reasonable and HH are regarded well. Many professional electric guitarists, however, still use tube amps from makers like Fender, Ampeg, Hiwatt, Vox and Sunn.

Bass Amplification

Bass players have tended not to use distortion, with the honorable exception of Jack Bruce and, at times, John Entwistle and Chris Squire. For this reason, many bass players were enthusiastic about the transistor amp. The lightness, versatility of tone control and cleanliness are not outweighed by the unnatural distortion when overdriven. Brands like Sunn, Acoustic, HH and Carlsbro are popular with bass players in their transistorized formats. But bass players want special tones in addition to a clean sound and although some have stayed with simple formats of two or four 15-inch speakers and a 100-watt amp, others have built what amounts to mini PA systems on stage with powerful clean-sounding amps designed for PA power amp use running through three- or even four-way speaker systems with various different-sized speakers handling different parts of the audio spectrum. To some extent, this is a result of the emergence of lead bass players such as Stanley Clarke (a notable exponent of this bass PA approach).

The recent trend among bass players has swung over to cheaper integral amplifiers than the Amcron (Crown) or BGW powered bass rigs. Carlsbro's new Pro Bass range of integral amplifiers includes such features as compression (a limiting technique which increases sustain and dynamic tightness), variable electronic crossovers (to direct the output to one or two different speaker cabinets with different speakers in each) and various other useful facilities. Amplifiers like these will eventually bring the Stanley Clarke approach within the reach of the semi-professional bass player who could not otherwise afford it.

Left Amplifier cabinets are made in a variety of different materials from plywood, pine, and various hardwoods to molded plastic. This packing crate style pine cabinet houses the compact Crate 60-watt bass amplifier which incorporates a specially designed 12-inch speaker.

Below There are many compact amplifiers now available that are powered by several batteries: the first of these was the Pignose. Examples shown below are the Mouse, Birdie, Vox Escort, Magna Voice Briefcase, John Hornby Skewes, Intermusic and SMS. These small portable amps are often used by street musicians. Even smaller amps have been built and these are often used for tuning up. Rory Gallagher has a custom-built amp that is only four inches high and two inches wide.

Above Stanley Clarke uses what amounts to a mini PA system on stage for his bass amplification. He is shown here in the studio with a Kramer bass.
Below The Rickenbacker Transonic Series 200 amplifier was an unusually shaped amp first produced in the late 1960s. A special version of this model was made for Led Zeppelin. Chris Squire of Yes also had a custom-built Rickenbacker amp.

Keyboard Amplification

There are very few specific keyboard amplification systems marketed today. Manufacturers seem to expect keyboard players to either build up their own systems to their own requirements, from available bass and instrument amplification equipment, or to use some of the hardware from PA rigs.

There are several problems uniquely associated with the amplification of keyboards: the first being the wide range of frequencies that a keyboard produces. The best reproduction of an amplified, electric or electronic keyboard is possible only with amplifier and speaker systems that have not only a flat frequency response down to the lowest frequency the instrument produces, but also a flat power response.

The phenomenon of virtual bass, whereby the ear and brain compensate for lack of low frequency response, can be used to great advantage when amplifying keyboard instruments. However, there is a distinct difference between hearing the virtual bass of an instrument and actually feeling the bass response of a full-range system. To get such a response, the speaker/driver must be capable of moving large quantities of air.

Although many of today's loudspeakers have an excellent frequency response, covering almost the entire audio spectrum, any keyboard amplification system should have separate drivers for bass and treble. In such a two-channel system, a crossover network is required to keep the powerful bass frequencies away from the tweeter (or high frequency driver), so they are not blown apart; and also to ensure that the high frequency signals do not cause any intermodulation in the woofer (or bass driver). The usual crossover frequency for a keyboard rig should be around 300 Hz.

The treble frequencies are far less of a problem and even inexpensive cone drivers produce acceptable results. For synthesizers and electric or electronic pianos, the relatively new high frequency piezo horns can be employed to give that extra high frequency lift to the sound at a reasonable cost. Many electric organs, however, notably the Hammond, which only produces audio signals up to 6,000 Hz, are not intended to have extended treble reproduction and have special amplification systems designed with a tailored response. Amplification above this frequency would just highlight the key clicks – although many rock and jazz players like to use these clicks to emphasize the harmonic percussion.

Intermodulation is one of the prime areas of concern. Hugh Banton, Van Der Graaf Generator's organist, was rumored to have special low frequency bass drivers for his bass pedalboard, which was polyphonic in design. The speakers he used were designed for testing aircraft for metal fatigue, and could handle frequencies down to a couple of cycles per second. If two adjacent notes were accidentally pressed at the same time, a beat frequency of 5 to 10 Hz was set up and the resulting signal was so powerful that the speakers had to be nailed to the stage and plaster would be shaken from the ceiling and walls of the auditorium.

As a rough guideline, most players prefer a tube amplifier for electric and electromechanical instruments and a transistor amp for electronic instruments. The warmth of the tube is particularly suited to electromechanical pianos such as the Rhodes and the Wurlitzer, and the distortion caused by overdriving these amplifiers is often used to great effect.

The most impressive keyboard amplification system must be the Moog Synamp. This consists of two 200-watt Bi-amps, a four-channel mixer, three-band parametric equalization for each channel, a ten-band graphic equalizer for the mixed signal, two compressors, and, on the loudspeaker side, two 15-inch low frequency drivers, a midrange horn and a high frequency horn with acoustic lens. This is specifically designed for synthesizers, but will handle any keyboard with aplomb.

The Leslie Organ Speaker

This unique loudspeaker arrangement was designed by Don Leslie of Electro Music Inc., and is used to give organ tones extra life and depth. To do this, the Leslie system employs a rotating drum which directs the output of the loudspeaker continuously around a full circle at two rates – seven times a second giving a tremelo effect, and once every 1.3 seconds, giving a choral effect. The rotating drum throws out the sound in all directions, producing, for the stationary listener, a Doppler phase shift. This gives the mechanical tones generated by the organ more charisma and presence and means that the actual point of origin is difficult to judge

The Leslie speakers were originally intended for use with the Hammond organs, but more recent models include a rotating high frequency horn to handle the higher frequencies produced by other keyboard instruments.

Recent Developments

Towards the end of the 1960s the audibility problem started plaguing musicians once again. The problem this time was the outdoor festival

Above A Peavey Backstage combo amp, designed for use as a portable practice amp. It is sometimes used on stage, however, because it can be made to reproduce the popular overdriven sound.

or the giant American auditorium seating thousands of people. No one could try to fill a hall that big by standing in front of a 20,000-watt amplifier/speaker stack, so mikes were placed in front of instrument amps and these were blended together with the vocals and drums via a mixing desk and put through the PA system. Used thus (and with the blended signal fed back to the musician through a monitor system) many felt stacks were no longer needed. Today, quite a number of musicians are using small combo amps, once again. Particularly favored are the exclusive brands like Burman (in Britain) and Music Man and Mesa Boogie (in the United States).

Nonetheless, there is something cosmetically titanic about a stack of amplifiers and such heavy rock bands as Judas Priest and Black Sabbath would look wrong without a physical demonstration of their might and power towered up behind them like a wall of threatening omens. Some bands even use their amps *purely* cosmetically, guitarists only using one of the three or four that they have on stage.

A stage setup today will reflect the nature of the music played, from an amplification point-of-view. Heavy metal bands will have wall-to-wall tube amplifiers; quieter bands will use a handful of combos: tubes if the guitarists want the tube sound for overload, transistor if not or if they prefer that icy edge of a crystal-clear HH, Peavey or Fender transistor amp.

As the tube is no longer used outside of a few very specialized applications (such as rock amplification) its production is being stepped down to the point where only a handful of makers are left in the world. In time, these makers will probably disappear altogether. By then a solid state device may have been developed to duplicate the tube sound properly. Peavey (arguably the biggest amp maker in the world) are working on it and some makers like the technically brilliant Mike Harrison of HH are experimenting with a new type of transistor, the MOS-FET, which, it is claimed, can sound as good as any tube amp. Whatever happens, the disappearance of the warm sounding tube will be lamented.

The amplifier has a symbiotic relationship with the electric guitar which ensures its survival. It may contain tubes or transistors, it may shrink to the size of those early radios without the receiver stage, it may leap up beyond the towering stacks or retain the form of the portable combos. It may have all types of built-in effects, such as phasing, reverb, distortion and flanging, but it keeps humming away, providing the power behind rock in all its forms.

THE PA SYSTEM

Although awe-inspiring in appearance, the massive equipment used at today's concerts has only a humble purpose: to allow musicians to communicate with their audience. For rock audiences, this rapport depends greatly upon the sense of intensity and physical presence provoked by loudness. Modern PA ("public address" or "power amplification") is essentially auxilliary amplification, a way of making the music loud enough when instrument amplifiers and drumkits cannot produce sufficient sound intensity to fill large halls or carry outdoors. Because drumkits and electric instruments are inherently loud, and the music of the late 1950s and early 1960s did not require exceptional sound levels, the early PAs were purely a means of projecting the vocals.

While PA equipment is adept at such amplification, in the process, it is also very easy to exchange clarity for dissonance, distortion and coloration. At high sound levels, the discrepancies can be very unpalatable with the ironic result that the PA can actually alienate audiences from the music. High fidelity is much more than just using high quality sound equipment: a lot of skill is needed to bring together the sounds of all the instruments to recreate a sound that is no more than purely a larger, louder version of the band without the PA. Bearing in mind the cost and complexity of technical excellence, it is best to accept that PA is imperfect. But provided the imperfections can be juggled to make them sympathetic to the music, the PA can become a musical instrument; an extension of the musicians themselves.

When major bands use a PA, they hand over much of their responsibility for the sound to a sound engineer. Rock tends to thrive when the people who design and operate the PA equipment have feeling for the music, empathy with the musicians and an insight into the music's relationship with the equipment. Today's sound engineers and electronics designers have become true musical craftsmen.

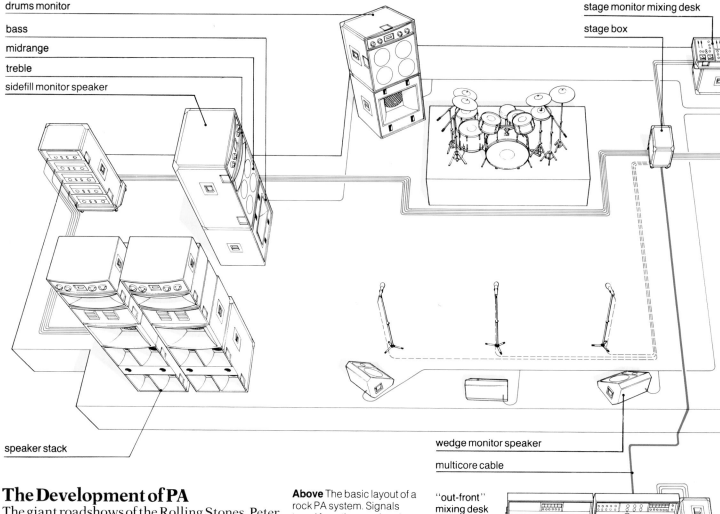

drums monitor

bass

midrange

treble

sidefill monitor speaker

stage monitor mixing desk

stage box

speaker stack

wedge monitor speaker

multicore cable

"out-front" mixing desk

effects unit

The Development of PA

The giant roadshows of the Rolling Stones, Peter Frampton and Wings epitomized the huge sound systems of the 1970s, but the origins of today's rock PA lies not only in the 1960s, but in the fledgling days of the first electric revolution which arrived with the talking motion picture.

Early microphones and Lord Rayleigh's treatise on sound had appeared in the 1870s. In the early 1920s, thermionic tubes were mass-produced, electronic amplification and the loudspeaker were developed and, in 1927, an early sound engineering company, Western Electric, pioneered mass "electric" entertainment with the first talkie, *The Jazz Singer*. The struggle to cover large audiences uniformly with high quality sound had begun.

The early speakers and amplifiers lacked sensitivity and power, so to increase the sound level, the speakers were coupled with gramophone horns, which had been used for the same purpose in earlier, purely acoustic systems. During the 1930s, 1940s and 1950s, these horn speakers were developed to a high level of sophistication

Above The basic layout of a rock PA system. Signals travel from the vocal and instrument microphones and direct injection boxes (not shown) to the stage box. At the stage box, the signals go to the "out-front" mixing desk and the stage monitoring mixing desk. On stage, an engineer mixes the sound for the musicians' monitors; the signals travel from there to stage monitor power amps and then to sidefill and wedge monitors. At the "out-front" mixing desk, the engineer mixes, equalizes and adds effects, the signals are split into three or more frequency bands at the crossover and then travel back along the multicore cable to the stage box. From the stage box they are routed to power amps (one for each frequency band) and then to the speakers.

by companies such as Altec (the successor of Western Electric), Vitavox and RCA and by pioneers like Paul Voigt, Percy Wilson and Harry Olson. They became the standard fitments in cinemas, theaters and halls throughout the United States; indeed, wherever a large audience had to be covered with high quality sound. Then television arrived, cinema audiences fell and the enormous development funds dried up.

Although American bands continued to benefit from superior speaker technology, the

stage monitor power amplifiers

"out-front" power amplifiers

sidefill monitor speaker

treble

midrange

bass

Below For their December 1980 UK tour, the heavy metal band Saxon used a 16,000-watt PA system. A flying speaker stack was used in the center to cover the upper tier seats.

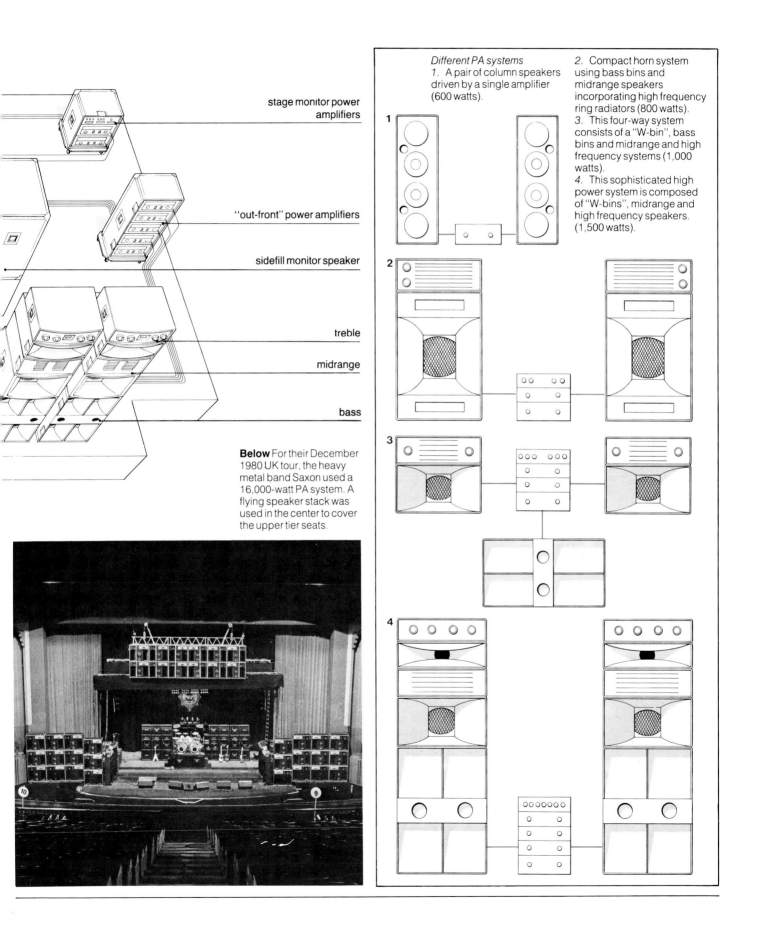

Different PA systems
1. A pair of column speakers driven by a single amplifier (600 watts).

2. Compact horn system using bass bins and midrange speakers incorporating high frequency ring radiators (800 watts).
3. This four-way system consists of a "W-bin", bass bins and midrange and high frequency systems (1,000 watts).
4. This sophisticated high power system is composed of "W-bins", midrange and high frequency speakers. (1,500 watts).

real development of rock PA took place in Britain. The story begins again in Liverpool, 1958. In those days of skiffle, the budget was tiny, but the vocalist had to be heard somehow above the guitars and screams and catwhistles. The ubiquitous Grundig tape recorder was borrowed from home and set up on stage with a microphone. A four-watt amplifier could be made by switching the machine to "record", and then pressing the "pause" button. A broom handle held up by bricks made a microphone stand. The microphone was taped onto the broom handle and the Grundig sat on a beer crate in front of the singer.

Beyond the turn of the decade, as the Merseybeat boom got underway, bands progressed to using equipment which, although primitive, was at least in part intended for the rigors of the road. One such setup used a WEM

Below Free concerts were held in London's Hyde Park in 1969. The most famous of these took place in July when the Rolling Stones performed shortly after the death of Brian Jones. Charlie Watkins of WEM provided 2,000 watts of power and miked up all the instruments – high power and sophisticated techniques for the time. Mick Jagger recited a poem by Shelley in memory of Brian Jones; the sound was so good that many of the 250,000 who attended could hear Jagger breathing.

25-watt Dominator tube guitar amplifier with two 10-inch loudspeakers. Linear Concorde and Vortexion amplifiers were also widely used.

The Vortexions had integral mixers: inputs for four microphones, giant bakelite volume control knobs for each and a pair of tone controls overall. The WEM Dominator did not boast these mixing facilities, but roadies discovered that the WEM Copicat (echo unit), with its two microphone inputs, could be used as a primitive mixer. At the same time, basic three- and four-channel microphone mixers were being pioneered on kitchen tables. In those days, nothing (except possibly the saxophone) was miked up: all the microphones would be used for vocals. British mikes, such as the square Reslos, were almost universally used.

There was no time for soundchecks: the gear was just thrown on stage and everyone helped everyone else to set up their instruments. In this way, bands could do three or four gigs in a night. Most of the clubs, cinemas and theaters had a house PA, which ought to have saved bands from carting their own around. Unfortunately, some of these house PAs were very poor. Sometimes there was only a facility for one microphone; often the puny speakers on either side of the stage were barely audible over the audience's screaming. The Cavern Club in Liverpool had one of the better PAs, with two 12-inch loudspeakers each side of the stage, operated by Brian Kelly. Kelly also hired out a PA (it was free of charge for The Beatles).

The Beatles brought Vox to the forefront; an early Vox PA system consisted of a four eight-inch column speaker used exclusively for vocals PA in conjunction with a 50-watt valve PA amplifier. This had an integral three input mixer, the big novelty being the provision of bass and treble controls on each input. The column speaker with its spindly legs was manifestly impractical. The idea was to raise the speaker above the heads of the crowd to aid sound projection, but roadies went one better: they hammered nails in the wall and hung the unstable contraptions upside down.

In 1965, Selmer produced a 100-watt PA amplifier, the TC300, with four microphone inputs, plus volume, bass, treble and "super treble" controls on each channel. ("Super treble" later became known as "presence". Its purpose was to adjust the level of the upper midrange frequencies.) The matching speaker was a four 10-inch column speaker, again, it sported ridiculous legs and was usually hung upside down like a bat. The roadies' toolkit during this period contained a hand drill, nails and a hammer so the speakers could be hung from the wall.

Left The development of rock PA was accelerated by the need for high quality sound at high levels; the type of sound needed at rock festivals. A musician closely associated with the heyday of large open-air pop concerts was Jimi Hendrix. His performance at the 1967 Monterey Festival brought him widespread acclaim; at Woodstock his version of *Star Spangled Banner* made rock history. A month before he died, in August 1970, he appeared at the second Isle of Wight Festival in Britain and received a mixed reception. For this concert, WEM provided 5,000 watts – more than had ever been used outdoors before – but the organizers were forced to use an unsuitable site for the concert and the sound was poor.

To compete with the Selmer TC300, Vox brought out a similar PA system, again with four 10-inch column speakers and a heavy-weight 100-watt amplifier.

A little later, Jim Marshall introduced his legendary guitar amplifiers. Overnight, instruments became very loud, exemplified by the Townshend "wall of sound". The vocals could not compete any longer. It was easy to lash together a number of 50-watt amplifiers to produce a notionally powerful PA capable of competing with the Marshall stacks, but the misused guitar amplifiers – or PA amplifiers using guitar speakers – were not really suitable for PA service because their peaky response aggravated feedback tendencies. Regardless of power, these early attempts were frustrated by the onset of

Right Charlie Watkins of Watkins Electric Music (WEM) was responsible for laying the foundations of British rock PA. WEM originally produced the Dominator guitar amplifier and another standard piece of early rock equipment – the WEM Copicat (echo unit). The Copicat first appeared in 1954 and during the early 1960s was sometimes used as a primitive mixer.

feedback at low levels, and the vocals remained subdued. New PA amplifiers continued to appear, but despite experimentation, PA remained much the same. Roadies had little time to think about improving the gear and the attitude of musicians was one of total lack of interest. Then in 1967, Pink Floyd astounded their peers by revealing that they had an 800-watt PA; they had enlisted the help of Charlie Watkins.

The WEM PA System

Charlie Watkins was something of a visionary, when, in 1953, he had set up to manufacture sound equipment with the firm conviction that electric music would one day reign supreme. The Watkins Electric Music (or WEM) Copicat and the Dominator guitar amplifiers were standard items of group equipment, but in the mid-1960s, WEM was hit by recession. In a desperate bid to retrieve lost business, Watkins mounted a disastrous publicity tour with The Byrds in 1966, in which he attempted to surmount the now very loud instrument amplifiers with a more powerful PA system: this attempt failed.

After the tour, Watkins was determined to solve the problem and began discussions with a French entrepreneur and a sympathetic Belgian engineer. The Belgian's view was that to provide PA power that could overcome the new instrument amplifiers would be to court danger to health. The view of the French businessman was that if it could be done groups would immediately accept the new technology.

The technology necessary to produce very high power transistor amplifiers was still in its infancy. Watkins' solution was to feed the microphone signals into many of his new 100-watt transistor amplifiers simultaneously. These amplifiers, and their associated column speakers, had a flat response and were purpose-built for PA. The result was that high power vocals amplification was no longer frustrated by acoustic feedback. Although the solution is obvious with hindsight, previous attempts had been along different and unfruitful lines.

The new WEM 1,000-watt PA system premiered with tremendous success at the 1967 Windsor Jazz and Blues festival. It was the world's first high clarity, high power PA system. Every British band now aspired to own a WEM PA, and groups like The Move and Pink Floyd vied to own the most power. Most important of all, the WEM factory became a meeting place where musicians who had suddenly developed an interest in PA could exchange ideas.

Around the same time, the WEM Audiomaster five-channel mixer appeared after three years of development. Although microphone mixers

Above When Jim Marshall brought out his legendary guitar amp – the Marshall stack – instruments could suddenly be played much louder. A new PA system designed for rock became essential to allow the vocals to be heard over the high volume guitar and keyboard amplification.

separate from the PA amplifiers had appeared before, they were treated as something of a nuisance by earlier bands, who could not be bothered to worry about PA. The Audiomasters were not only much more sophisticated than the mixers that had been built into tube amplifiers, but they could be linked together to provide as many input channels as were needed. Better microphones began to appear as well; the new music of 1967 celebrated sensitivity and vocalists sought smooth, clean-sounding microphones that could do it justice. German Beyer microphones found their way on stage. Touring American bands were seen using Shure microphones, and the Shure Unidyne III and 545, amongst others, rapidly found favor.

American Techniques

By 1969, many leading British bands had toured the United States and returned brimming with new ideas. At the Fillmore East, for instance, Bazz Ward, then road manager of The Nice was very impressed with the Altec "Voice of the Theater" (cinema-style) horn-loaded PA speaker system which was compact, yet loud for the power involved. All the instruments were miked

Above In the early 1960s, The Beatles toured with a Vox PA system and helped to popularize the company's products. The PA amplifier was only 50 watts, power that would be scorned by most bands today.

Right Pete Townshend of The Who was one of the first players to use a Marshall stack and soon became famous for his high volume guitar playing – later using Hiwatt amps for the Townshend "wall of sound".

up through the PA, via a mixer placed at the side of the stage; everything was reproduced through the PA. A roadie standing by the side of the stage did the mixing, periodically racing out into the audience to check the sound. There were also soundchecks – the musicians would play a few numbers before the gig to allow the roadie to set up the sound on the mixer.

Influenced by American techniques, roadies began to mike up the instruments and Audio-master mixers appeared in tandem to handle as many as twenty microphones. Miking up not only made the instruments louder, it also gave the musicians new sounds to play with. Miked-up drums were especially dramatic. Thanks to the dedication of conscientious roadies, bands became willing to spend more time setting up their sound system. In 1970, "Dinky" Dorson, engineer with Fleetwood Mac, brought back a Belden multicore cable from the United States and, using three Audiomasters, mixed "out front" in the middle of the audience for the first time. Previously mixing out front was considered too complicated – not to mention dangerous with the wilder audiences of the early 1960s.

Also in 1969, the idea of stage monitors was tentatively imported from the United States. Bobby Pridden, The Who's sound engineer, persuaded Charlie Watkins to modify his Audio-masters, adding an extra output for stage monitors. The signal then passed to a WEM 100-watt amplifier and a speaker cabinet was placed in front of Roger Daltrey so he could hear himself. But monitors cost money and it was so unusual and satisfying to have a good PA sound out front that stage monitors were largely disregarded until the novelty of high-power PA had been surpassed.

Horn-Loaded Speaker Systems
Between 1967 and 1970, Charlie Watkins pioneered successful festival sound systems that helped to make Britain the musical center of the rock world. After the second Isle of Wight festival and the death of Jimi Hendrix, the magical atmosphere soured. Other engineers took over from Watkins to complete the development of rock concert PA.

The WEM PAs had used column (direct radiator) speakers for the bass and midrange frequencies. Although their directional properties were not ideal when stacked in tandem, they were fairly efficient and, most importantly for projecting vocals, the WEM columns exhibited a subtle, delicate midrange sound which suited the music of the era. But soon PA began to suffer from the "power at all costs" syndrome. Bands suddenly wanted to use the horn-loaded

Above In the early 1970s, The Grateful Dead used their own gigantic and bizarre PA system. It took a large crew two days to set up and featured 450 direct radiator speakers arranged behind the band in towering 40-foot stacks. Each instrument had its own stack, an arrangement which potentially could provide a clean, unmuddied sound. The musicians had total control of the system but problems would arise when one member of the band increased the volume of his part of the PA, only to be followed by the others in turn, a process which resulted in a very loud, unbalanced sound. The group eventually dismantled and sold the system in the mid-1970s. Here they are shown using a more conventional PA setup.

cinema-style speaker systems they had seen in the United States. These were dubbed "bin and horn" because the huge bass horns were like bins – or bathtubs. Public address-style sound systems (announcement only) using "trumpet" horns had provided crude vocals PA in the early 1960s for bands such as The Beatles, when they played the giant Shea Stadium during their first US tour. American bands had always enjoyed the luxury of cinema-style horn-loaded house PAs which, while relatively low in power, were at least intended for music. By the mid-1960s, quiet, acoustic groups like Peter, Paul And Mary were touring clubs with portable high fidelity horn speakers such as Paul Klipsch's La Scala. But although the Americans had the technology, they lagged behind in applying it to high-power rock sound systems, especially to festival systems. The sound at the Woodstock festival in 1969 was so demure that one observer remarked that it seemed as if "at a large and spontaneous gathering of hippies, some bands just happened to come along and play some music".

Horn speakers were attractive to British bands and PA entrepreneurs because, although the units were bulky, they were very efficient and in the end, took up less room than an equally

Above Charlie Watkins of WEM with his 1971 Festival stack.

Below The original WEM Audiomaster, a five-channel mixer, appeared in the late 1960s and was used to mix the sound at all the early British pop festivals. Audiomasters could be linked together to provide as many input channels as required.

loud PA made of column speakers. In 1970 the quintessential heavy metal band Iron Butterfly toured Britain, bringing a horn speaker system to the country for the first time. Knowing that their breakup was imminent, Iron Butterfly sold the PA at the end of the tour to their support band, a group called Yes. The system consisted of one giant eight-foot RCA "W-bin", and one sectoral horn on each side of the stage. The size of these speaker stacks matched their loudness and they caused something of a sensation.

What had been good technology in the cinemas of the 1940s was found to be good technology in the concert halls of the 1970s. Bill Kelsey duly began to manufacture modified versions of cinema horns in Britain. Bands also turned to Vitavox, the indigenous manufacturer, who had been producing horn speakers for cinemas for years. At the same time, the new, very high-power American amplifiers such as Crown DC300 and models manufactured by Phase Linear and SAE became widely used, and to match the new aggrandizement of out-front power, musicians began to demand powerful stage monitoring systems so they could hear themselves singing and playing.

By 1972, the foundations of today's PA systems had been laid, but there were problems. Horn speakers could sound very harsh and without careful application, they could alienate audiences at high levels. Building big PA systems involved much more thought and skill than heaping up dozens of speakers and deafening everyone in the first six rows. From 1970, it has taken nearly a decade to learn amidst countless decibels of ear-ripping, feedback-enhanced, muddy and nauseous sound how to achieve clarity, balance and precision in rock sound systems: in short, how to make the PA work as a real aid in communications between musicians and their audiences. Changes made over the past ten years have been mainly cosmetic; the basic components of the PA have remained the same.

The Modern PA System
Microphones

First of the many links in the PA chain is the microphone. The job of a microphone – to convert sound waves into equivalent electrical vibrations – seems quite simple; after all, the ordinary telephone has used microphones successfully for over 80 years. However, with live sound microphones, the stress is on the word equivalent. The carbon microphones used in telephones, although tough and reliable, are horrendously noisy and only reproduce a fraction of the range of audible frequencies. On the other hand, a live sound microphone must not generate any audible noise, it must be equally sensitive to all the frequencies it will be asked to reproduce and it must not produce spurious harmonics (or distortion) regardless of the intensity of the sound it is asked to handle. Such microphones exist; indeed, the best microphones convert sound into electricity much more accurately than their opposite numbers, loudspeakers. Regrettably, subtlety and finesse in converting sound into electricity tends to go hand in hand with fragility and rock performers are not renowned for fastidious relationships with microphones. Phil Lewis, for instance, vocalist of Girl, smashed a $200 (£100) microphone against the stage each night as part of his act.

Somehow, fidelity has to be consolidated with robustness, and only two of the many methods of converting sound into electricity are practical for the stage. The dynamic or moving coil microphone is the heavy duty, high fidelity equivalent of the toy microphones which accompany oriental cassette recorders. This microphone works rather like a speaker in reverse. Because the moving coil mike is inherently tough and was already highly developed when rock and roll began, it became the standard. However, its reproductive qualities are not as accurate as the alternative: the capacitor microphone. This requires a DC voltage, which can be a nuisance, but otherwise, modern versions are probably superior to moving coil microphones in all respects excepting ruggedness. Ironically, although the capacitor microphone was developed nearly 60 years ago, the only practical head amplifiers available until the late 1960s used tube and these made the microphone impossibly heavy, bulky and delicate for stage use. As a result, only in the latter half of the 1970s did the capacitor microphone find a place on the stage, when its new sturdiness made it acceptable to the habitual users of moving coil microphones.

Capacitor microphones exhibit a very flat frequency response, while moving coil mikes are often peaky in the upper midrange. This peakiness adds character, particularly to vocal sounds, and microphones are often chosen on the basis of such character or coloration.

The simplest way of miking up a band is to place a single microphone (mono) or a crossed pair of microphones (stereo) in front of the stage. This technique is admirably suited for purist recording, but it does not work at all for PA. The microphone has to be a fair distance from the musicians for it to "hear" in perspective. This separation between the sound source and the mike lowers the sound level heard by the mike,

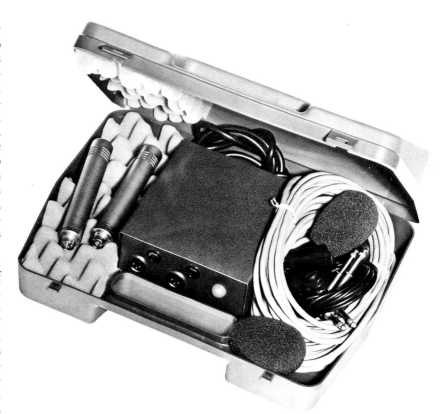

Above Microphone carrying case containing two condenser mikes, windshields, clamps, leads and a transformer.

which in turn means the signal has to be amplified to a greater degree than is strictly necessary. To achieve this separation the microphone must be positioned out front, dangerously close to or even in line with the sound from the PA speakers. The inevitable result of this arrangement (aggravated by the need for extra microphone gain) is that acoustic feedback occurs long before any useful amplification of the original sound can be attained. In any case, the balance in the sound level of the individual instruments is totally out of the sound engineer's control, and the musicians themselves cannot hear what cacophonous sound is being suffered by the audience. Finally, this simple miking method produces a very reverberant sound, full of ambience, which, although realistic, includes audience noise and lacks both "tightness" and the all-important feeling of spontaneity.

For these reasons, the best and most popular way to mike up is to give each instrument its own close-seated microphone, a technique called "close miking". Because rock instruments are quite noisy, stage microphones are almost exclusively unidirectional, that is, they are especially sensitive in one direction only. Careful positioning of the myriad microphones on the drumkit is essential to limit the degree of sound spill from, say, adjacent toms and snares.

These two diagrams contrast the miking up arrangement for a five-piece band in a small venue (1) with the miking arrangement for a major venue (2). The symbols indicate mike placement. Despite the fact that amps and drumkits are usually loud enough on their own in small clubs, most groups mike up bass and lead amps and the bass drum.

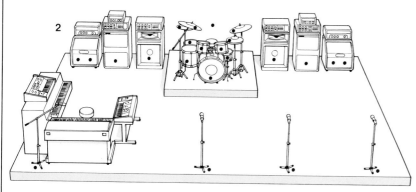

Close miking means that the microphones are subjected to very high sound levels. Therefore the microphone gain required is very small and the likelihood of acoustic feedback is neatly deflated. Because each instrument has its own microphone, the sound engineer can control the overall balance of the band's sound, as heard by the audience, by mixing the microphone signals out front. The emphasis in PA microphone techniques, then, is to capture each instrument as a discrete entity.

Direct Injection, Stage Box and Multicore

Apart from the purely acoustic instruments, guitars and keyboards have to be fed into the PA. Since these instruments are electric, microphones can be avoided by tapping off the electrical signal somewhere between the guitar or keyboard and the instrument amplifier's loudspeaker. If the sound is a clean one (electric bass or keyboards) the signal is tapped off as close to the instrument as possible for the sake of clarity. If the sound is a dirty one, which includes the sound of an overdriven amplifier and speaker, a microphone can be placed in front of the instrument amplifier's speaker to capture the raunchy sound in its entirety. Nonetheless, direct injec-

Left Joni Mitchell surrounded by microphones. Subtle acoustic sounds are difficult to capture: the solution is to place mikes as close to the sound source as possible. The sound engineer can then control the balance by mixing the signals from the various mikes to achieve the desired effect.

tion can be added to supplement this sound to taste, and with both types of signal sources to hand, the mixing engineer can reproduce both clean and dirty styles of playing without compromise. The direct injection (DI) box is simply a means of connecting amplifiers on stage to the PA without creating unhealthy hums and buzzes. The DI box also frequently incorporates an attenuator which cuts the signal and an amplifier to allow minute voltages from guitar pickups and the large voltages driven into instrument amplifier speakers to be fed into the PA at a fairly standard level and without overload, noise or loss of clarity.

Cables lead from each microphone and DI box and are collated at the stage box. Then a very thick cable, affectionately termed "multicore" or "snake", containing 80 wires or more leads the signals to the mixing desk, which is sited somewhere in the center of the auditorium, usually toward the rear.

The Desk
Although the mixing desks seen at major concerts look dauntingly like mission control, once the functions of one of the channels are grasped, operating the desk becames mainly repetitive. The signal from each microphone and DI box is allocated a channel. The desk is designed to route and control the level and tonality of a large number of signals, both singly and in groups, without spurious interaction, or the addition of distortion, hiss or other noises. Big rock concert desks are broadly similar to their counterparts in film and recording studios, but the emphasis is on ruggedness, the subgrouping accords with the number of instruments typically encountered in bands and the inputs are designed to handle the high level signals that originate from wild rock performers and close miking techniques. In the smaller PA setups, fewer channels are required and the desk shrinks into a mixer, with perhaps four or six channels, and the facilities reduced to the bare essentials – volume, bass, midrange and treble controls for each microphone and a master volume control. Although cosmetically different, such mixers are essentially similar to their forerunner, the WEM Audiomaster.

Size or complexity regardless, the desk is the control center of the PA. The sound engineers or musicians can aim to reproduce the music *per se*, or can add their own interpretation. Mixing a band is much more than merely summing the signals from all the microphones or twiddling knobs. Despite all its advantages, close miking does not reproduce the natural sound of many instruments; skilful use of the equalization (or

Below The moving coil microphone is the mike most often used for rock vocals. It works in a similar way to a generator or dynamo. Sound waves vibrate the diaphragm *(right)* which is curved for rigidity and connected to a voice coil. The voice coil moves through a strong magnetic field and generates a tiny electrical current (although at the high sound levels encountered on stage, the output voltage can reach one volt, 10,000 times greater than the output from mikes in a broadcasting studio). Air vents at the rear of the diaphragm make the microphone most sensitive to sound arriving from the front (directional). The windshield prevents "popping" noises when the microphone is held close to the singer's mouth. The transformer adjusts the signal to match the mixing desk input, preventing unwanted hums and ensuring the treble response is not limited.

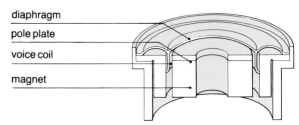

diaphragm
pole plate
voice coil
magnet

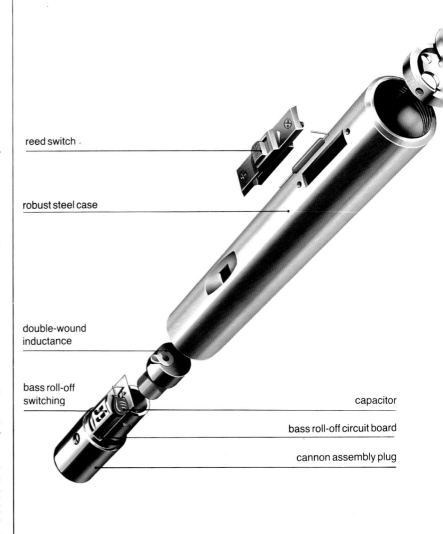

reed switch

robust steel case

double-wound inductance

bass roll-off switching

capacitor

bass roll-off circuit board

cannon assembly plug

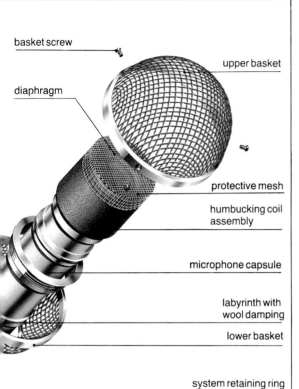

basket screw

upper basket

diaphragm

protective mesh

humbucking coil assembly

microphone capsule

labyrinth with wool damping

lower basket

system retaining ring

Above Roger Daltrey of The Who is noted for his energetic stage presence, expressed, typically, by swinging microphones. Stage microphones have to be sturdy to accommodate this type of treatment.

The major manufacturers of microphones include Electrovoice (1, 2, 7), Shure (3), AKG (4), Audio-Technica (5) and Calrec (6). The Electrovoice RE15 is one of the strongest mikes ever made; the Shure SM58 is the "industry standard" rock PA mike.

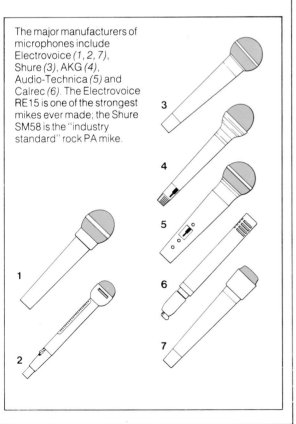

Below The direct injection (DI) box allows signals to be taken from the instrument itself and routed directly to the mixer, eliminating problems of sound "spill" between mikes. DI boxes are often used for capturing the "clean" sounds of bass and keyboards, if the amplifier's tone is not part of the overall sound.

tone) controls is necessary to counteract this deficiency. A good engineer must also have rapport with the audience and know how to make the musicians come through to the best of their ability: success in PA is largely a matter of the person on the desk being in accord with the musicians on stage. A complex desk provides a great versatility in control, but without unique human attributes such as creativity, wit and skill, the desk is merely an expensive showpiece.

Hall Equalization

Hall equalization is the use of specialized equipment to match the sound of the PA to the acoustic qualities of a particular venue. The left and right (stereo) output signals lead from the desk to yet another equalizer. Each channel and each subgroup has already suffered equalization, primarily to account for deficiencies in close miking techniques, or to counteract or accentuate the qualities of each instrument. Although the signal emanating from the desk is then nearly perfect, hall acoustics and loudspeaker systems contrive to add coloration, thereby destroying the quality of the sound. Further equalization is needed to restore the original quality. Ex-cinemas tend to be "dead" (lacking reverberation), and an overall treble boost is needed. A certain bass frequency may set up a sepulchral boom, in which case this frequency must be attenuated. Similarly, an otherwise excellent midrange speaker may sound harsh at certain frequencies. Again, the solution is to "notch out" the offensive sound using an equalizer. In order to counteract these deficiencies without com-

Right A typical channel from a 12-channel mixer. Each instrument or microphone is assigned a channel; for example lead vocals may be assigned the first channel, bass the second, and so on. At the rear of each channel is an input socket and a slide switch which selects the appropriate input sensitivity – "line" or mike signals. Input gain adjusts the level of the input signal. Some amplification is necessary to maintain a large ratio between hums and desirable sounds, but too much level will cause overload. The equalization controls (bass, midrange and treble) are an extension of the bass and treble controls found on domestic hifi equipment. These are used for cutting and boosting the different frequencies in the different frequency bands. High midrange can be used to accentuate vocal "presence" or to harden the drum sound. Boosting the low midrange gives the sound warmth. The echo send level control determines the level sent to an auxiliary submixer used to feed effects units; it is also sometimes used to provide an additional mix for the monitors. The foldback level control allows the engineer to set up a separate mix for the stage monitors. The panpot deploys the signal between the left and right speaker stacks (similar to a domestic stereo's balance control). Turning the control knob creates the impression of a sound image moving across the stage, particularly effective for drums. Otherwise, the panpots are set up to position each sound according to the relevant instrument's position – drums center, bass stage right, and so on. The channel fader is used as a volume control, unlike the input gain which is usually disregarded once set up. The normal position for the fader is "¾ up". After the channel fader and panpot, the signals from each channel are mixed down and pass to the left and right output sockets via a pair of master faders. These allow the overall level fed to each

side of the stage to be adjusted easily. Sometimes a master equalization section is also provided in the output section. Two meters show whether the output levels are overloading any part of the system. The outputs for echo send and foldback are in mono

Terms for mixing desks
Desks are termed according to how many channels, subgroups and outputs they have. A 12/2 or "twelve into two" has 12 channels (inputs) and two (stereo) outputs. A 12/4/2 has four subgroups before the outputs.

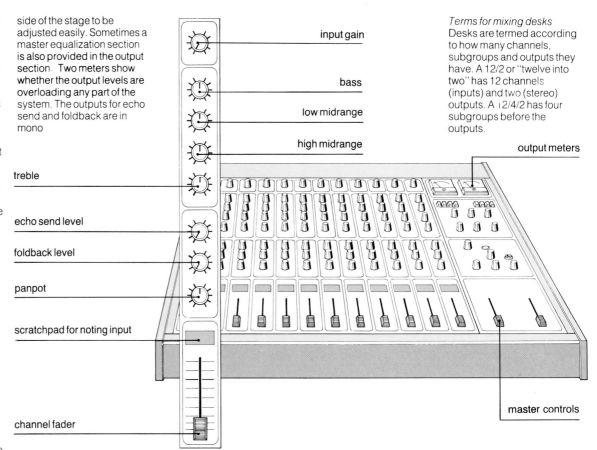

input gain

bass

low midrange

high midrange

treble

echo send level

foldback level

panpot

scratchpad for noting input

channel fader

output meters

master controls

pletely upsetting the sound quality, the equalization must be restricted to a very narrow band: if a tenfold attenuation at 1kHz is attempted using a normal three- or four-band equalizer, most of the midrange frequencies will end up being lost. For equalizing the acoustics of concert halls and deficiencies in speaker systems, the multichannel (also called the graphic or third-octave equalizer) is used. The range of audio frequencies is split into around 27 bands (each one-third octave apart – hence the name). With this number of bands, fairly aggressive adjustments to any spot frequency can be made without grossly upsetting the adjacent frequencies.

The Crossover
The only way to achieve high quality in high-power sound systems is to use specialized loudspeakers to cover segments of the audio band. The crossover's job is to split up the signals into several frequency bands to feed the appropriate loudspeakers with bass, midrange and treble frequencies. In domestic hifi systems, the crossover is wired between the amplifier and speakers. This arrangement (known as a passive crossover), a not-too-useful legacy from 1930 cinema

sound systems, gives fair results at low power levels, but wastes a lot of power. For this reason alone, passive crossovers are the *bête noire* of sound systems and are studiously avoided in most of the larger PA systems.

Instead, active crossovers find almost universal use. The signal is routed to the crossover before going to the amplifiers. If the crossover splits the signal into three bands (bass, midrange and treble) three amplifiers are needed, whereas a passive crossover would only use one. However, this rather perverse arrangement makes the best use of the power available and greatly improves the sound quality. Such systems are frequently called "tri-amplified".

Most of the energy in music lies in the bass regions. Power is rarely to spare at rock concerts, and from time to time, it is inevitable that the bass will overload the PA. One of the prime advantages of using an active crossover is that the gross distortion caused by occasional bass end overload will be limited to the bass speakers. Thus the clarity of the midrange and treble frequencies will remain unaffected, and since the ear is not unduly upset by bass distortion, regardless of its severity, the end result is cleaner sound at higher levels than would otherwise

Above This 32-channel Soundcraft series 3B desk is typical of large rock concert desks. Large desks not only have more channels but also feature more sophisticated controls. They also have four to eight subgroups so that instruments which are miked up in a complex way can be controlled as a whole regardless of the number of mikes or DI boxes involved.

Above The Peavey Mark 2 eight-channel mixer is the type of desk used by a small band in a small venue.

be possible. After the third-octave equalizer, lies the active crossover. Once split up, the signal is ready to be amplified. It travels back to the stage along the same multicore cable that brought the microphone signals to the desk.

In smaller PAs using passive crossovers, the signal will usually travel directly from the desk to the power amplifiers. In this case, there will frequently be only one power amplifier per side, feeding the speakers in each stack via the (passive) crossovers.

The Paradox of Power

The essence of the PA is to encourage rapport between musicians and audience. Creative aspects apart, rapport thrives on the sound in the auditorium being sufficiently loud to make the music come alive, or for a quarter of a million people to hear Mick Jagger breathing in Hyde Park. For this reason the power amplifiers are the backbone of the PA, and not surprisingly, the machismo of a band is sometimes assessed according to the megawattage of their PA.

A loud domestic hifi system typically uses 100-watt power amplifiers, a deafening Marshall stack might total 300 watts, yet the PA used by The Jam is 15,000 watts, while Status Quo

have used 30,000 watts indoors. Powers of 100,000 watts have been used outdoors at festivals. In practice, however, 100,000 watts of PA is disappointing. Our hearing encompasses a vast range – the quietest sounds we can hear are ten million million times quieter than the loudest rock bands. To accommodate this huge range without undue distress, our brain interprets tenfold increases in power as a mere doubling in loudness: in other words, 15,000 watts is only about four times louder than 150 watts. Another psychoacoustic principle is that certain types of distorted sound can appear much louder than power alone would suggest, while clean amplification can make even raunchy music appear relatively quiet.

When the power of a PA is talked about, it is always the electrical power fed to the speakers which is referred to. Although PA speakers are very efficient, only a fraction of the electrical power is converted into acoustic energy for consumption by our ears. Even the acoustic power fed into the auditorium bears little relationship to loudness: a large, reverberant auditorium tends to magnify the sound, while 1,000 watts in an over-carpeted, acoustically "dead" nightclub can be surprisingly quiet. Loudness also depends on the directional characteristics of the loudspeakers: obviously, a very powerful speaker array that sprays music out over a wide angle will tend to sound quieter than one that directs the sound in a very tight beam – assuming you are sitting in line with the speakers. For all these reasons loudness is only very loosely determined by power, but nevertheless, rock PA powers can be classified roughly as follows:

300-1,000 watts – Small halls, clubs, pubs and bars.

1,000-5,000 watts – Large halls (also jazz, easy listening and cabaret-style performances in major auditoriums).

5,000-30,000 watts – Major auditoriums.

25,000-80,000 watts – Outdoor concerts.

Power Amplifiers

Back on stage, the signals from the crossover are routed via the stage box to the power amplifiers. Up to now, the signals originating from the microphones will have remained at substantially the same power level, usually amplified around ten times so they will not be swamped in noise as they pass through the desk and other processing gear. The job of the power amplifiers is to turn the milliwatts arriving from the crossover into the kilowatts of power required to drive stacks of loudspeakers.

Although very high power amplifiers (up to 1,000 watts) have been available for some years,

Left Two amplifier chassis from amplifiers made by WEM. The EL84 chassis *(top)* was used in the first Dominator amplifier, originally produced in 1959. The 100-watt slave amplifier chassis *(bottom)* was first produced in 1966. These amplifiers could be connected up and used in conjunction with the WEM Audiomaster.

Below Horn loading a speaker helps the speaker cone to couple efficiently with the outside air. The compression chamber is a limited volume of air which counteracts the high pressure in the throat. The high air pressure in the small throat matches the stiff diaphragm. The expansion of waves reduces air pressure and at the mouth the pressure of the sound waves matches that of the air outside.

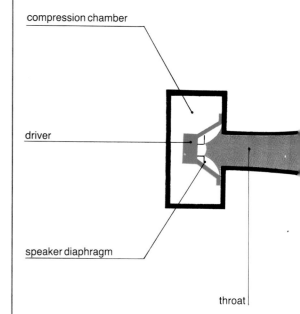

compression chamber

driver

speaker diaphragm

throat

it is preferable to pair one amplifier with only one or two speakers – if the amplifier fails, you cut your losses. As few speakers can handle more than a few hundred watts, the majority of power amplifiers provide relatively moderate amounts of power, typically 100 to 500 watts. Therefore a large number of amplifiers are required to provide kilowatts of power. The amplifiers are grouped in flight cases (racks) according to the frequency band handled by their associated speakers.

Speakers

The loudspeaker is basically a microphone in reverse: electrical signals are converted into equivalent sound vibrations. In order to make the speaker diaphragm do useful work, the sound waves must be channeled to prevent them reaching the other side of the cone, otherwise they would cancel out. A simple way to do this is to enclose the speaker in a box: this is the direct radiator, the everyday enclosure used for radios, hifi systems and guitar amplifiers. Unfortunately, to obtain high sound quality from such an enclosure, efficiency must be sacrificed. For instance, exotic hifi speakers deliver a mere 0.5 per cent of the power from the amplifier to the air. Using such inefficient speakers is impractical when high sound levels need to be generated in a large auditorium: most of the seats would have to be filled with speakers to produce a reasonable sound level. Placing several speakers side

Below Power amplifiers used for rock PA include the Crown (Amcron) DC300 and the Altec 9440A. Introduced in 1967, the Crown DC300 was the first reliable high power transistor audio amplifier. Mark II versions of this legendary "industry standard" are still widely used today.

Right Today, many bands have as much as half the amount of out-front power coming back through the on-stage monitor speakers. The Jam, shown here on stage with wedge monitors, use 5,500 watts of foldback.

166

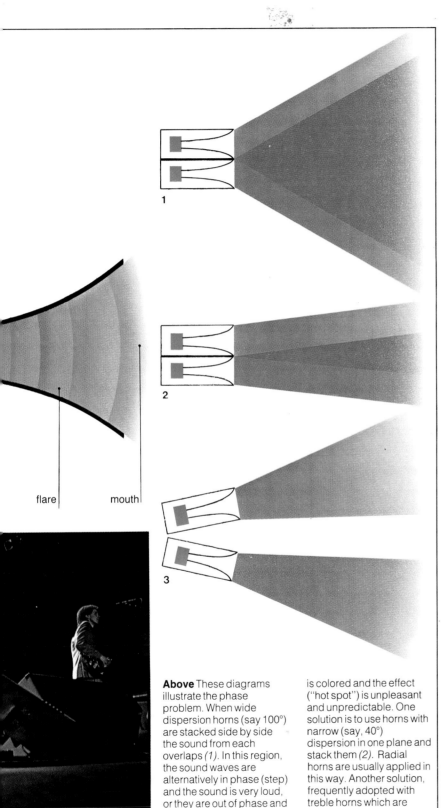

flare | mouth

Above These diagrams illustrate the phase problem. When wide dispersion horns (say 100°) are stacked side by side the sound from each overlaps *(1)*. In this region, the sound waves are alternatively in phase (step) and the sound is very loud, or they are out of phase and the level will be below average. These phase distortion effects occur at different points. The sound is colored and the effect ("hot spot") is unpleasant and unpredictable. One solution is to use horns with narrow (say, 40°) dispersion in one plane and stack them *(2)*. Radial horns are usually applied in this way. Another solution, frequently adopted with treble horns which are small and can be easily angled, is to place them side by side and point them in different directions *(3)*.

by side in a box raises the efficiency to around 5 per cent; this arrangement gives the column speaker of the 1960s. Unfortunately, apart from the fixed dispersion characteristics and none-too-wide frequency range, the column speaker is also simply not efficient enough.

The solution is to use a completely different approach. The direct radiator speaker is inefficient because the speaker's stiff cone does not match the compliance (floppiness) of the surrounding air it is trying to vibrate. Horn-loading the speaker overcomes this problem and raises the efficiency of the speaker to between 20 and 40 per cent. This means that for any given amount of power input, a horn-loaded speaker will be louder than a column speaker.

For low frequency reproduction, an ordinary cone speaker is used but for high, midrange and treble frequencies, the horn is paired with a compression driver. This is a driver (or speaker) designed especially and solely for horn-loading. Horn speakers intended for high quality sound reproduction have critical and well-defined minimum dimensions. They are large yet efficient specialized speakers that come into their own when cavernous auditoriums have to be filled with loud music. For these large-scale applications, these speakers are relatively smaller, cheaper and lighter than any other type and arguably provide the best sound quality at high levels.

Horn speakers work best when they are limited to specific frequency bands. At least three horns are required to cover the audio band; a fact not appreciated in the original two-way horn-loaded PAs of the early 1970s. More than other speakers, the dimensions of horns are closely related to the wavelength of the sound they handle. Bass horns (nicknamed "bins") are large (a 50Hz note has a wavelength of 22 feet 7 inches/6.8 m) while treble horns are much smaller (a 10kHz note has a wavelength of 1½ inches/3.8 cm). Horn speakers have another attribute which makes them ideal for concert PA systems and accounts for their bizarre shapes – the horn flares can be contoured to control the dispersion of the sound waves as they emerge from the mouth. Dispersion control is extremely important because power costs a lot of money, and it is obviously desirable to ensure that most of the sound is beamed directly at the audience. Sound which travels elsewhere will be wasted. Outdoors, sound which travels in this way annoys anti-rock campaigners; indoors, it will bounce off walls and ceilings to cause unpleasant slapback echoes or meet up with the microphones on stage to aggravate tendencies toward acoustic feedback.

Positioning Speakers

To simulate "real sound" the PA should magnify the sound of the band without altering the apparent position of the musicians on stage. In other words, if the keyboard player is to the right of the stage, the audience should hear the sound of the keyboards coming from the right. To achieve this effect, short of placing speakers behind or in front of the band, the most practical method is to place them on each side of the stage.

The horns are stacked predominantly in a vertical fashion, with the largest, the bass bins, at the bottom. This statuesque arrangement not only saves space, it also has definite acoustic advantages. Tall stacks tend to obviate phase distortions. Since high frequencies are easily absorbed by crowds of people packed together, treble horns are placed at the top of the speaker stack so they can beam the high frequencies well over head height. Midrange horns come next and, finally, the heavyweight bass bins provide stability at the bottom of the stack. The midrange and treble horns stacked on top of the bass bins form a wall which helps the bins to project low frequencies into the auditorium.

The flown stack, where the midrange and treble horns are suspended in the center above the band, is a recent development. Flying takes advantage of the ears' insensitivity to vertical displacement – the sound appears to come from the band even though the speakers are many feet above them. Flying PAs also enhance the sound for the audience sitting in the upper tier seats of split-level auditoriums. Bass bins are rarely flown, partly because they are so heavy, but also because there is no real need. Low frequencies can permeate an entire building without any assistance.

In small halls and clubs, the bare minimum – a stack of three horns (bass, midrange and treble) – usually provides ample sound level. In this case, horns with a wide angle dispersion pattern will be used to cover the entire audience.

In larger venues, the sound level produced by a single driver becomes inadequate. An obvious way of augmenting the power is to use additional speakers in each frequency band – for instance, placing a pair of three horn stacks side by side. Unfortunately, to double the loudness, ten times the power is required. To make the PA twice as loud, roughly ten times as many cabinets would be needed. Another more insidious problem is the unpleasant coloration which results when the sound waves emanating from speakers operating in the same frequency band interact. Building high power PA stacks without this phase distortion is a skilled task: horns with well-specified dispersion character-

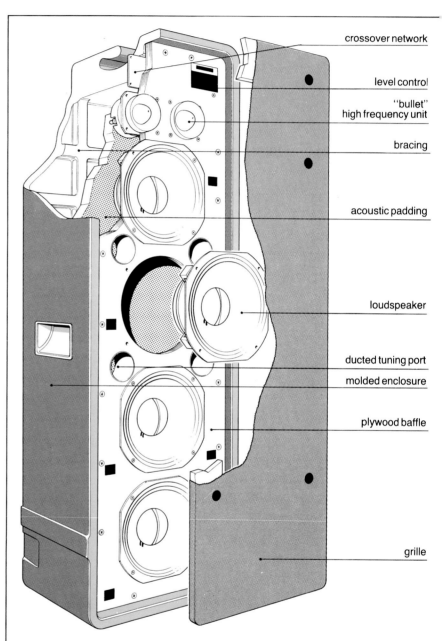

crossover network

level control

"bullet" high frequency unit

bracing

acoustic padding

loudspeaker

ducted tuning port

molded enclosure

plywood baffle

grille

Above The JBL strongbox column speaker. The direct radiator is the common speaker enclosure used for radios, hifi systems and guitar amplifiers: placing several speakers side by side gives the column speaker, popular in 1960s rock PA systems. Column speakers are not efficient enough for rock music although they project a delicate midrange sound.
Right Horn-loaded speakers are more efficient than columns. At least three horns are needed to cover the audio spectrum properly. For low frequencies, an ordinary cone speaker is used, but for high midrange and treble frequencies, a driver is paired with the horn. The Vitavox 4kHz treble horn (1) gives wide dispersion in the horizontal plane and is useful for small venues. The T35 treble horn (2) provides clean, sweet-sounding treble. Radial horns (3) for high midrange and treble have a narrow dispersion and can be stacked vertically. The Vitavox multicellular midrange horn (4) is fitted with two compression drivers to increase the power handling capacity. The Electrovoice 1823 high power compression driver (5) is widely used for midrange frequencies. The Martin 115 bass bin (6) is a semi-folded horn designed to deliver more "punch" than conventional bins.

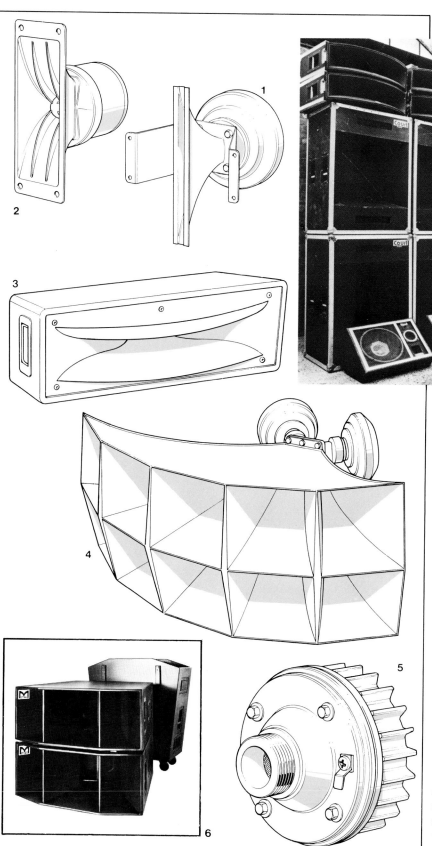

Above A range of PA equipment from Court Acoustics, a PA hire company. Wedge monitors are in the foreground; the bass bins are stacked in the first and second rows and the mid and high frequency horns are on top.

istics have to be judiciously stacked and subtly angled to avoid interaction, yet at the same time cover the audience evenly. This goes some way to explaining the seemingly untidy arrangement of many PA speaker stacks.

Monitors

Musicians on stage need mutual rapport to play well just as much as they need rapport with their audience. Apart from skill, tight musicianship is the result of being able to hear other members of the band clearly. This is the purpose of the stage monitors. It is not surprising to learn, then, that the monitors are often regarded as the most important part of the PA; if the musicians can not play properly because of inadequate monitors, the remainder of the PA is superfluous.

In small PA setups, the monitor signals are derived from the desk via the foldback or cue sends (outputs on the mixing desk). There may only be one or two monitor mixes available – in this case, the needs of the vocalist are usually given precedence. The monitor mix travels from the desk to a power amplifier and then to a speaker cabinet, known as a wedge monitor, placed in front of the musician.

In large PA setups, all the musicians are treated to stage monitoring. The signals from the microphones are split off from the stage box, fed simultaneously into the out-front desk and a monitor mixer, which is placed in the stage wings. The monitor mixer is usually a less sophisticated version of the main desk. Instead of a stereo mixdown however, the monitor mixer has a number of output groups, similar in essence to the subgroups on a large out-front desk. These output groups, one for each musician, are routed to adjacent crossovers and power amplifiers, which in turn feed the monitor speakers beside each musician. The monitor mixing engineer can then route any combination of instruments to each monitor speaker, according to what each musician wants to hear.

Compared to the immensity of the main PA, the monitors often appear to be a casual afterthought. In early monitor systems, it was not thought necessary to reproduce the whole frequency range, just the bare essentials. The midrange frequencies (for example, the vocals) were emphasized to cut through the ambient racket. Unfortunately, the result sounded like an unbearably loud telephone and was obnoxious and fatiguing at high sound levels. The best modern systems cover most of the audio frequency band, with more bass and treble than their predecessors, and the results are more tolerable. However, wedge, as opposed to sidefill and drum monitors, must be small, to avoid obscuring the band. Thus a wide frequency range is often eschewed, because this would necessitate bulky bass cabinets.

Each musician must hear substantially only his own monitor as he moves around stage. As the proximity of the monitors to the microphones can easily precipitate acoustic feedback, the monitors must have a very flat, uncolored response: any peaks will send the system into howls of feedback long before a useful sound level can be achieved. Third-octave equalizers can be used to smooth out any gross coloration created by poor stage acoustics, but it helps if the monitor speakers have a basically smooth response.

Effects Units

Some sound engineers justly feel that there are enough problems to worry about and knobs to turn without the addition of effects units. But, some people love gimmicks, and skilfully used effects can be enjoyable for everyone. Effects are often on stage, under the musician's control, but

voice coil

coil form

magnet

vent

frame

treble cone

cone

Above The loudspeaker is basically a microphone in reverse: electrical signals are converted into equivalent sound vibrations. A varying electrical impulse reaches the speaker's magnet, altering the magnetic field by varying amounts, which in turn moves the voice coil, attached to the cone. The coil makes the cone, mounted in a frame, move in and out, displacing air and so causing sound waves.

1

2

4▲ 5▼

3▲ 6▼

Setting up a PA system
Trailers carrying equipment are backed up in front of the stage to offload *(1)*. The stage monitors are checked *(2)*. Speakers are arranged according to the space available. This system was arranged with 10,000 watts on either side of the stage. The illustration shows the rear view of the stage right setup. *(3)*. The bass bins were stacked at either end and in the middle, flanked by the high frequency and midrange speakers. The backline – the band's amplification – is then assembled on stage *(4)*. Mixing and lighting desks are usually positioned out front in the middle of the hall *(5)*. In split-level auditoriums, with seating in the upper tiers, some of the speakers will be "flown", or suspended above *(6)*.

when a band is trying to recreate a sound originally made in the studio with the help of a producer and engineer, it makes sense to hand over responsibility for predetermined live effects to the mixing engineer: the musician can then concentrate wholly on his instrument.

For their "Wall" concerts, Pink Floyd were backed with almost an entire recording studio's worth of tape machines and effects units, while bands less dependent on sound contrived in the studio may use nothing more than an echo unit to enhance the vocals or a compressor to tighten the bassist's sound. Effects for individual musicians can be linked in at the mixer – or if the effects refer to the band as a whole, they can be taken across the stereo outputs, before the equalizer and crossover.

Future Developments

The foundations of rock music were built upon the punishment and abuse of primitive equipment, Jimi Hendrix-style. The very early PAs were terrible by today's standards, but the music of the 1960s did not seem to suffer; and, not surprisingly, the much improved PAs of the late 1970s did not automatically bring forth correspondingly better music, although certain styles of jazz-rock, funk and reggae thrive on high quality sound. The only reason for developing even better PA systems is that most people are today familiar with high quality sound at home, and expect to hear equal clarity at concerts.

An interesting trend is the specialization of the larger PA systems. The rigs used by Pink Floyd, The Jam and Steve Hillage are all idiosyncratic yet near perfect systems within the context of the music to which they are attuned. In a sense, each type of music now defines its own sound system. Perhaps this is a process which has been going on surreptitiously since 1958.

Right Britain's most popular heavy metal band, Status Quo, have been playing together for 20 years. In the 1970s they became popular on the club circuit for their driving rock based around loud, simple chords. To be effective, this type of music relies on the sense of presence that loudness provokes.

PLAYING LIVE

For music which has grown out of a tradition of raw, spontaneous entertainment, it is ironic that the staging of a live show should have become fraught with pitfalls and complexities. At the same time as audiences have become accustomed to seeing and hearing groups in live performance, they have also come to expect a sound which is clearly audible from all parts of the auditorium (whatever its shape and size) as well as some sort of visual spectacle.

Expectations were lower when The Beatles, back in the early 1960s, took on hysterical audiences in such venues as Shea Stadium, armed only with 30- and 50-watt Vox amplifiers and a paltry PA system. It seems unlikely the audience heard a note of what was played and The Beatles themselves admitted as much afterward. Just being in the same auditorium with their idols was enough for early rock'n'roll audiences, but as rock music has grown into a multibillion, multinational industry, change has been inevitable and inexorable.

The progress of rock music since the mid-1960s has been toward providing a complete audio-visual package. As recording techniques have become ever more elaborate – from The Beatles' four-track sleight of hand on *Sergeant Pepper* to the later electronic collages of David Bowie – live performances have had to update themselves to keep pace. Similarly, more sophisticated music and presentation has speeded the growth of packaging and merchandising. The elaborate kitsch of Roger Dean's album cover designs for Yes, the ubiquitous work of Hipgnosis, or Peter Saville's chilling artwork for Joy Division are matched by the growth of video promotion to sell a group's image to a mass television audience. These are all aspects of the process designed to impress the potential customer with something more than just sound.

Right Ian Dury And The Blockheads bring the atmosphere of the music hall to rock, preserving the intimacy of small club gigs even when performing in larger venues. Ian Dury was originally with Kilburn And The High Roads, one of the better known of the British "pub rock" bands of the mid-1970s.
Below Dire Straits rose to fame with their hit single, *Sultans Of Swing*, emerging at the same time as many "new wave" bands. Their musical style reflects older traditions, however, and the lead guitarist, Mark Knopfler, has since been in demand as a session player for such

rock luminaries as Bob Dylan and Steely Dan. The band's increasing popularity has taken them a stage further from the club circuit, to larger venues and American tours.
Bottom American rockers, Blue Oyster Cult, make extensive use of lasers to highlight their performances. Extravagant lighting is a feature of many rock shows which take place in football stadiums and other huge auditoriums where visual exaggeration is necessary.

Small Venues

From The Grateful Dead playing at the Egyptian Pyramids to the local band at the steamy club around the corner, live rock music has always existed on several levels. At the most basic level, there will always be the pubs, clubs and bars where groups can get up and play with abandon, dripping with sweat and face to face with the front row. Plenty of bands never make it further than this, but most of the ones who end up appearing in football stadiums had to put in time in just these places. The small clubs are, essentially, the heartland of rock; places where groups can get used to the feel of live audiences (more often than not pushing, shoving, spitting and throwing things). Many experienced followers of rock music insist that only in a small club can a band deliver that intimate electric feeling which is the essence of good live music.

This is not to say that there are no drawbacks to playing in small venues and most bands encounter a number of serious problems at one time or another which prevent them from delivering their best performance. These problems usually concern sound. In some small clubs, bands are not allowed to bring their own PA system and must hire the club's PA and the sound engineer who goes with it. These systems can be poor or not really suited to the music. Soundchecks may be inadequate or nonexistent; a sound mixed in an empty room might change drastically when the room fills up with people. Dressing rooms are invariably awful and access to the stage limited, frustrating any desires to put on an elaborate show. Although a well-established residency at a well-known club can be profitable, most bands only find playing small venues lucrative if it sparks off a major recording interest and leads to bigger things.

Left There is a strong tradition of rock performers whose acts are notable primarily for their flamboyance and outrageous theatricality. The flashy "glitter rock" of the early 1970s, Elton John's absurd stage gear and The Tubes' manic cavortings with chain saws are all aspects of this type of rock "glamor". The American group Kiss are notorious for their extraordinary costumes and makeup, to the extent that the band try not to be photographed as they really are. One of a new wave of "technorock" groups, Kiss' music appears to take second place to their overall presentation.

The "punk revolution" which began in 1977 seemed to mark a change in attitude toward small venues, both in New York and London. A fierce rapport with the audience was the chief requirement of a live performance for these new groups and the energetic fans who followed them. To achieve this, it was vital to play in a club small enough for the audience to be (literally) within spitting distance of the group, where frantically "pogoing" dancers could ricochet onto the stage without being intercepted by bouncers. There will always be groups who want this sort of contact with their fans, but the punk heyday represented a rare occasion when this approach was at the core of a widespread musical movement. It had happened before in the mid-1970s in England, when the "pub-rock" groups like Brinsley Schwarz, Ducks Deluxe and Doctor Feelgood rediscovered the joys of drinking and playing, but that remained on a small scale and never fired the imagination of a cross-section of the music-loving populace. The punk movement faded almost as quickly as it had begun; with the closure of such punk venues as London's Roxy club, dozens of groups disappeared without trace. Others changed: The Clash, for example, emerged as a broadly based

Above The British pub rock band of the mid-1970s, Ducks Deluxe, playing in London's Hard Rock Cafe. Small venues – clubs, bars, pubs and restaurants – allow close contact between musicians and audience.

eclectic rock group with an ever-growing American following.

Medium-sized Venues

Some medium-sized venues, for example, London's Lyceum or Hammersmith Palais and New York's Ritz, can still accommodate the type of atmosphere beloved by devotees of small clubs. In these places, the audience can be reasonably certain of being near enough to the stage to recognize the performers. Many are ex-ballrooms with open space downstairs for those who like standing or dancing close to the stage and seating upstairs for those who would rather sit down. Others are university or college halls more specifically designed for live performances. As with small clubs, sound can be a problem, but if a good PA system is used and time taken over the mixing, the results can be quite good. At their best, medium-sized venues can provide a happy combination of small-club atmosphere and the facilities (and earning potential) of larger venues.

Large Venues

The trend toward playing in football stadiums, conference centers and arenas began in the

Above The opening night at The Venue in London with Graham Parker And The Rumour. At this concert, the band used the house PA, but after widespread criticism about the quality of the sound, The Venue increased the quality of components for subsequent performances.
Left The late Bob Marley, the first "Third World superstar", played to ever-increasing audiences toward the end of his life. His last major concert took place at New York's Madison Square Garden in 1979 where he appeared with Stevie Wonder. His popularity and importance in his native Jamaica went far beyond the realms of rock stardom.

United States in the early 1970s, probably inspired by such enormous occasions as the 1969 Woodstock Festival (half a million people in a sea of mud), the festivals at the Isle of Wight in 1969 and 1970, and Watkins Glen in 1973.

The giant rock event began with the 1967 Monterey Festival in California which featured Jimi Hendrix, Otis Redding, The Byrds and Buffalo Springfield. Woodstock was the apogee of the festival spirit, in legend if not in uncomfortable reality, with its extraordinary lineup of the hottest acts of the day – The Who, Jimi Hendrix, Crosby, Stills, Nash And Young, Jefferson Airplane, Creedence Clearwater Revival and The Band, amongst others.

When Woodstock was followed with sinister swiftness by the stark horrors of Altamont, where a fan was murdered by Hell's Angels as the Rolling Stones played, the idea of one nation under a tent quickly took a dive. It was substituted by the fashion for staging shows in giant venues. Plainly audiences existed in sufficient numbers to pack out large stadiums, and there were plenty of bands keen to trade the rigors of touring for a handsome profit.

The 1970s became the decade when rock groups suddenly turned into megastars. Queen, The Who, Led Zeppelin, the Electric Light Orchestra, Yes and Genesis developed lavish stage presentations; in the United States, older rockers like Blue Oyster Cult and Ted Nugent were superseded by a new wave of "technorockers" like Styx, Rush, Kiss and Kansas. These acts certainly had drawing power but the music was not always interesting or fresh. Peter Gabriel, who quit his lucrative job as singer with Genesis in 1975, described the increasing move among bands to get the flashiest and most expensive onstage accessories as "a million-dollar arms race".

It is inevitable that as a group becomes increasingly popular, it is only profitable to appear live in large auditoriums where enough tickets can be sold to recoup the costs of dragging both the group, crew and the vast heaps of hired PA equipment from one major city to another. In their heyday, Emerson, Lake And Palmer used to tour with one huge truck each.

It still seems disproportionately harsh that the more fans a group has, the worse it treats them. Fans have to pay more money to see a group in a huge venue like London's Earl's Court or New York's Madison Square Garden than they do to see a group in a bar, and they are usually lumbered with a ticket labeled "Row 93 Block X (Restricted View)". Given that it is impossible to see a group like Pink Floyd in anything smaller than a stadium, often with a

Above left The Swedish pop group, Abba, who have grown to be one of Sweden's major exports, give a carefully orchestrated and choreographed performance, which would be equally at home in a television studio as on a rock concert stage.

Left From humble beginnings singing folk songs in the clubs and bars of Greenwich Village, Bob Dylan has become one of the legendary figures of rock. Today, his appearances in huge auditoriums are special occasions, and tickets are usually only available on subscription, months ahead.

Above "Along we go, we play through our LP tracks and we do our commercial numbers and we do our movements. And then it comes to the end and we do *My Generation* and we smash everything up." *Pete Townshend, The Who,* 1968. In the 1960s, The Who were noted for on-stage violence – smashing guitars, drumkits and mikes. Today, they are more restrained but their reputation as spontaneous, enthusiastic rock and rollers remains.

Right Spandau Ballet on BBC's *Top Of The Pops.* Spandau Ballet reflect a current preoccupation with style: audiences often dress to match. The group are reputed to have spent more on their video promotion than on actual recording.

Far right A sequence of stills from the video made for Blondie's *Eat To The Beat* album showing Debbie Harry, the lead singer.

giant echo and a distinct lack of intimacy or ambience, the devotee is left with the choice of either going and putting up with these problems or staying at home with the records.

The Who's bass player John Entwistle commented on this state of affairs to *New Musical Express* during the band's 1980 British tour. The Who had played at London's Rainbow theater, a reasonably sized hall which holds 3,000 people, but Entwistle complained that he hated playing in such "small" places. He said, "The Who aren't geared to play them. Our sound system was built up over years to stadium level and once you get into that way of playing you can't suddenly scale down. The Who don't sound like The Who in those places."

ELO's 1979 world tour featured a stage act with a five-ton spaceship and a laser lightshow. After the tour was over, Bev Bevan, the drummer, agreed that playing huge stadiums was generally unsatisfactory for the fans. However, he justified the tour by saying, "If you haven't got any sort of stage show, the people in the bad seats – which is like three-quarters of the auditorium – can hardly see you and the sound is bad. So at least with this big stage set, the further away from the stage you are, the better the visuals become." Nevertheless, it remains questionable whether a laser show can compensate for not being able to see or hear the band properly.

Touring

Touring encompasses a wide range of activity from small-time bands' regular visits to regional venues on the club circuit to massive roadshows involving complicated itineraries and specialist crews. Whatever the scale, touring is invariably arduous, but no one has come up with a better way of bringing a band's performance, as distinct from their music, to the attention of a scattered public. Some groups have always enjoyed life on the road and grow impatient during enforced intervals in the recording studio. Others, notably The Beatles, were only too glad to give up touring in order to devote their energies to exploring new musical avenues away from the demands of live audiences. Some bands undergo tours periodically, to promote a new release; for others it is a way of life which has little to do with marketing strategy.

Bands who are not particularly well-known or financially successful often find tours especially punishing. Lack of money means that such groups cannot afford either their own road crew or a more comfortable means of transportation than a large van. Too many dates too far apart from each other mean that traveling often has to

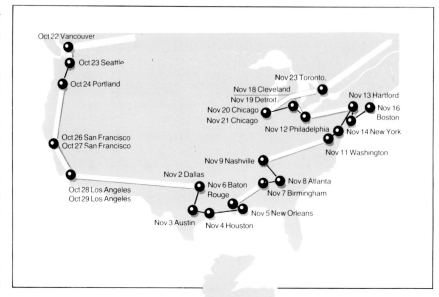

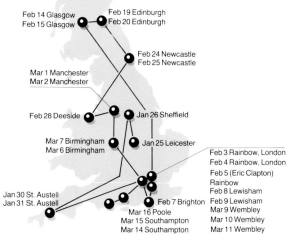

Above Touring maps from Dire Straits' American tour, October to November 1980 and The Who's U.K. tour, January to March 1981. Dire Straits toured with six road crew, two drivers and a tour manager. The group used house PAs in all their venues; the backline was driven from city to city in a small truck. The crew and five band members either flew between locations or drove; toward the end of the tour a mobile home was hired for all the touring party. The Who's tour was composed of four stage crew, six sound crew, five lights crew, three laser crew, a "supertrooper" operator, four truck drivers, a bus driver and a production manager. The band members traveled to gigs in their own transport. Three cars and a bus took the crew; four trucks transported the equipment: two for lighting, one for the PA system and one for the band's equipment and backline. The dates were spaced at generous intervals because Roger Daltrey's wife was having a baby.

take place at night after the gig is over and the equipment has been dismantled, a routine which leaves the band progressively more exhausted as the tour wears on. In such cases, members of the band take turns to drive, move and set up the equipment: all this apart from actually playing. When the distances are great, as in an American tour, the demands on individual performers are very high indeed.

Tours for the major rock groups impose less strain on the members of the band but they require an enormous amount of organization and administration to coordinate the equipment, PA and lighting paraphernalia needed for sophisticated stage shows. Some idea of the logistics involved in such a tour can be gleaned

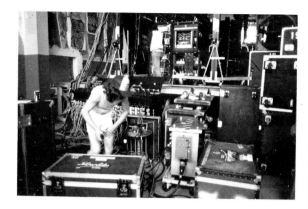

from the figures from the last American tour undertaken by Styx, one of America's top album sellers since the release of *Paradise Theater*. Styx were scheduled to appear in 90 cities across the country in little over four months. The size of venues ranged from 12,000 seaters to 50,000 seaters, and at any one gig, 8,000 seats had to be filled before the band started to make any profit. Styx's equipment demands five big rigs; another two carry the band's own specially designed portable stages. While the first of the two stages is being used by the group in one city, the second is already being assembled in the next by some of Styx's 42-strong entourage. Their two-hour show always started at 8.15 p.m. and finished at 10.15.

Apart from a great deal of money, these tours also require the expertise of a road crew. Obviously the crew will vary according to each band's requirements and resources, but all major groups have a number of roadies whose jobs include all or some of the following: driving, shifting equipment, taking care of instruments and being on call during performances in case anything goes wrong. If the band has their own PA, they will also have a sound technician for mixing; when the PA is hired, the sound technician usually comes from the hire company. This "package deal" arrangement is also standard for lighting: lighting rigs are nearly always hired and the lighting crew are supplied by the lighting company. The trend today is for more specialized personnel to look after specific aspects of the show. Keith Richard of the Rolling Stones, a band noted for its large entourage on tour, has his own guitar roadie who looks after Richard's many instruments and makes sure they are in tune for each performance.

Video Promotion

An alternative to the hard physical labor of touring is the much-touted video promotion. ELO, for example, now make a videotape of

Above left Apart from traveling, a large proportion of the time spent touring is taken up by putting the sound system together. Here the crew assemble the PA for a Van Halen concert.
Above Gerry Cott of the Boomtown Rats, playing an Aria Gerry Cott, sets up the levels during a soundcheck.

every track of a new album which can then be cycled to all the world's television networks to promote either the whole album or any singles which happen to be taken from it. There have been numerous cases of a memorable promotional videotape helping a band to push a record to huge sales. Queen's *Bohemian Rhapsody* (1975) benefited enormously from a lavish videotape made by Jon Roseman Associates and directed by Bruce Gowers. This was the first time video had been used so spectacularly. The Boomtown Rats struck gold with another Roseman videotape for their hit *I Don't Like Mondays*, and Buggles availed themselves of Roseman's skills to boost their single *Video Killed The Radio Star*.

Promotional videotapes have only a limited application on television, nevertheless, since they can only be used on the few programs dedicated to rock music. In Britain, in particular, record companies are reluctant to spend money on expensive videotapes when only a few regional TV shows can use them. On top of that, a videotape only really makes a discernible impact if it appears on BBC's *Top Of The Pops*, which boasts a nationwide viewing figure of some 19 million. Companies are likely to get more mileage out of promotional video in Europe or Japan than in Britain.

The stylistic incarnations of David Bowie *(above, below, right)* match his progression through different musical areas. From early days on the folk circuit, he rose to stardom with his most theatrical creation, Ziggy Stardust *(right)* which marked a transition to rock. After a much-publicized retirement, he reemerged to experiment with soul, disco, funk and electronics. Lately his work seems to integrate many of his previous musical directions.

Below Queen represent one of the more commercially successful attempts to appeal to a cross-section of the rock audience. With strong emphasis on the posing of lead singer Freddie Mercury and a skilfully produced blend of heavy rock, orchestral arrangements and straight pop, Queen continue to enjoy a wide popularity.

Right Electric Light Orchestra's (ELO) 1979 world tour featured a five-ton spaceship and a laser show. The "spaceship", constructed from huge lighting gantries, opened and rose gradually at the beginning of each concert in simulated takeoff, amid swirling dry ice. The band were revealed underneath, ready to begin their first number. The rig housed a variety of lights and lasers which provided a light show throughout each concert.

Television

Television itself remains a potent marketing tool in rock music. With the ever-increasing number of people buying or renting video recorders, it is becoming worthwhile for groups to make video cassettes which can be bought or rented by the home video user. Blondie's *Eat To The Beat* cassette, which contained all the tracks from the album, each with a specially shot video accompaniment, marked a major step in that direction, though other artists have not rushed to follow suit. Blondie's guitarist and songwriter, Chris Stein, believes that a satisfactory balance between the detached and cold medium of videotape and the raw voltage of a live performance can be obtained by combining the two – by playing a live concert and broadcasting it simultaneously on television. When Blondie were last in Britain, in 1980, they played in Glasgow and broadcast the performance on radio and TV. Evidently, it was a great improvement on Blondie's previous British television appearance, which took place in the studios of the BBC's *Old Grey Whistle Test*. "The last time we appeared on *Whistle Test*," Stein remarked, "it sounded like the Sex Pistols with Debbie (Harry) singing. They didn't have any of the instruments turned on except the guitar and drums, and the vocals. But if you can do something like Glasgow – a good exciting TV show – it's great."

European viewers can regularly switch on their TVs to watch one of the marathon *Rockpalast* shows from Germany on a Saturday night. These consist of bands playing live before a sizable concert audience, the entire show being beamed across Europe via Eurovision. The Police, The Who and The Grateful Dead are just a few of the well-known rock names to have appeared on *Rockpalast*.

In the United States, nationwide programs which present live rock performances include *Saturday Night Live* (NBC, New York) and *Fridays* (ABC, Los Angeles). *Fridays* has shown less well-known groups than *Saturday Night Live* but it also features established groups like The Grateful Dead. Prerecorded music or videotaped performances are used on such shows as *Solid Gold* (chart acts), *Rock World* and *Soul Train* (exclusively rhythm and blues or disco performed by black groups). *American Bandstand* (ABC), which began in the mid-1950s, has a nationwide audience and features dancers, canned music and artists miming to their current hits.

Television and music still remain uneasy partners. Television sound cannot cope with the sophisticated PA systems favored by modern rock bands and it is not unusual to find that the sound has been badly mixed anyway. During The Grateful Dead's *Rockpalast* appearance, for example, it was only possible to hear one of their two drummers and the bass guitar was completely inaudible. Even live television is very far removed from the real emotional contact which only a successful live show can offer.

Using Technology

The modern rock musician, whatever his or her claims to being raw, natural and spontaneous, has to acknowledge a debt to technological innovations. It is easy to overlook the extent to which gadgetry of various kinds has infiltrated the modern rock repertoire, but most modern sounds are the product of carefully worked-out effects and extras, and these are being used more and more successfully on stage. The Clash's guitarist, Mick Jones, uses a Mesa Boogie amp and a minefield of footswitches; Dexy's Midnight Runners achieve their unique new soul sound with the help of an extremely sharp PA. The Jam have 5,500 watts of foldback to go with their hired Muscle Music PA.

The Police have been less abashed than most about incorporating up-market electronics into their live sound. Though on stage Andy Summers uses a brace of 100-watt Marshall amps (the working musician's amplifier), he also has a custom-built Pete Cornish effects board which houses those familiar gadgets – phasing, compression and the like. Summers is very wary of effects: his attitude is to use only as many artificial additives as the music can stand. Referring to *Walking On The Moon*, Summers said, "Half of that number is the sound of the guitar."

Evidently, there is a correct level for every group's sound, a level where form complements content. Emerson, Lake And Palmer adopted a complex technological form that tended to overpower the creative content of their material with the extravagance of their equipment and performance. On the other hand, the electronic jazz group, Weather Report, use a bewildering variety of instruments and types of amplification but extract a range of tonal expression that justifies the presence of so much equipment on stage. Their keyboard player, Joe Zawinul, surrounds himself with a circular bank of instruments, but he uses these instruments to create a sound like a whole Duke Ellington brass section or to give the impression of Rio de Janeiro in the rush hour.

From Acme PA to Zenith lighting, the world of the live performance has become a jungle of confused options for aspiring bands. At the top of the scale, there is always the best that money can

Right. One of the earliest punk bands in Britain, The Slits were originally an all-women lineup. "Girl groups" have always been a novelty in rock; while female vocalists are common, it has been rare to find women actually playing instruments on stage. Punk and the new wave music which followed heralded a change in this area and an increasing number of groups are now emerging where women are no longer just peripheral members of the band. Since the days of punk, The Slits' music has moved on and is now based heavily on reggae rhythms. Their live performances have the air of stage parties with friends joining the band to dance to the music.

buy, but there remains the problem of deciding what is the right sort of equipment for a particular sound.

One of the more interesting groups to emerge in Britain in the last few years has been a three-piece band called The Cure. They toured Britain in the spring of 1981 and decided that since the tour would not make any money anyway, they would hire the best PA they could afford to present their music in as direct and uncompromising a way as possible. They ended up hiring a 6,000-watt Court PA system from Pink Floyd's Britannia Row company and assembled their road crew after spending weeks auditioning 50 potential candidates. In addition, they introduced a sophisticated lighting system which provided subtle, simple tones and spotlights of brilliant clarity. The whole package proved ideal for the band and their music. The Cure also substituted a half-hour film in place of the usual support group, which enabled them to set up and control both the look and the sound of the whole evening.

The live performance is rock's foundation. Despite the increasing use of sophisticated hardware – drum machines, sequencers, polyphonic synthesizers and even microprocessors – to recreate live the complex sounds that are usually achieved in a studio, there will always be something special about playing live. The British Musicians' Union slogan, "Keep Music Live", echoes a sentiment shared by most rock musicians.

RECORDING

The inside of a modern, state-of-the-art recording studio can be an intimidating and bewildering place. Musicians are quite often shut away in a cavernously large, dry acoustic – where sound travels only a few feet before being totally soaked up by the thick layers of absorbent material lining the walls – their only communication with the engineer and producer in the control room being the disembodied voices which talk to them through headphones. Wonders of technology lurk in the control room: mixing consoles eight feet long, covered in literally hundreds of knobs, faders, switches, pushbuttons, indicator lights and flickering meters, and which are linked by miles of cable to equally sophisticated tape machines, effects devices, gigantic monitor loudspeakers, and even computers. It is hardly surprising that quite a few bands and musicians that are new to the multitrack recording process find their first experience in a studio to be somewhat overwhelming and, as a result, often fail to give their best performance. At the other end of the scale, successful sounds have originated from much smaller setups. Punk brought with it both a tolerance and a demand for a rougher, less orchestrated quality and many interesting recordings emerged from studios with comparatively limited facilities – perhaps just a four-track recorder, a mastering machine, a mixer, monitors and a couple of effects units. It would be hard to imagine a typical Abba hit such as *Money, Money, Money* being produced without the benefits of 24 tracks or more, but the equally successful *Money* from the Flying Lizards makes good use of the primitive, hollow effect of home recording. Such limitations are not for every artist, but by using prerecorded tapes during the actual recording session, a surprisingly full sound can be created.

Early Recording

A great deal has changed since the first recordings were made by Thomas Edison onto specially coated wax cylinders in the late nineteenth century. In those halcyon days, groups of musicians would gather around a single horn "microphone", which would capture the sounds and transfer them acoustically to the surface of the record or wax cylinder. Electromagnetic cutting heads and amplifiers were gradually introduced to enable higher, more dependable levels to be cut into the shellac recording blank. This basic direct-cut recording technique remained virtually unaltered right up to the end of the Second World War.

One obvious drawback of the direct-to-disc process is that the musician needs to be able to record a song or performance in its entirety. In other words, once the cutting stylus has been lowered onto the recording blank, it cannot be lifted off again until it reaches the center because it would be virtually impossible to lower the stylus again in exactly the same place. It is hardly surprising that little development work was carried out by manufacturers of disc-cutting systems to extend the playing time of a 78-RPM record much beyond the available 15 to 20 minutes. Being able to play for that long without making a single mistake is sufficiently difficult, without putting further strains on a performer.

Although several companies had been working on experimental recording systems using various forms of oxide-covered wire, paper and metal tapes, it was the German company Telefunken which pioneered development of the modern tape machine during the 1930s. (In fact, some of their early prototype machines were so good that contemporary recordings dating from the Second World War still sound perfectly respectable today.) Several Magnetaphon machines were subsequently captured by American forces during 1945, and taken back to the United States. Despite a lack of decent supplies of recording tape, these machines were soon pressed into service to record, amongst other things, Bing Crosby's weekly radio programs. Further development work was undertaken by the fledgling Ampex company who, in the late 1940s, began to market the first commercial single-channel tape decks.

The overriding advantage of tape was that it was possible to edit together several takes, or remove the odd false start and similar "funnies". It was also possible to record part of a song on one machine – say the background melody – replay the tape while adding another part – the vocal solos, perhaps – and then record the resul-

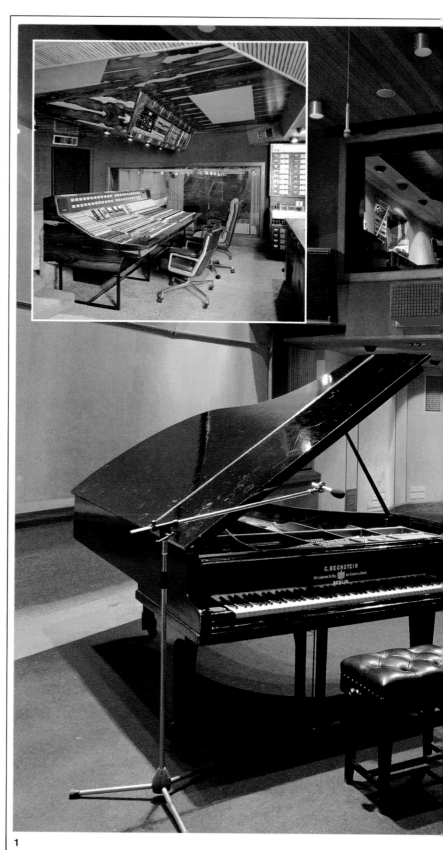

1

2

3

4

Trident Studios in London is an independent studio which first opened in 1969 and has expanded since then to provide a full range of facilities. The large acoustically treated studio *(1)* has both "live" and "dead" sound areas; special acoustic screens can also be used to isolate different instruments. The control room is unusually situated above the studio *(inset)*. Control room facilities include a custom-designed 28 into 48 console, JBL 4350 monitors and two Studer A80 24-track tape machines which can be locked together to provide 46 tracks. The reduction suite *(2)* is where mixdown takes place and is equipped with a range of effects, some of which are built into an overhead rack. At the front of this suite is an overdub room. The disc-cutting room *(3)* has a Neumann VMS 66 computer controlled cutting lathe and JBL 4343 monitors. The copy room *(4)* where tape copies are made for members of the group and record companies is sometimes used for editing and compiling albums. Many major groups have recorded at Trident: The Beatles recorded part of *The White Album* there; David Bowie made three albums including *Ziggy Stardust* at Trident; Elton John, Rod Stewart, Queen and Peter Gabriel have also been among the studio's customers.

tant mix on a second machine. Just such a process could be repeated time after time, or until tape hiss became too noticeable. (This technique – usually referred to as "sound-on-sound" – can also be achieved using a modern stereo tape machine, by alternating between left and right track as each instrument or vocal is added to the previous mix.)

One of the first performers to make extensive use of multitracking was Leslie Polfuss, better known as Les Paul, a guitarist associated with the Gibson guitar bearing his name. Many Les Paul recordings were built up layer by layer by bouncing tracks back and forth between two or more mono tape machines. The best example is probably his 1948 release, *Lover*.

These basic developments and techniques paved the way for the advances which came in the 1960s. Technological progress gave rise to stereo machines, four-track, eight-track and eventually the 24- and 32- track tape recorders of today. Recording not only improved in quality, benefiting the home listener, but also became more accessible to a wider variety of musicians and groups, enabling fairly sophisticated effects to be realized even in small studios.

Tape Recording

Sound recording is basically the process of transforming energy from one state to another for use at a later date. No matter how many tracks are involved, all tape recorders use the same principle to coax sounds onto lengths of magnetic tape. Sound vibrations are first converted into electrical vibrations, by means of a microphone, for example. These fluctuating voltages, when fed into a tape recorder, are transformed to magnetic vibrations by the record head, which, in simple terms, consists of coils of wire wrapped around an iron core. The changing patterns of magnetic field are laid into the ferric oxide coating on the tape. At the playback head, these patterns are reconverted to minute voltages, which in turn are amplified and reach our ears via loudspeakers or headphones.

Early mono tape recorders were soon followed by stereo, three-track and then, in the early 1960s, by four-track recorders. These developments arose out of technological advances which made it possible to record tracks in parallel on the same tape via gaps in the recording head spaced at equal intervals. More tracks meant that each component part or instrument could be recorded separately before being mixed down to stereo.

The common tape widths are ¼-inch (four-track), ½-1-inch (eight-track), 1-inch (16-track) and 2-inch (16 ,24- and 32-track). The master

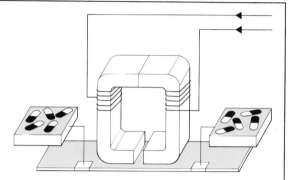

Right The record head on a tape recorder is basically an iron core wrapped with coils of wire. Electrical signals applied to the head are converted to magnetic patterns: the gap at the bottom sets up a magnetic field which fluctuates with the strength of the signals and leaves its imprint on the magnetic particles coating the tape.

Above This Teac 16-track tape machine has a built-in dbx noise reduction system and uses 1-inch tape, which makes it cheaper to run than the standard 16-track recorders using 2-inch tape.

Right EMI's Studio Control Room 3 at Abbey Road. The mixing desk is a 36 input/24 output EMI Neve console with computer-assisted mixdown facility. There are four Studer tape recorders: 24-, 16- and two-track. The inset shows the same control room in the mid-1960s, at the time when The Beatles were recording at Abbey Road.

stereo tape, onto which all the tracks are mixed, is ¼-inch wide.

Noise Reduction

All sound equipment is designed to reproduce or transform sound as faithfully as possible without distortion, additional noise or the loss of either certain frequencies or dynamic range, and tape recorders are no exception. Special features must be built in to preserve the original

characteristics of the sound being recorded and various techniques employed during recording to ensure the same result. A special bias signal is applied to the record head together with the signal to be recorded: this is an inaudible tone which prevents distortion. Various other features are also built in to prevent high frequencies from being lost. These involve boosting the high frequencies to a certain extent during recording and cutting them back slightly during playback.

To achieve a high quality recording, the sound must be recorded at as high a level as possible without overloading the magnetic tape. Due to inherent limitations in the recording process itself, all tape machines produce a high frequency hiss. Consequently, the higher the level at which the sound is recorded, the further removed the music will be from this irritating background noise. Since each additional track will increase the tape noise anyway, the less hiss added at each stage the cleaner and quieter the final result will be.

If the amount of noise produced by each tape

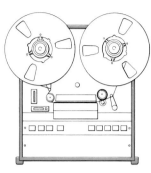
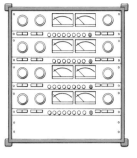

Right The Otari MX-5050 eight-track recorder is designed for use in smaller studios and uses the cheaper ½-inch tape rather than 1-inch. With this size of tape, some form of noise reduction system must be used and greater care taken when tracks are bounced down since the space between the tracks is much narrower.

Left A tape machine that offers many creative possibilities for small studios is the Teac Model A-3440 four-track recorder. A row of "safe"/"ready-to-record" pushbuttons allow different instruments to be recorded on any or all of the available tracks. During overdubs the tracks which are not being used are switched automatically to the record/sync head so that all tracks are synchronized.
Below The Brenell Mini-8 eight-track machine is popular with demo studios and uses 1-inch tape. Separate front panel controls are provided for setting up input and output levels and adjusting record; equalization and bias levels.

track is known, it is possible to calculate the dynamic range of a tape machine using a particular brand of tape. Sounds outside this range will either end up distorted through tape overload, or lost in the ever-present tape hiss.

By the mid-1960s, manufacturers like Ampex, Studer and 3M had developed eight-track machines using one-inch tape but could not progress any further until someone devised a means of reducing tape hiss. At this time, Dolby Laboratories came up with their now world-famous Dolby-A noise reduction process. In essence, by means of a band-splitting process, the Dolby system boosts low-level, high frequency signals during recording and then reduces them during replay. This improves the dynamic range radically and up to 24 tracks can be remixed to stereo with little additional hiss.

The dbx system, developed a few years later, is simpler: it compresses or "squashes" the dynamics of the music during recording and then expands them again on replay. Although these systems are sometimes criticized for giving the music a slightly artificial sound, they have opened up the creative possibilities of multitracking.

Multitracking

With the development of multitracking, producers and engineers began to take advantage of the enormous potential it offered. Rather than having to decide on the balance between instruments during a live mix, or as each sound-on-sound pass was made (and being forced to go back a stage or two if the eventual sound was not satisfactory), with multitrack it became possible to record each individual instrument or group of instruments on different tracks, and then try out various mixes or balances during the subsequent remix stage. In addition, if the producer did not like a particular vocal track, for example, it was now possible to re-record over just that one part, without having to start from scratch.

Just as important, was the practically limitless opportunities for building up a sound in stages. In a similar fashion to making a succession of sound-on-sound passes, tracks could be recorded one or two at a time, and then remixed at a later date. To enable musicians to hear what had been recorded on previously recorded tracks – an essential requirement if they are expected to sing or play in synchronization with them – the "sel-sync" (selective-synchronization) technique was evolved. This involves nothing fancier than arranging for the off-tape signal to be taken from the record rather than the replay head. With this arrangement, since

Above One of the most popular stereo tape recorders is the Revox B77. Built-in facilities for sound-on-sound recording enable multitrack performances to be built up layer by layer as each new instrument or vocal part is added.
Left A familiar sight in larger studios is the Studer A-800 multitrack, available with either 16- or 24-track headblocks for recording on 2-inch tape.
Below Island's studio at Basing Street.

Right The Solid State Logic (4000 Series) mixing console uses computer technology to provide the interface between tape machines and the desk. Information about each track is stored in the computer and can be called up on a visual display screen for reference.
Inset Virgin Records' studio, Townhouse, has a Helios desk and Telefunken tape recorders. Artists such as Kate Bush, Joan Armatrading, The Jam and Adam And The Ants have recorded there.

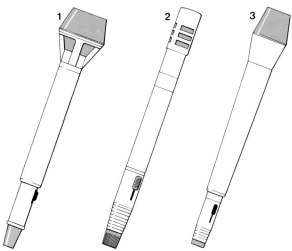

Left A selection of good microphones is essential for any recording session. AKG make a wide range including the D190 *(1)* a dynamic model suited for handling high levels from a guitar or bass amp; the C451 *(2)*, a capacitor mike; and the D222 *(3)*, a good choice for cymbals, acoustic guitar and vocals. The Neumann U87 *(4)* is a capacitor mike used in many larger studios and is particularly favored for vocals.

the tape is being monitored at exactly the same point at which the new or overdubbed material is being recorded – rather than a fraction of a second later, as would happen if the signal came from the conventional playback head – both the old and new tracks will be in perfect synchronization with one another.

There is another advantage in using a multi-track recorder equipped with sel-sync. If track space is running out – maybe seven out of eight tracks have been filled up with backing instruments, and four solo guitars still need to be added before mixdown – it is possible to "bounce" some of the tracks down. Four drum tracks, for example, could be submixed to mono (or stereo if there is more than one track left) and recorded on the remaining tracks. So long as the

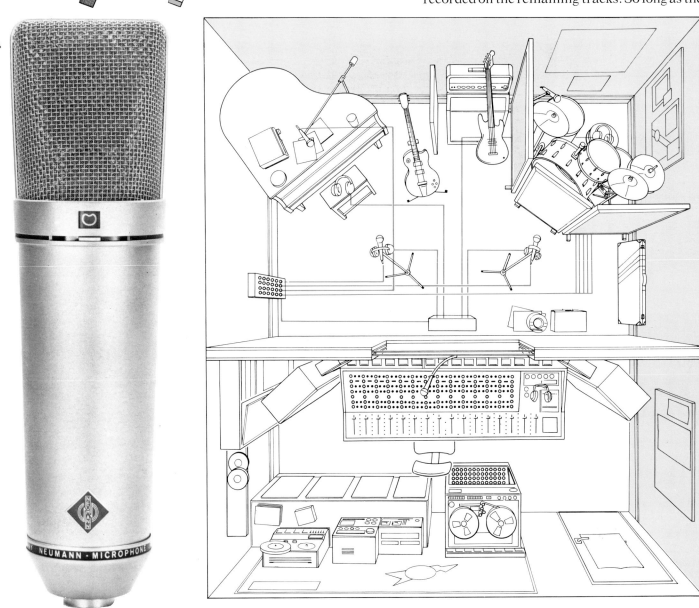

tracks to be bounced are monitored off the record or sel-sync head rather than the replay head, the submixed track or tracks will still be synchronized with the other material.

Few groups require more than the facilities offered by 24-track recording. Nevertheless, it is possible to create 46 tracks by tying two 24-track machines together by means of pulses which are recorded onto a track of each machine to lock them in synchronization.

The Studio

All studios are designed to ensure that recording takes place in as non-reverberant an environment as possible and one from which all extraneous sounds – such as traffic noise – have been excluded. They must also provide for

Below The Teac Model 5 *(top)* is a good basic mixing desk, suitable for small studios. It has eight inputs and four outputs; each input has a gain control, mike/line selection switch, simple two-band equalization, foldback and echo send controls, routing to four output groups, solo pan and channel fader. Four large meters monitor the recording levels sent to the multitrack and a smaller fifth meter displays either foldback or echo send output levels. A master fader is located on the right. The Teac Model 3 *(bottom)* is also an 8/4 desk.

acoustical separation or isolation between instruments so that each microphone only picks up the sound of its own instrument and there is no sound spillage between adjacent mikes. Most studios look fairly similar, although facilities vary considerably from the basic four-track setup specializing in demo tapes to the large 24-track studio full of sophisticated gadgetry and special effects units.

The recording area where the musicians play is usually acoustically treated to cut down on unwanted sound reflections and can be fitted with absorbent screens to enclose areas for different instruments. Large studios often have a purpose-built drum booth and may feature special areas for recording strings and vocal overdubs.

A separate, soundproofed control room enables the producer and engineer to monitor the sounds being picked up in the studio without it feeding back to the mikes. Inside the control room will be a mixing console, a multitrack machine, a stereo mastering tape deck, monitor loudspeakers and a selection of effects units. Engineers can hear what is being played by using headphones, but a far better indication of the subtleties of sound quality and balance can only be achieved with monitor loudspeakers, usually either Tannoy or JBL.

Left The basic equipment used in any recording studio includes a mixing console, multitrack machine, stereo mastering deck, monitor amplifiers and loudspeakers, together with a selection of effects – artificial reverb and echo, compressor-limiters, flangers, delay lines and so on. The diagram shows how the major elements in the control room and recording area are set up.

Tape recorders for studios come from a variety of manufacturers. The Teac A-3440 is a commonly used four-track machine; Teac also make eight-track recorders. Lyrec, 3M, MCI, Studer and Ampex are well known for 24-track machines and the Revox B77 is used as the stereo mastering tape deck in most smaller studios. Ampex, Scotch, Agfa and BASF are the most frequently used brands of tape.

The Mixer

With so many tracks at his disposal, the studio engineer needs both a convenient means of connecting each mike to its allocated tape track and a way of feeding the track or tracks to the control room monitors and the musicians' foldback headphones. All this, and more, is achieved with

the mixing console. Modern recording consoles can accept as many as 48 simultaneous microphone and line inputs; these can then be routed to up to 24 group outputs. At the same time, a separate stereo or quadraphonic monitor mix can be set up in the control room, taking various contributions from the group outputs during the recording stage or from the tape tracks during overdubbing. A different mix can be routed to the musicians' headphones.

Recording consoles are generally arranged in one of two ways. The most popular design, the "split" console, is composed of identical vertical rows of knobs. Each instrument is allocated one of these rows, or input modules; the knobs control volume, foldback, pan (left and right) and equalization. On split consoles, each input mod-

ule has its own bank of group output and monitor modules, which not only enable different instruments to be added together, but also allow adjustment of the combined sound.

When mixing consoles grew in size – a 32-input/24-output split console could easily measure eight feet across – several manufacturers decided to incorporate the group output and monitor sections within each input module to save space. These "in-line" consoles are much more compact, but take some getting used to since each row controls both the signal coming in and the adjusted sound going out.

Consoles obviously vary in sophistication as well as varying in size, but several other features are commonly found. The equalization section can range from simple bass and treble boost and

Below For studio monitoring, a large-diameter bass drive unit is usually considered essential, as in the Tannoy Super Red monitor loudspeakers.

Left Phoenix is an eight-track studio in London, with a range of facilities typical of most smaller studios. The recording area *(top)* has an acoustic screen set up beside the drumkit. The control room contains a 3M eight-track recorder using 1-inch tape and a custom-built console.

Top Perhaps the most popular transistorized stereo power amplifier used in larger recording studios, the Amcron DC300A has a pair of LEDs that light up to show when overload-induced distortion occurs anywhere in the unit.
Above The Soundcraft Series 800 mixing console is the type of large desk used in major recording studios. It has 32 inputs and 8 outputs.

cut controls to elegant and versatile four-band parametric equalizers, which enable the center-frequency, filter shape and degree of cut and boost to be altered independently. Such a wide range of adjustment is needed because when a mike is placed close to a sound source, it tends to be more sensitive to bass frequencies – the "proximity effect". To restore the sound to its natural form – or to create a bizarre special effect – recording engineers like to work with as wide a range of equalization control as possible.

It is often important to be able to select just one channel or group output to check the sound quality and make changes without disturbing the overall balance. Rather than having to pull down all the other faders or turn off the output from unwanted channels, most consoles have some form of solo system, usually a pushbutton or switch for each channel or group.

To enable different parts of the console to be connected together, to bypass a particular section of the circuitry, or to insert an external processing unit into the signal path at a certain point, most mixing desks come complete with some form of patch-bay or jack field – a row of jack sockets fitted with internal switches that disconnect a signal when a plug is inserted.

As well as the foldback circuits, a second auxiliary or echo-send output is also provided. This enables artificial reverberation or echo to be added to an instrument while it is being remixed.

Since the engineer will be riding levels of up to 24 multitrack channels during mixdown, as well as several echo return inputs, it is hardly surprising that he or she quickly runs out of fingers with which to operate the faders. Careful notes may also need to be taken – and wax pencil marks made beside each fader – if complicated balancing sequences are to be preserved for the final mixdown. All of this is made a great deal simpler with some form of console automation. Several different types exist, but all of them use voltage controlled amplifiers within each channel or group module to detect the changing levels during an early mix attempt. These changes are recorded or "written" on a spare tape track and then used to control the VCAs during subsequent mixes. Most automated consoles also allow several channel faders to be linked together so that subgroups of tracks can be controlled by just one or two "master" faders.

Manufacturers include Teac for small desks and Soundcraft and Trident for larger desks. EMI's Abbey Road Studios use a 36-input/24-output EMI-Neve mixing desk; another popular desk is the Harrison. Desks are often custom made to the buyer's specifications.

Left A mixdown session in Studio Control Room 3 at EMI's Abbey Road studios. The engineers are remixing a 24-track recording down to stereo using a 36-input/ 24-output EMI-Neve mixing desk. The desk has a Necam computer-assisted mixdown facility whose data entry panel can be seen to the center left.

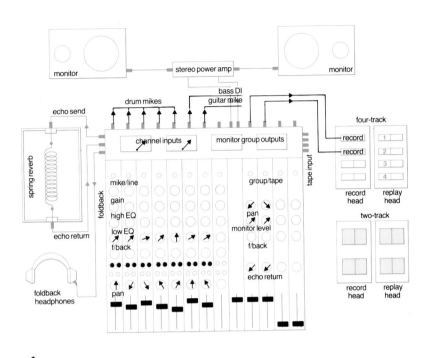

1

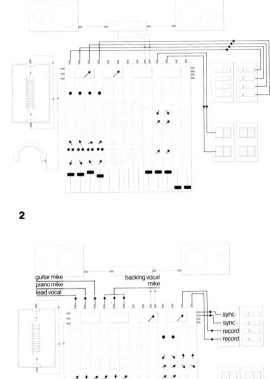

2

3

The Recording Session

The resources that different bands or record companies have at their disposal vary, as does the extent of the facilities offered by different studios, but most recording sessions follow much the same procedure. Usually the basic rhythm tracks – drums, bass and keyboards – perhaps with the addition of a guide vocal, are recorded first. The next stage, overdubbing, is when the guitar tracks and the lead vocals are recorded. String passages or any other extra instrument tracks are also recorded at this point to complete the number of tracks the engineer and producer will have at their disposal during mixdown. Mixdown, when all the tracks are remixed to stereo, is the stage when the creative potential offered by multitrack recording comes into its own. Different balances are tried out and special effects added until the right sound is achieved.

Before recording can begin, the first step is for the musicians to set up their instruments in the recording area and begin to mike up. With multitracking, each microphone is usually assigned its own tape track; while this means an almost limitless number of balances can be tried out during mixdown, it can cause problems of acoustical separation. Imagine that half a dozen mikes have been placed around a drumkit with one in front of the bass amp to record the basic rhythm section of drums and bass, and that the output from each microphone is recorded on a

Above The three stages of recording consist of laying down the backing or rhythm tracks, overdubbing solos and vocals and then remixing the multitrack tape to stereo. These three diagrams show how a recording console's input, output and monitor channels would be set up differently for basic tracklaying *(1)*, overdubbing *(2)* and mixdown *(3)*.

separate track. During the remix stage, it is important that the producer or engineer should be able to increase or decrease the contribution from individual tracks; otherwise, it would hardly be worth recording them separately. Consequently, as far as is technically possible, the engineer will try to ensure that the particular microphone picks up only the sounds of the instrument near which it has been placed. The studio itself provides the non-reverberant environment necessary for acoustical isolation but further measures also have to be taken. First, each microphone is placed as close to its instrument as possible; each instrument is then surrounded by absorbent screens to prevent sound leakage from nearby microphones – particularly bass frequencies, which are far less directional than high frequencies. Microphones for studio use come from such manufacturers as AKG, Shure, Neumann and Sennheiser.

Control room personnel usually includes a producer, a sound engineer and a tape operator The producer acts as musical director and is responsible for what happens during the session. He or she aims to come up with a certain

overall sound and can suggest ways of achieving this – perhaps by adding extra instruments, synthesized sounds or special effects. The engineer "plays" the desk, ensuring, first of all, that the recorded sound is of the right quality. The tape operator changes reels, threads the tape and may be asked to find an earlier take for subsequent remixing and adjustment.

During recording, whether the tracks are backing tracks or overdubs, the engineer's role is to equalize, adjust the levels, pan and route the signals from the various microphones: basically, to capture the band's best musical effort on tape and make sure that the sound of each instrument is recorded at its optimum level. During these early stages, a stereo mix will be set up in the control room monitors to act as a rough guide to the way the performance is coming together. At the same time, the musicians can listen to what they are doing via their headphones. For overdubs, the previous tracks are routed to the monitors and the musicians are also supplied with a mix of these tracks to enable them to play along with what has already been recorded.

The mixdown stage is the most creative of the entire recording process and it is often the stage which takes the most time to complete. Records like Fleetwood Mac's *Tusk* and *The River* by Bruce Springsteen only emerged from the studio after months of remixing and adjustment. Once the sounds of the individual instruments

Above The first Yes album to feature Rick Wakeman on keyboards was *Fragile*, released in 1971. The album was a big seller and established Yes as one of the leading exponents of "technorock" – technically accomplished, highly orchestrated and arranged music. Here lead guitarist Steve Howe and vocalist Jon Anderson record during one of the sessions for *Fragile*.

are safely committed to the multitrack tape, balances are tried out and the sounds are altered until the required effect is achieved. At this point special effects are also added.

Special Effects
Echo and Reverberation

One of the most common effects units found in a recording studio is a gadget for creating artificial echo or reverberation. Echo – or the simple repetition of a sound – can be produced by either a tape machine or, more normally, with a delay unit. Artificial reverberation, however, is usually produced by passing the signal through a spring or plate reverb unit. These are made up of transducers mounted at one end of a softly-coiled spring or large steel plate. Pickups placed at the other end detect the changing sound pattern as it moves back and forth along the spring or plate, before gradually dying away – and thus mimics the way in which sound is reflected around the inside of a room, before finally being absorbed by the walls, floor and ceiling.

Tape tracks are normally recorded "dry" – that is, without any added echo – to keep all the options open until the mixdown stage. The non-reverberant acoustic of most studios unfortunately often results in a dull, somewhat unnatural sound, so to put warmth and life back into an instrument or vocal track, the signal will be passed through an external reverberation unit before being added to the final mix.

Delay-related Effects

A variety of interesting effects can be achieved by first delaying a sound, mixing it with the undelayed signal, and then feeding it back on itself. At very short delay intervals, this will result in flanging and phasing, as different frequency bands cancel each other out giving that metallic or hollow sound which characterizes the effect. As the delay time is lengthened, however, separate repeats can be heard, resulting first in ADT (or artificial double-tracking) and then, with sufficiently delay, distinct echoes. By gently varying a short delay time, dynamic flanging can be produced, while at longer delays the variation will give rise to a chorus or vibrato effect. If the delay time is altered as a particular signal is passing through the unit, a Doppler shift in frequency will occur (not unlike that produced when a fire-engine passes in the street). Harmonizers or pitch-shifters work on much the same principle, except they sample the frequency of the mote to be processed and then quickly alter the delay to produce a specified number of semitones' change in pitch.

Most inexpensive delay-based effects units make use of bucket-brigade or charge-coupled devices (CCDs), and are capable of producing up to several hundred milliseconds of delay. Their one drawback though, is that at longish delay times such analog units are prone to be rather noisy, and have a restricted bandwidth. Digital delay lines, on the other hand, are quite a bit more expensive, but are capable of creating several seconds of delay at perfectly respectable bandwidths and add very little noise to the processed signal. Some manufacturers have even developed reverberation units based on multiple-output digital delay lines, and which can be used to produce some extremely realistic reverb effects – albeit at rather a high price.

Compressors and Limiters

Having gone to all the trouble of ensuring that a tape track will handle as wide a dynamic range as is technically possible – by recording at a high level, and making use of noise-reduction systems – it may seem somewhat bizarre to deliberately compress or restrict a signal's dynamic range. Compressors detect the level of the input signal and then reduce or boost it according to a preset rate. This effect can be very useful for putting extra bite and punch into a guitar or vocal track, for example.

An expander works in a reverse fashion, by opening out or increasing the dynamics of a chosen track, and can be particularly useful for cleaning up slightly noisy sounds – by pushing

Right MXR graphic equalizer. Graphic equalizers have a number of band pass filters which are used to adjust the tone of a signal. Sophisticated units are usually used to smooth out minor anomalies in the acoustics of a control room. These units would be connected between the output from a console and the power amplifiers driving the monitors.

Below Parametric equalizers are more flexible than graphic equalizers and enable the frequency area to be adjusted to be selected more precisely. Parametric equalizers can cut or boost at a variable bandwidth.
Far right This diagram shows how flanging or phasing is produced. Two tape recorders with the same distance between the record and playback heads are

required; one must have a variable speed control. A signal is fed into both tape machines at the same time, with both machines set up to record. By slowly changing the speed of the variable-speed recorder, a time delay is created between the two outputs. When the two signals are added together, some frequencies are in phase, others are out of phase.

Far right The MXR Flanger/Doubler is a unit which combines the effect of flanging with doubling (making one instrument or voice sound like two).
Right Two other effects units include the MXR Pitch Transposer and the MXR Digital Delay. The pitch transposer creates harmonies at preset intervals. The digital delay line gives longer delay times than can be achieved with analog delay units and can be used to create echo, doubling and chorus effects.

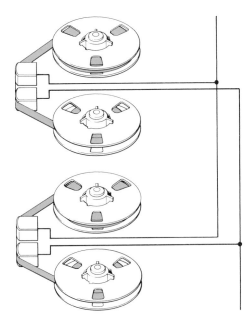

down the noise floor – or for increasing, for example, the ring of a cymbal.

Limiters simply prevent signals from rising in level beyond a chosen threshold point. By setting this threshold a dB or two below a tape's saturation point, higher levels can be recorded without running the risk of overload distortion.

Compressors, limiters and expanders need to be carefully adjusted to give the best results. It often takes a certain degree of experimentation before the correct combination of slope, threshold, attack and release time (the latter to determine the speed at which the circuits operate) can be set up to achieve to a desired result.

Making a Record

Once the producer, engineer and the band (and the record company that is paying for the album) are happy with the final stereo mix, the master tape will be sent off to a cutting room. Here the tape will be replayed through a smaller console, levels checked and, more often than not, small changes made in the overall equalization. When the cutting engineer has made all the necessary adjustments, the recorded material is cut into the surface of a circular sheet of cellulose material – or recording blank – mounted on a special cutting lathe. This is a particularly skilled operation, since the amount of groove spacing is critical. In fact, a special "preview" head mounted on the replay machine enables the spacing to be worked out before the audio signals to be cut arrive at the normal replay head. The spiral being cut must not collapse upon itself as the grooves move closer together during particularly loud passages but at the

Mobile recording There is no reason why the hardware found in a recording studio cannot be used to record a live concert. There are some differences in the way the actual recording is made: separate split feeds will be taken from the PA mikes; more mikes might have to be added. Since there will be no chance of a retake, the engineer has to be careful that the levels are set properly and the tape does not overload. Most mobiles have at least two multitrack machines so that the tape does not run out before the end of the concert. Mobiles seldom have as good acoustics as control rooms and the tapes are usually remixed at a recording studio. Unless the band wants to release a truly live album, one or two tracks will usually be overdubbed to patch up a bad recording or imperfect performance. Mobile One is one of the most versatile mobile recording units in Europe with its 46-track facility and has recorded Yes, Genesis, Dr. Hook and The Kinks; the unit also recorded Toots And The Maytals at London's Hammersmith Odeon – the album was available in record stores the following afternoon.

1. Outside view of the mobile showing main cables and stage boxes. Mobile One consists of just one truck – most other mobiles have a second truck for cables.

2. Mobile One recording Barclay James Harvest on the steps of the Reichstag at the Berlin Wall.

3. The effects rack, featuring limiters, compressors, digital echo, noise gates, harmonizer and sweep equalizers.

4. Inside the mobile, looking toward the monitors. The walls, floor and ceiling are acoustically treated.

5. Inside view toward the studio. The equipment includes two 24-track machines, stereo mastering deck and a 52-input main desk.

1

2▲ 4▼

3

5

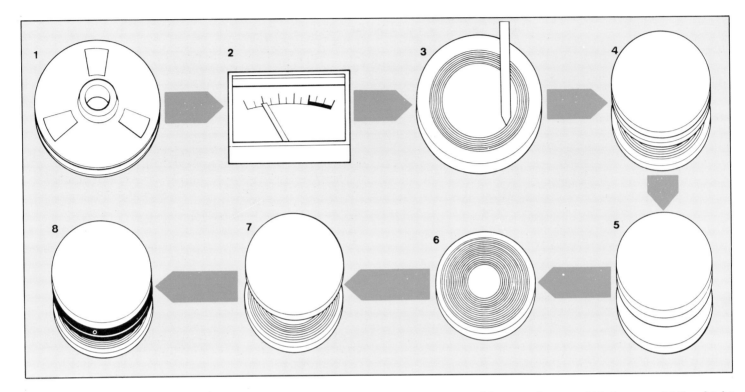

same time, all the material must fit onto an album side. Most of these adjustments can now be controlled by a small computer, but an experienced eye is still needed to watch out for problems during the critical final cut.

After the cutting stage has been completed to everyone's satisfaction, the finished lacquer will be taken to the plating and pressing plant. Here it is first electroplated with a very thin layer of silver. This enables a layer of nickel to be "grown" on the surface of the disc when it is immersed in a special bath of electrolyte, through which a direct current is passed. The nickel layer or "master" is then removed and, by a similar electrolytic process, used to produce a nickel replica of the original lacquer, called a positive or "mother". From this mother several "stampers" are made, which are used in the record presses to mold a lump of molten vinyl into the shape of a gramophone record. Every stage in the process from lacquer to stamper – one for each side of the finished record – has to be checked meticulously, since the smallest particle of dust would cause an imperfection in the playing surface.

Digital Recording

The equipment and techniques described in this chapter concern analog recording, whereby fluctuating voltages are converted into magnetic patterns on tape, or grooves in a record. Over the last couple of years, several manufacturers –

Above The diagram illustrates how a record is made. The master tape (1) is sent to a cutting room where it is played and the levels are checked (2). The recorded material is cut into a recording blank (3) and the finished lacquer is taken to the plating and pressing plant where it is plated with a thin layer of silver, on which a nickel layer is grown (4). The nickel layer is used to produce a replica (5), called a positive or "mother" (6). The mother is used to produce several "stampers" (7) which are used to press molten vinyl into the shape of a record (8).

notably Soundsteam, 3M, Sony and Mitsubishi – have been developing digital recording equipment that makes use of an entirely different process. A digital tape machine samples the input signal at up to 50,000 times a second, and then converts the shape of the signal into a complex series of on/off pulses which are recorded on tape. By means of some very advanced jiggery-pokery, the process is capable of producing a frequency response practically flat from DC to 20kHz, radically improved transient response, virtually no wow and flutter and distortion, and enables a 96dB dynamic range to be coaxed onto magnetic tape.

At present, however, except in the case of one or two experimental designs, it still is not possible to edit tape by cutting and resplicing it. Instead, different sections of a tape have to be copied from one machine to another. Nevertheless, within a few years a growing number of the bigger studios will almost certainly go digital. The advantages of digital recording are already apparent in the crystal-clear sound of Ry Cooder's *Bop 'Til You Drop*, recorded in 1979 on a 3M 32-track 1-inch digital tape recorder.

Now that video discs have become a commercial reality, the audio digital disc, based on similar technology, cannot be far away. With this development it may be possible for listeners at home to experience for themselves the kind of quality that the band, producer and engineer heard during the recording session.

DISCOGRAPHY

INTRODUCTION

Beach Boys "Good Vibrations" 1966 (Capitol)
The Beatles *Sergeant Pepper's Lonely Hearts Club Band* 1967
    (Capitol)
Buggles "Video Killed The Radio Star" 1980 (Island)
Eric Clapton (Derek And The Dominos) *Layla And Other Assorted*
    Love Songs 1970 (Polydor)
Gerry And The Pacemakers "Ferry Across The Mersey" 1964
    (Laurie/Columbia)
John McLaughlin on Miles Davis' *Bitches' Brew* 1970
    (Columbia/CBS)
Elvis Presley "Heartbreak Hotel" 1957 (RCA Victor/HMV Pop)
Santana *Abraxas* 1970 (Columbia/CBS)
Simon And Garfunkel *Bridge Over Troubled Water* 1970
    (Columbia/CBS)
The Who *Tommy* 1970 (MCA/Track)

THE ACOUSTIC GUITAR

Joan Armatrading *Joan Armatrading* 1976, *Show Some Emotion*
    1977 (A&M)
Judy Collins *So Early In The Morning* 1977 (Elektra)
Bob Dylan *The Freewheelin' Bob Dylan* 1963 (Columbia/CBS)
The Everly Brothers "Wake Up Little Susie" 1957
    (Cadence/London)
Emmylou Harris *Pieces Of The Sky* 1975 (Reprise)
Richie Havens "Freedom" from *Woodstock* 1970
    (Cotillion/Atlantic)
Leo Kottke *Six And Twelve String Guitar* 1971 (Takoma/Sonet)
Joni Mitchell "Big Yellow Taxi" from *Ladies Of The Canyon* 1970
    (Reprise)
Paul Simon *There Goes Rhymin' Simon* 1973 (Columbia/CBS)
James Taylor *Mud Slide Slim And The Blue Horizon* 1971 (Warner
    Bros)
The Who "Pinball Wizard" 1969 (Decca/Track)
Dobro
Manfred Mann "Pretty Flamingo" 1966 (United Artists/HMV Pop)
Mandolin
Lindisfarne "Lady Eleanor" 1970 (Elektra/Charisma)
Sitar
George Harrison (The Beatles) "Love You Too" from *Revolver* 1966
    (Parlophone)
"Within You Without You" from *Sergeant Pepper's Lonely Hearts*
    Club Band 1967 (Parlophone)
Denny Dias (Steely Dan) "Do It Again" from *Can't Buy A Thrill*
    1972 (ABC/Probe)
Banjo
Crosby, Stills And Nash *Crosby, Stills And Nash* 1969 (Atlantic)
Pedal Steel
Red Rhodes on Mike Nesmith's *And The Hits Just Keep On Comin'*
    1972 (RCA/–)
Lloyd Maines on Joe Ely Band's "Boxcars" from *Honky Tonk*
    Masquerade 1979 (MCA)

THE ELECTRIC GUITAR

The Beatles *The Beatles 1962-66* 1973 (Apple)
    The Beatles 1967-70 1973 (Apple)
Jeff Beck *Truth* 1968 (Epic/Columbia-EMI), *Beck-Ola* 1969
    (Epic/Columbia-EMI), *Blow By Blow* 1975 (Epic)
George Benson *Breezin'* 1976 (Warner Bros)
Larry Carlton *Larry Carlton* 1978 (Warner Bros)
Eric Clapton *Layla And Other Assorted Love Songs* 1970 (Polydor)
    461 Ocean Boulevard 1974 (RSO)
The Clash *London Calling* 1979 (Columbia/CBS)

The Cure *Seventeen Seconds* 1980 (Polydor)
Bo Diddley "Bo Diddley" 1955
Duane Eddy *Twenty Terrific Twangies* 1981 (RCA)
Robert Fripp *Exposure* 1979 (Polydor)
Peter Green (Fleetwood Mac) "Oh Well" 1969 (Reprise)
    "The Green Manalishi" 1970
    (–/Reprise)
George Harrison *All Things Must Pass* 1970 (Apple)
Jimi Hendrix *The Essential Jimi Hendrix* (vol. 1 and 2) 1976
    (Polydor)
Buddy Holly *Buddy Holly's Greatest Hits* 1974 (Coral/–)
B.B. King *Indianola Mississippi Seeds* 1970 (Probe)
Hank Marvin (The Shadows) *20 Golden Greats* 1976 (–/EMI)
Roger McGuinn (The Byrds) *Turn! Turn! Turn!* 1966
    (Columbia/CBS)
    Younger Than Yesterday 1967
    (Columbia/CBS)
John McLaughlin (The Mahavishnu Orchestra) *My Goal's Beyond*
    1971 (Douglas), *The Inner Mounting Flame* 1972
    (Columbia/CBS)
Steve Miller *Sailor* 1968 (Capitol) *Fly Like An Eagle* 1976
    (Capitol/Mercury)
Ted Nugent *Free-For-All* 1976 (Epic)
Lee Ritenour *The Captain's Journey* 1978 (Elektra)
Roxy Music *Roxy Music* 1972 (Reprise/Island)
Carlos Santana (Santana) *Abraxas* 1970 (Columbia/CBS)
Sex Pistols *Never Mind The Bollocks* 1978 (Virgin)
Siouxsie And The Banshees *Juju* 1981 (Polydor)
Paul Weller (The Jam) *All Mod Cons* 1978 (Polydor)
Johnny Winter *First Winter* 1970 (Buddah)
The Youngbloods *Elephant Mountain* 1969 (RCA)

THE ELECTRIC BASS GUITAR

Ralphe Armstrong (The Mahavishnu Orchestra) *Visions Of The*
    Emerald Beyond 1975 (Columbia/CBS)
Family Man Barrett (Bob Marley And The Wailers) *Burnin'* 1973
    (Island)
Stanley Clarke *Stanley Clarke* 1974 (Nemperor)
Rick Danko (The Band) *The Band* 1969 (Capitol)
"Duck" Dunn (Booker T. And The M.G.s) *The Best Of Booker T. And*
    The M.G.s 1968 (Stax/Atlantic)
Bernard Edwards (Chic) *Chic's Greatest Hits* 1979 (Atlantic)
John Entwistle (The Who) *Meaty, Beaty, Big And Bouncy* 1971
    (MCA/Track)
Andy Fraser (Free) "All Right Now" 1970 (A&M/Island)
Larry Graham (Sly And The Family Stone/Graham Central
    Station) *There's A Riot Going On* 1971 (Epic),
    Graham Central Station 1974 (Warner Bros)
Bill Haley "Shake, Rattle And Roll" 1954 (Brunswick)
    "Rock Around The Clock" 1955 (Brunswick)
    "See You Later Alligator" 1956 (Decca/Brunswick)
Colin Hodgkinson (Back Door) *Back Door* 1973 (Warner Bros)
James Jamerson on Four Tops' "Reach Out, I'll Be There" 1966
    (Motown/Tamla Motown)
Alphonso Johnson *Spellbound* 1979 (Epic)
Carole Kaye on Beach Boys' "Good Vibrations" 1966 (Capitol) and
    Glen Campbell's "Wichita Lineman" 1969
    (Capitol/Ember)
Paul McCartney (The Beatles) "Taxman" from *Revolver* 1966
    (Parlophone) "Paperback Writer/Rain" 1966
    (Parlophone) (Wings) "Silly Love Songs" 1976
    (Parlophone)
George Murray (with David Bowie) *Low* 1977 (RCA), *Heroes* 1977
    (RCA)

Neil Murray (National Health, Whitesnake) *Of Queues And Cures* 1978 (Charly)

Jaco Pastorius (Weather Report) "Birdland" from *Heavy Weather* 1977 (Columbia/CBS); (solo) *Jaco Pastorius* 1976 (Epic)

Robert Popwell (The Crusaders) *Images* 1978 (MCA)

Mike Rutherford (Genesis) *Selling England By The Pound* 1973 (Charisma)

Chris Squire (Yes) *The Yes Album* 1971 (Atlantic)

Robbie Shakespeare (Peter Tosh) *Legalize It* 1976 (Virgin)

Bruce Thomas (Elvis Costello And The Attractions) *My Aim Is True* 1977 (Stiff)

John Wetton (Family, King Crimson) "Burlesque" 1972 (Reprise) *Lark's Tongues in Aspic* 1973 (Atlantic/Island)

Tina Weymouth (Talking Heads) *Fear of Music* 1979 (Sire) *Remain In Light* 1980 (Sire)

DRUMS AND PERCUSSION

Acuna (Weather Report) *Heavy Weather* 1977 (Columbia/CBS)

Carmine Appice (Vanilla Fudge) "You Keep Me Hangin' On" from *Vanilla Fudge* 1967 (Atlantic)

Chepito Areas (Santana) *Abraxas* 1970 (Columbia/CBS)

Ginger Baker (Cream) *Wheels Of Fire* 1968 (Atco/Polydor)

John Bonham (Led Zeppelin) *Led Zeppelin IV* 1971 (Atlantic)

Bill Bruford (Yes) *The Yes Album* 1971 (Atlantic)

David Byrne And Brian Eno *My Life In The Bush Of Ghosts* 1981

Billy Cobham (The Mahavishnu Orchestra) *The Inner Mounting Flame* 1972 (Columbia/CBS), *Birds Of Fire* 1973 (Columbia/CBS)

Victor Feldman (Steely Dan) *Countdown To Ecstasy* 1973 (ABC/Probe)

Steve Gadd on Paul Simon's *Still Crazy After All These Years* 1975 (Columbia/CBS), Chick Corea's *Leprechaun* 1977 (Polydor)

Quincy Jones' *Stuff Like That* 1978 (A&M)

Al Jackson Jnr (Booker T. And The M.G.s) *The Best Of Booker T. And The M.G.s* 1968 (Stax/Atlantic)

Landscape *From The Tearooms Of Mars To The Hell-holes Of Uranus* 1981 (RCA)

Little Feat *Feats Don't Fail Me Now* 1974 (Warner Bros), *Dixie Chicken* 1973 (Warner Bros)

Harvey Mason on Herbie Hancock's *Headhunters* 1973 (Columbia/CBS)

Mitch Mitchell (Jimi Hendrix Experience) *Are You Experienced?* 1967 (Reprise/Track)

Keith Moon (The Who) *My Generation* 1965 (Decca/Brunswick) to *Who Are You* 1978 (Polydor)

Bernard Purdie on Steely Dan's *Aja* 1977 (ABC)

Rolling Stones "Not Fade Away" 1964 (London/Decca) "Honky Tonk Women" 1969 (London/Decca)

Ringo Starr (The Beatles) *Abbey Road* 1969 (Apple)

Bill Summers on Herbie Hancock's *Man Child* 1975 (Columbia/CBS)

Talking Heads *Remain In Light* 1980 (Sire)

Ruth Underwood (Mothers Of Invention) *Roxy And Elsewhere* 1974 (DiscReet)

Charlie Watts (Rolling Stones) *Get Yer Ya-Ya's Out!* 1970 (London/Decca)

KEYBOARDS

The Acoustic Piano

Chick Corea on Miles Davis' *Bitches' Brew* 1970 (Columbia/CBS)

Elton John *Tumbleweed Connection* 1970 (MCA/DJM)

Chrstine McVie (Fleetwood Mac) "Sara" from *Tusk* 1980 (Warner Bros)

Joni Mitchell *Blue* 1971 (Reprise)

Steve Naive (Elvis Costello's Attractions) *This Year's Model* 1978 (Columbia/CBS)

Randy Newman *Sail Away* 1972 (Reprise)

Leon Russel *Carney* 1972 (Shelter)

Joe Sample *Rainbow Seeker* 1978 (CBS)

Robert Wyatt *Rock Bottom* 1974 (Virgin)

The Hammond Organ

Keith Emerson (The Nice) *Elegy* 1971 (Mercury/Charisma)

Argent "Hold Your Head Up" 1972 (Epic)

Electronic Organs

The Animals "House Of The Rising Sun" 1964 (MGM/Columbia)

Pink Floyd "Set The Controls For The Heart Of The Sun" from *A Saucerful Of Secrets* 1968 (Capitol/Columbia)

Mellotron/Novatron

The Beatles "Strawberry Fields Forever" 1967 (Parlophone)

Julie Driscoll With The Brian Auger Trinity "This Wheel's On Fire" 1968 (Marmalade)

King Crimson *In The Court Of The Crimson King* 1969 (Atlantic/Island)

Mike Pinder (Moody Blues) *Days Of Future Passed 1967 (Deram)*

Replay Keyboards

Rick Wakeman *The Six Wives Of Henry VIII* 1973 (A&M)

Electric and Electronic Pianos

Chick Corea *Return To Forever* 1979 (Polydor)

Peter Hammill (Van Der Graaf Generator) *H To He Who Am The Only One* 1970 (Dunhill/Charisma)

Herbie Hancock *Headhunters* 1973 (Columbia/CBS)

Queen "You're My Best Friend" 1976 (Electra/EMI)

Supertramp "Dreamer" 1975 (A&M)

Stevie Wonder "Superstition" from *Talking Book* 1972 (Tamla) "Higher Ground" from *Innervisions* 1973 (Tamla)

SYNTHESIZERS

British Electric Foundation *Music For Stowaways* 1981 (Virgin)

Buggles *The Age Of Plastic* 1980 (Island)

Walter Carlos *Switched On Bach* 1968

George Duke *Feel* 1974 (BASF/–) *Follow The Leader* 1979 (Epic)

Brian Eno *Another Green World* 1974 (Island), *Discreet Music* 1975 (Obscure), *Possible Musics* (Editions EG)

Larry Fast on Peter Gabriel's *Peter Gabriel* 1977 (Atco/Charisma),

Jan Hammer (The Mahavishnu Orchestra) *Birds Of Fire* 1973 (Columbia/CBS)

Herbie Hancock *Sunlight* 1978 (Columbia/CBS)

Jean-Michel Jarre *Equinoxe* 1978 (Polydor)

The Human League *Reproduction* 1979 (Virgin) *Travelogue* 1980 (Virgin)

Kraftwerk *Autobahn* 1974 (Vertigo) *Trans Europe Express* 1977 (Capitol)

New Musik *Anywhere* 1980 (GGO)

Orchestral Manoeuvres In The Dark *Organization* 1980 (Din Disc)

Roger Powell (Utopia) *Back To The Bars* 1978 (Bearsville) (solo) *Air Pocket* 1980 (Bearsville)

Morton Subotnick *Silver Apples Of The Moon* (Nonesuch)

Tangerine Dream *Phaedra* 1974 (Virgin)

Isao Tomita *Snowflakes Are Dancing* 1975 (RCA) *The Planets* 1977 (RCA) *Bermuda Triangle* 1979 (RCA)

Ultravox *Vienna* 1981 (Chrysalis)

Yellow Magic Orchestra *Yellow Magic Orchestra* 1969 (Parlophone)

David Vorhaus (White Noise) *White Noise* 1977 (Island) *Concerto For Synthesizer* (Virgin)

Rick Wakeman *The Six Wives Of Henry VIII* 1973 (A&M)

EFFECTS UNITS

Jeff Beck "Beck's Bolero" from *Truth* 1969 (Columbia/CBS)
"Goodbye Pork Pie Hat" from *Wired* 1976 (Epic)
Al DiMeola *Elegant Gypsy* 1977 (Columbia/CBS)
Fleetwood Mac *Rumours* 1977 (Warner Bros)
Peter Green (John Mayall) "The Supernatural" from *A Hard Road* 1967 (London/Decca)
Jimi Hendrix "Purple Haze" 1967 (Reprise/Track)
"Voodoo Chile" from *Electric Ladyland* 1968 (Reprise/Track)
Rolling Stones *Some Girls* 1978 (Rolling Stones Records)
The Who *Who Are You* 1978 (Polydor)

WOODWIND, BRASS AND STRINGS

Flute
Ian Anderson (Jethro Tull) *This Was Jethro Tull* 1968 (Reprise/Island)
Stand Up 1969 (Reprise/Island)
Thijs van Leer (Focus) "House Of The King" from *Focus 3* 1973 (Sire/Polydor)
Raphael Ravenscroft (Gerry Rafferty) "Night Owl" 1979 (United Artists)

Saxophone
Clarence Clemens (Bruce Springsteen) *The Wild, The Innocent And The E-Street Shuffle* 1973 (Columbia/CBS), *Born To Run* 1975 (Columbia/CBS)
Lol Coxhill (with Kevin Ayers) *Shooting At The Moon* 1971 (–/Harvest)
Elton Dean (Soft Machine) *Fourth* 1971 (Columbia/CBS)
Mel Collins (King Crimson) *In The Wake Of Poseidon* 1970 (Atlantic/Island)
David Jackson (Van Der Graaf Generator) *The Least We Can Do Is Wave* 1969 (Mercury/Charisma)
Phil Kenzie on Al Stewart's "Year Of The Cat" 1977 (RCA)
Jim King (Family) *Music In A Doll's House* 1968 (Reprise)
Madness *Absolutely* 1981 (Stiff)
Davey Payne (Ian Dury And The Blockheads) "Hit Me With Your Rhythm Stick" 1978 (Stiff)
Rudy Pompelli (Billy Haley And The Comets) *Golden Hits* 1974 (MCA)
Raphael Ravenscroft on Gerry Rafferty's "Baker Street" 1978 (United Artists)
Saxa (The Beat) "Mirror In The Bathroom" 1979 (2 Tone)

Brass
Blood, Sweat And Tears *Blood, Sweat And Tears* 1969 (Columbia/CBS)
Chicago *Chicago II* 1970 (Columbia/CBS)
Graham Parker And The Rumour *Parkerilla* 1978 (Vertigo)
Otis Redding *Live At Monterey* (Reprise)
Tower Of Power *In The Slot* 1975 (Warner Bros)
Wings *Wings Over America* 1976 (Capitol/EMI)

Harmonica
Bob Dylan *Highway 61 Revisited* 1965 (Columbia/CBS)
Mick Jagger (The Rolling Stones) "Not Fade Away" 1964 (London/Decca)
Stevie Wonder "For Once In My Life" 1968 (Tamla/Tamla Motown)

Violin
Dave Arbus (East of Eden) *Snafu* 1970 (Deram)
Papa John Creach *Playing My Fiddle* 1974 (Grunt)
David Cross (King Crimson) *Starless And Bible Black* (Atlantic/Island)
George Csapo (Bethnal) *Crash Landing* 1978 (Vertigo)
Rick Grech (Family) *Family Entertainment* 1969 (Reprise)
Don "Sugarcane" Harris on Frank Zappa's *Hot Rats* 1969 (Bizarre/Reprise)
Jean-Luc Ponty *Imaginary Voyage* 1976 (Atlantic)
Cosmic Messenger 1979 (Atlantic)
Darryl Way (Curved Air) "Vivaldi" from *Air Conditioning* 1970 (Warner Bros)

String Section
The Beatles "Yesterday" from *Rubber Soul* 1965 (Capitol)
"Eleanor Rigby" 1966 (Capitol/Parlophone)
"She's Leaving Home" and "Day In The Life" from *Sergeant Pepper's Lonely Hearts Club Band* 1967
"Strawberry Fields Forever" 1967 (Capitol/Parlophone)
ELO "Look At Me Now" and "First Movement" from *Electric Light Orchestra* 1971 (United Artists/Harvest)
Love *Forever Changes* 1967 (Elektra)
Van Morrison *It's Too Late To Stop Now* 1974 (Warner Bros)

AMPLIFICATION

Jeff Beck "She's A Woman" from *Jeff Beck With The Jan Hammer Group Live* 1977 (Epic)
Blondie "Heart Of Glass" from *Parallel Lines* 1978 (Chrysalis)
Kate Bush "Delius" from *Never For Ever*
Eric Clapton (Cream) "Sunshine Of Your Love" 1968 (Atco/Polydor)
"Politician" from *Heavy Cream* 1973 (Polydor)
Lol Creme And Kevin Godley *Consequences* 1977 (Mercury)
Peter Frampton *Frampton Comes Alive* 1975 (A&M)
Isaac Hayes "Theme From 'Shaft'" 1971 (Enterprise/Stax)
Jimi Hendrix *Electric Ladyland* 1968 (Reprise/Track)
John Martyn *Bless The Weather* 1971 (–/Island)
Solid Air 1973 (Island)
Inside Out 1973 (Island)
Jaco Pastorius on Joni Mitchell's *Hejira* 1976 (Asylum)
Elvis Presley "Heartbreak Hotel" 1957 (RCA Victor/HMV Pop)
Roxy Music "Same Old Song" from *Flesh And Blood* 1980 (Polydor)
The Small Faces "Itchycoo Park" 1967 (Immediate)
Supertramp *Breakfast In America* 1979 (A&M)
Stevie Winwood (Spencer Davis Group) "Keep On Runnin" 1965 (Atco/Fontana)
"Gimme Some Loving" 1966 (United Artists/Fontana)

PLAYING LIVE

Blondie *Eat To The Beat* 1979 (Chrysalis)
The Boomtown Rats "I Don't Like Mondays" 1979 (–/Ensign)
Buggles "Video Killed The Radio Star" 1980 (Island)
Dire Straits "Sultans Of Swing" 1979 (Vertigo)
The Police "Walking On The Moon" 1979 (A&M)
Queen "Bohemian Rhapsody" 1975 (Elektra/EMI)
The Who "My Generation" 1965 (Decca/Brunswick)
Woodstock 1970 (Cotillion/Atlantic)

RECORDING

Abba "Money, Money, Money" 1976 (Epic)
The Beatles *The Beatles* (The White Album) (Apple) 1968
David Bowie *The Rise And Fall Of Ziggy Stardust And The Spiders From Mars* 1972 (RCA)
Ry Cooder *Bop 'Til You Drop* 1979 (Warner Bros)
Fleetwood Mac *Tusk* 1980 (Warner Bros)
Flying Lizards "Money" 1979 (–/Virgin)
Bruce Springsteen *The River* 1980 (Columbia/CBS)
Yes *Fragile* 1971 (Atlantic)

SELECTED MANUFACTURERS

ACOUSTIC
Acoustic Control Corporation, 7949 Woodley Avenue, Van Nuys, Ca 91406, USA.

AGFA-GEVAERT
Agfa-Gevaert AG, Kaiser Wilhelm Allee, D-5090 Leverkuden-Bayerwerk, West Germany.
Agfa-Gevaert Ltd, Great West Road, Brentford, Middlesex, UK.
Agfa-Gevaert Inc, 275 North Street, Teterboro, NJ 07608, USA.

AKG
AKG GmbH, Brunhildengasse 1, A-1150 Vienna, Austria.
AKG Acoustics Ltd, 191 The Vale, London W3 7QS, UK.
AKG Acoustics Inc, 77 Selleck Street, Stamford, CT 06902, USA.

ALEMBIC
Alembic Guitars, 45 Foley Street, Santa Rosa, Ca 95401, USA.

ALLEN & HEATH BRENELL
Allen & Heath Brenell Ltd, Pembroke House, Campsbourne Road, London N8, UK.
Audio Marketing, 652 Glenbrock Road, Conn 06906, USA.

ALTEC LANSING
Altec Corporation, 1515 South Manchester Avenue, Anaheim, Ca 92806, USA.
Theatre Projects Sound Ltd, 10 Long Acre, London WC2 9LN, UK.

AMPEG
The Ampeg Company, Box 310, Elkhart, IN 46515, USA.

AMPEX
Ampex Corporation, 401 Broadway, Redwood City, Ca 94063, USA.
Ampex GB Ltd, Acre Road, Reading RG2 0QR, UK.

ARIA
Aria & Co Inc, 41 1-chome, Kandacho, Chikusaku, Nagoya, Japan.
Gigsville, South Drive, Phoenix Way, Heston, Middlesex TW5 9ND, UK.
Aria Music (USA) Inc, 1201 John Reed Court, City of Industry, Ca 91745, USA.
Music Distributors Inc, 3400 Darby Avenue, Charlotte, NC 28216, USA.

ARP
Arp Instruments Inc, 45 Hartwell Avenue, Lexington, Mass 02173, USA.
London Synthesiser Centre, 22 Charlton Street, London W1, UK.

BALDWIN
Baldwin Piano & Organ Co, 1801 Gilbert Avenue, Cincinnati, OH 45202, USA.
Baldwin (UK) Ltd, Unit 4, Sterling Industrial Estate, Rainham Road South, Dagenham, Essex, UK.

ERNIE BALL
Ernie Ball, Box 217, Newport Beach, Ca 92663, USA.
Strings and Things Ltd, Unit 2, Chapel Road, Portslade, Brighton, Sussex BN4 1PF, UK.

BARCUS-BERRY
Barcus-Berry Inc, 15461 Springdale Street, Huntington Beach, Ca 92649, USA.

BASF
BASF Aktiengesellschaft, Carl Bosch Strasse 38, D-6700 Ludwigshafen am Rhein, West Germany.
BASF (UK) Ltd, Haddon House, 2-4 Fitzroy Street, London W1F 5AD, UK.
BASF Systems Inc, Crosly Drive, Bedford, Mass 01730, USA.

BECHSTEIN
Bechstein Pianofortefabrik GmbH, Reichenbergerstrasse 124, D-1000 Berlin 36, West Germany.

BEYER
Beyer Dynamic, PO Box 1320, D-7100 Heilbronn, West Germany.
Beyer Dynamic (GB) Ltd, 1 Clair Road, Haywards Heath, Sussex RH16 3DP, UK.
Burns Audiotronics Inc, 505 Burns Avenue, Hicksville, NY 11801, USA.

BOSE
Bose Corporation, 100 The Mountain Road, Framingham, Mass 01701, USA.
Bose (UK) Ltd, Sittingbourne Industrial Park, Crown Quay Lane, Sittingbourne, Kent, UK.

BOSENDORFER
Bösendorfer Klavierfabrik AG, Bösendorferstrasse 12, AS-1010 Vienna, Austria.
Bösendorfer Pianos Ltd, 38 Wigmore Street, London W1, UK.
Kimball International Inc, 1549 Regal Street, Jasper, IN 47546, USA.

BOSS as **ROLAND**

BURMAN
Burman Amplification, Handyside Arcade, Percy Street, Newcastle-upon-Tyne, Tyne and Wear NE1 4PZ, UK.
Burman Amplification (USA) Inc, PO Box 463, Gracie, New York, NY 10028, USA.

BURNS
Actualisers Ltd, Padnal Road, Littleport, Ely, Cambs, UK.

CARLSBRO
Carlsbro Sound Equipment, Cross Drive, Lowmoor Road Industrial Estate, Kirkby-in-Ashfield, Nottinghamshire, UK.

CASIOTONE
Casio Computer Co Ltd, 2-6-1 Nishishin Juku, Shinjuku-ku, Tokyo 160, Japan.
Casio Electronics, 28 Scrutton Street, London EC2, UK.
Casio Inc, 15 Gardner Road, Fairfield, NJ 07006, USA.

PETER COOK
Peter Cook Guitars, 17 Perimead Road, Perivale, Greenford, Middlesex, UK.

PETE CORNISH
Cornish Musical Accessories, 38 Long Acre, London WC2, UK.

COURT ACOUSTICS
Court Acoustics, 35-39 Britannia Row, London N1 8QH, UK.

CROWN/AMCRON
Crown International Inc, 1718 West Mishawaka Road, Elkhart, IN 46514, USA.
HHB, Unit F, New Crescent Works, Nicoll Road, London NW10 9AX, UK.

CRUMAR
Crumar SpA, PO Box 98, I-60022, Castelfidardo, Italy.
Trevor Daniels, 49 Potters Lane, Kiln Farm, Milton Keynes, Bletchley, Bucks, UK.
Music Technology Inc, 105 Fifth Avenue, Garden City Park, NY 11040, USA.

CUSTOM SOUND
Custom Sound Ltd, Custom House, Arthur Street, Oswestry, Salop ST11 1JN, UK.

DAION
Daion Co Ltd, 3-5-20 Motomachi, Naniwa-ku, Osaka 556, Japan.
Rosetti Ltd, 138-140 Old Street, London EC1, UK.
MCI Inc, 7400 Imperial Drive, Waco, TX 76710, USA.

DIMARZIO
DiMarzio Musical Instrument Pickups Inc, 1388 Richmond Terrace, Staten Island, NY 10301, USA.
Rose-Morris & Co Ltd, 32-34 Gordon House Road, London NW5 1NE, UK.

DOD
Dod Electronics Corporation, 242 West 2950 South, Salt Lake City, UT 84115, USA.
Strings and Things, Unit 2, Chapel Road, Portslade, Brighton BN4 1PF, UK.

DOLBY
Dolby Laboratories Inc, 346 Clapham Road, London SW9, UK.
Dolby Laboratories Inc, 731 Sansome Street, San Francisco, Ca 94111, USA.

SEYMOUR DUNCAN
Seymour Duncan Pickups, Box 4746-H, Santa Barbara, Ca 93103, USA.
Doug Chandler, 199 Sandycombe Road, Kew, Richmond, Surrey, UK.

DYNACORD
Dynacord Electronic GmbH, Sienmensstrasse 41-43, D-8440 Strubing, West Germany.
Dynacord Electronics, PO Box 26038, Philadelphia, Penn 19128, USA.

EKO
Eko Musical Instruments SpA, via Ceccaroni 1/3, Cas Postale 53, I-62019 Recanati, Italy.
Rose-Morris & Co Ltd, 32-34 Gordon House Road, London NW5 1NE, UK.

ELECTRO-HARMONIX
Electro-Harmonix, 27 West 23rd Street, New York, NY 10010, USA.
Electro-Harmonix (UK), Unit F24, Park Hall Trading Estate, Martell Road, London SE21 8EN, UK.

ELECTRONIC DREAM PLANT
Electronic Dream Plant (Oxford) Ltd, Red Gables, Coombe, nr Stonesfield, Oxfordshire, UK.

ELECTRO-VOICE
Electro-Voice Inc, 600 Cecil Street, Buchanan, Michigan 49107, USA.
Electro-Voice (Gulton Europe) Ltd, Maple Works, Old Shoreham Road, Hove, Sussex BN3 7EY, UK.

EMS
Datanomics Ltd, 7 Westminster Rd, Wareham, Dorset, BH20 4SP, UK.
EMSA, 269 Locust Street, Northampton, Mass 01060, USA.

EPIPHONE
Norlin Music, George Yard, Braintree, Essex, UK.
Norlin Music Inc, 7373 North Cicero Avenue, Lincolnwood, IL 60646, USA.

EVANS
Evans Corporation, 5-21-5 Higashiryoke, Kawaguchi-shi, Saitama Pref. 332, Japan.
John Hornby Skewes, Salem House, Garforth, Leeds LS25 1PX, UK.

EVENTIDE
Eventide Clockworks Inc, 265 West 54th Street, New York, NY 10019, USA.
Feldon Audio Ltd, 126 Great Portland Street, London W1N 5PH, UK.

FAIRLIGHT
Fairlight Instruments Pty Ltd, Boundary Street, Rushcutters Bay, Sydney, Australia.
Syco Systems, 20 Conduit Place, London W2, UK.
Fairlight Instruments USA, 1610 Butler Avenue, Los Angeles, Ca 90025, USA.

FARFISA
Farfisa SpA, Aspio Terme di Camerano, Cas Postale 204, I-60100 Ancona, Italy.
Farfisa UK Ltd, 2 Denbeigh Hall, Bletchley, Milton Keynes, Bucks, MK2 7QT, UK.
Farfisa Music Inc, 135 West Foster Avenue, Bensenville, IL 60106, USA.

FENDER
CBS Musical Instruments, 1300 East Valencia Drive, Fullerton, Ca 92634, USA.
CBS/Arbiter, Fender House, Centenary Estate, Jeffreys Road, Brimsdown, Enfield, Middlesex, UK.

FOSTEX
Fostex Corporation, 512 Miyazawa-cho, Akishima-shi, Tokyo 196, Japan.
Bandive Ltd, 10 East Barnet Road, New Barnet, Herts EN4 8RW, UK.
Fostex Corporation of America, 15431 Blackburn Avenue, Norwalk, Ca 90650, USA.

FRAP
Strobotronix Inc, PO Box 40097, San Francisco, Ca 94140, USA.
Peavey (UK) Ltd, Unit 8, New Road, Ridgewood, Uckfield, Sussex TN22 5SX, UK.

FYLDE
Keith Hand, 219 Walmersley Road, Bury, Lancs BL9 6RU, UK.

G & L
G & L Music Sales Inc, 2548 East Fender Avenue, Unit G, Fullerton, Ca 92631, USA.

GIBSON
Norlin Music Inc, 7373 North Cicero Avenue, Lincolnwood, IL 60646, USA.
Gibson Division, Norlin Music, George Yard, Braintree, Essex, UK.

GRETSCH
Gretsch Guitars, 908 West Chestnut, Chanute, Kansas 66720, USA.
Baldwin (UK) Ltd, Unit 4, Sterling Industrial Estate, Rainham Road South, Dagenham, Essex, UK.

GUILD
Guild Guitars, 225 West Grand Street, Box 203, Elizabeth, NJ 07207, USA.
Guild Division, Summerfield Brothers, Saltmeadows Road, Gateshead, Tyne and Wear NE8 3AJ, UK.

GUITAR MAN
Stuyvesant Music Inc, 174 West 48th Street, New York, NY10036, USA.

GUYATONE
Rose-Morris & Co Ltd, 32-34 Gordon House Road, London NW5 1NE, UK.

HAMER
Hamer Guitars, 835 West University Drive, Arlington Heights, IL 60004, USA.

HAMMOND
Hammond Organ Company, 4200 West Diversey, Chicago, IL 60639, USA.
Hammond Organ Company, 19 Denbeigh Hall, Bletchley, Milton Keynes MK3 7QT, UK.

HARRISON
Harrison Systems Inc, PO Box 22964, Nashville, TN 37202, USA.
F W O Bauch Ltd, 49 Theobald Street, Boreham Wood, Herts WD6 4RZ, UK.

HELPINSTILL
Helpinstill Designs, 5808 South Rice Avenue, Houston, TX 77081, USA.
London Synthesiser Centre, 22 Charlton Street, London W1, UK.

H/H
H/H Electronic, Viking Way, Bar Hill, Cambridgeshire, CB3 8EL, UK.

HIWATT
Hiwatt Equipment Ltd, Park Works, 16 Park Road, Kingston-upon-Thames, Surrey, UK.

HOFNER
Karl Hofner oHG, Schobacherstrasse 56, D-8521 Bubenreuth, West Germany.

HOHNER
M Hohner AG, Hohnerstrasse, Postfach 160, D-7218 Trossingen, West Germany.
M Hohner Ltd, 39-45 Coldharbour Lane, London SE5, UK.
Hohner Inc, Andrews Road, Hicksville, NY 11802, USA.

HONDO
John Hornby Skewes, Salem House, Garforth, Leeds LS25 1PX, UK.
Hondo Guitars, International Music Corporation, PO Box 2344, Fort Worth, TX 76113, USA.

IBANEZ
Fuji Gen-Gakki Mfg Co Ltd, 793 Yoshikawa Hirata, Matsumoto-shi, Nagana Pref. 499-65, Japan.
Summerfield Brothers, Saltmeadows Lane, Gateshead, Tyne and Wear NE8 3AJ, UK.
Ibanez, PO Box 469, Bensalem, PA 19020.
Ibanez, 327 Broadway, Idaho Falls, ID 83401, USA.

JBL
James B Lansing Sound Inc, 8500 Balbao Boulevard, Northridge, Ca 91329, USA.
Harman (Audio) UK Ltd, St John's Road, Tylers Green, High Wycombe, Bucks HP10 8HR, UK.

KAWAI
Kawai Musical Instrument Ltd, 2-8-8 Shinbashi, Minato-ku, Tokyo 105, Japan.

KORG
Keio Electronic Laboratory, 15-12 Shimotakaido 1-chome, Suginamu-ku, Tokyo 168, Japan.
Rose-Morris & Co Ltd, 32-34 Gordon House Road, London NW5 1NE, UK.
Unicord, 89 Frost Street, Westbury, New York, NY 11590, USA.

KRAMER
Kramer Guitars, BKL International Corporation, 1111 Green Grove Road, Neptune, NJ 07753, USA.

LAB SERIES
Norlin Music Inc, 7373 North Cicero Avenue, Lincolnwood, IL 60646, USA.
Gibson Division, Norlin Music, George Yard, Braintree, Essex, UK.

LATIN PERCUSSION
Latin Percussion Inc, PO Box 88, Palisades Park, NJ 07650, USA.
Rosetti Ltd, 138-140 Old Street, London EC1, UK.

BILL LAWRENCE
Bill Lawrence Products, 1003 Saunders Avenue, Madison, TN 37115, USA.
Fletcher Coppock and Newman, Morley Road, Tonbridge, Kent, UK.

LINN
Linn Electronics Inc, 3249 Tareco Drive, Hollywood, Ca 90068, USA.
Scenic Sounds Equipment, 97-99 Dean Street, London W1, UK.
Syco Systems, 20 Conduit Place, London W2, UK.

LUDWIG
Ludwig International Ltd, 1728 Damen Avenue, Chicago, IL 60647, USA.
Rose-Morris & Co Ltd, 32-34 Gordon House Road, London NW5 1NE, UK.

MAINE
Maine Electronics, Maine House, 193 Rickmansworth Road, Watford, Herts, UK.

DEAN MARKLEY
Dean Markley Strings, 3350 Scott Boulevard No 29, Santa Clara, Ca 95051, USA.
Dean Markley (UK) Ltd, 296 Charminster Road, Bournemouth, Dorset, UK.

MARSHALL
Marshall Amplification Ltd, First Avenue, Bletchley, Milton Keynes, Bucks, UK.
Unicord, 89 Frost Street, Westbury, NY 11590, USA.

MARTIN
C F Martin Organization, Box 8968, S-40274 Gozeborg, Sweden.
Phil York, Kinchyle, Church Lane, Great Holland, Frinton-on-Sea, Essex, UK.
C F Martin Organization, Box 329, Nazareth, PA 18064, USA.

MCI
MCI, 1400 West Commercial Boulevard, Fort Lauderdale, FL 33309, USA.
MCI Ltd, 54-56 Stanhope Street, London NW1 3EX, UK.

MESA BOOGIE
Mesa Engineering, Box 116, Lagunitas, Ca 94938, USA.
ML Executives Ltd, Shepperton Studio Centre, Squires Bridge Road, Shepperton, Middlesex, UK.

MIGHTY MITE
Mighty Mite Mfg, 4809 Calle Alto, Camarillo, Ca 93010, USA.
Rosetti Ltd, 138-140 Old Street, London EC1, UK.

MM/PACE
MM Electronics/PACE, Lampas House, 63 Kneesworth Street, Royston, Herts SG8 5AG, UK.

MOOG
Moog Music Inc, 2500 Walden Avenue, Buffalo, NY 14225, USA.
Roy Goudie, 11 Forth Wynd, Port Seton, East Lothian, Scotland, UK.

MORLEY
Tel-Ray Electronics, 6855 Vineland Avenue, North Hollywood, Ca 91605, USA.
Rosetti Ltd, 138-140 Old Street, London EC1, UK.

MUSIC MAN
Music Man Inc, 1338 State College Parkway, Anaheim, Ca 92803, USA.
Music Man Division, Unit 2, Chapel Road, Portslade, Brighton, Sussex BN4 1PF, UK.

MXR
MXR Innovations, 740 Driving Park Avenue, Rochester, NY 14613, USA.
Atlantex Music Ltd, 34 Bancroft, Hitchin, Herts SG5 1LA, UK.

NEUMANN
Georg Neumann GmbH, Charlottenstrasse 3, D-1000 Berlin 61, West Germany.
F W O Bauch Ltd, 49 Theobald Street, Boreham Wood, Herts WD6 4RZ, UK.
Gotham Audio Corporation, 741 Washington Street, New York, NY 10014, USA.

NOVATRON
Streetly Electronics, 388 Aldridge Road, Streetly, Sutton Coldfield, West Midlands B74 2DT, UK.

OBERHEIM
Oberheim Electronics Inc, 2250 South Barrington Avenue, Los Angeles, Ca 90064, USA.
London Synthesiser Centre, 22 Charlton Street, London NW1, UK.

OHM
Ohm Amplification Ltd, Unit 1, Knutsford Industrial Estate, Parkgate Lane, Knutsford, Cheshire, UK.

OTARI
Otari Electric Co, Otari Building, 4-29-18 Minami, Ogikubo, Suginami-ku, Tokyo, Japan.
ITA, 1-7 Harewood Avenue, London NW1, UK.
Otari Corp, 1559 Industrial Road, San Carlos, Ca 94070, USA.

OVATION
Ovation Instruments Inc, Blue Hills Avenue, Bloomfield, CT 06002, USA.
Rose-Morris & Co Ltd, 32-34 Gordon House Road, London NW5 1NE, UK.

PAISTE
Paiste AG, CH-6207 Nottwil, Switzerland.
CBS/Arbiter, Fender House, Centenary Estate, Jeffreys Road, Brimsdown, Enfield, Middlesex, UK.

PEARL
Pearl Musical Instrument Co, 16-6 4-chome, Narihira, Sumida-ku, Tokyo 130, Japan.
Pearl UK, Unit 5, 29-35 North Acton Road, Park Royal, London NW10, UK.

PEAVEY
Peavey Electronics, 711 A Street, Meridian, MS 39301, USA.
Peavey (UK) Ltd, Unit 8, New Road, Ridgewood, Uckfield, Sussex TN22 5SX, UK.

PREMIER
Premier Drum Company, Blaby Road, Wigston, Leicester LE8 2DF, UK.

RANDALL
Randall Instruments Inc, 1132 Duryea, Irvine, Ca 92714, USA.
Stewart Field, Everbimes, 2A Bath Road, Mansfield, Nottinghamshire, UK.

REMO
Remo Inc, 12804 Raymer Street, North Hollywood, Ca 91605, USA.

REVOX
Studer International AG, Althardstrasse 150, CH-8105 Regensdorf, Switzerland.
F W O Bauch Ltd, 49 Theobald Street, Boreham Wood, Herts WD6 4RZ, UK.
Studer Revox America Inc, 1819 Broadway, Nashville, TN 37203, USA.

RHODES
CBS Musical Instruments, 1300 East Valencia Drive, Fullerton, Ca 92634, USA.
CBS/Arbiter, Fender House, Centenary Estate, Jeffreys Road, Brimsdown, Enfield, Middlesex, UK.

B C RICH
B C Rich Guitar Co, 4770 Valley Boulevard, No 117, Los Angeles, Ca 90032, USA.

RICKENBACKER
Rickenbacker, 3895 South Main, Santa Ana, Ca 92707, USA.
Wing Music, 15 London Road, Bromley, Kent, UK.

RMI
RMI Inc, Macungie, PA 18062, USA.
Allen Organ Studios (London) Ltd, 177 Hook Road, Hook, Surbiton, Surrey, UK.

ROGERS
CBS Musical Instruments, 1300 East Valencia Drive, Fullerton, Ca 92634, USA.
CBS/Arbiter, Fender House, Centenary Estate, Jeffreys Road, Brimsdown, Enfield, Middlesex, UK.

ROLAND
Roland Corporation, 7-13 Shinkithaima 3-chome, Suminoe-ku, Osaka 559, Japan.
Roland (UK) Ltd, Great West Trading Estate, 983 Great West Road, Brentford, Middlesex, UK.
Roland Corporation US, 2401 Saybrook Avenue, Los Angeles, Ca 90040, USA.

SCHALLER
Schaller Electronic, Pfinzingstrasse 2, D-8501 Feuch, West Germany.
Rosetti Ltd, 138-140 Old Street, London EC1, UK.

SCHECTER
Schecter Guitar Research, 6164 Sepulveda Boulevard, Van Nuys, Ca 91411, USA.
Doug Chandler, 199 Sandycombe Road, Kew, Richmond, Surrey, UK.

SENNHEISER
Sennheiser Electronic, D-3002 Wedermark 2, Hanover, West Germany.
Hayden Laboratories Ltd, Hayden House, Chiltern Hill, Chalfont St Peter, Gerrards Cross, Bucks SL9 9UG, UK.
Sennheiser Electronic Corporation, 10 West 37th Street, New York, NY 10018, USA.

SEQUENTIAL CIRCUITS
Sequential Circuits, 3051 North First Street, San Jose, Ca 95134, USA.
Rod Argent's Keyboards, 20 Denmark Street, London WC2, UK.

SHERGOLD
Shergold Guitars, 9 Avenue Industrial Estate, Southend Arterial Road, Harold Wood, Romford, Essex RM3 0BY, UK.

SHURE
Shure Brothers Inc, 222 Hartrey Avenue, Evanston, IL 60204, USA.
Shure Electronics Ltd, Eccleston Road, Maidstone, Kent ME18 6AU, UK.

SIMMONS
Musicaid, 176 Hatfield Road, St Albans, Herts, UK.

SLINGERLAND
Slingerland, 6633 North Milwaukee Avenue, Niles, IL 60648, USA.

GORDON SMITH
Keith Hand, 219 Walmersley Road, Bury, Lancs BL9 6RU, UK.

SOLID STATE LOGIC
Solid State Logic Ltd, Stonesfield, Oxfordshire, UK.
Washington Musicworks Inc, 3421 M Street NW, Washington, DC 20007, USA.

SONOR
Sonor Percussion, Zum Heilbach 5, D-5920 Bad Berleburg-Aue, West Germany.
Charles Alden Music Co, Industrial Park, Westwood, MA 02090, USA.

SOUNDCRAFT
Soundcraft Electronics Ltd, 5 Great Sutton Street, London EC1V OBX, UK.
Soundcraft North America, PO Box 2023, Kalamazoo, MN 49003, USA.

STEINWAY
Steinway & Sons, Steinway Hall, 1 St George's Street, London W1, UK.

STUDER as **REVOX**

SUNN
Sunn Musical Equipment Co, Amburn Industrial Park, Tualatin, OR 97062, USA.

SUPERWOUND
Superwound Ltd, Unit 1, Morewood Close, London Road, Sevenoaks, Kent, UK.

TAMA
Summerfield Brothers, Saltmeadows Lane, Gateshead, Tyne and Wear, NE8 3AJ, UK.
Chesbro Music Co, 327 Broadway, PO Box 2009, Idaho Falls, ID 83401, USA.

TANNOY
Tannoy Products Ltd, St John's Road, Tylers Green, High Wycombe, Bucks HP10 8HR, UK.
BGW Systems, 13130 South Yukon Avenue, Hawthorne, Ca 90250, USA.

TEAC
Teac Corporation, 3-7-3 Naka-cho, Musashino, Tokyo 180, Japan.
Harman Audio (UK) Ltd, Mill Street, Slough SL2 5DD, Bucks, UK.
Teac Corporation, of America, 7733 Telegraph Road, Montebello, Ca 90640, USA.

TEISCO
Teisco Co Ltd, Ohaza Shimokayama 2712, Shobu-machi, Minami Saitama-gun, Saitama Pref, Japan.
John Hornby Skewes, Salem House, Garforth, Leeds LS25 1PX, UK.

TELEFUNKEN
AEG-Telefunken, Postfach 2154, D-7754 Konstanz, West Germany.
Hayden Laboratories Ltd, Hayden House, Chiltern Hill, Chalfont St Peter, Bucks, SL9 9UG, UK.
Gotham Audio Corporation, 741 Washington Street, New York, NY10014, USA.

TRAVIS BEAN
Travis Bean Inc, 11671 Sheldon Street, Sun Valley, Ca 91352, USA.

TRIDENT
Trident Audio Developments Ltd, PO Box 38, Studio Road, Shepperton, Middlesex WW17 0QD, UK.
Studio Maintenance Services, 12438 Magnolia Boulevard, North Hollywood, Ca 91607, USA.

VANTAGE
Matsumoku Industrial Co Ltd, 11-4 Namiyanagi, Matsumoto-shi, Nagano Pref 390, Japan.
Stack Music, 9 Stapleton Road, Orton Southgate, Peterborough, Cambs, UK.

VOX
Vox Ltd, 32-34 Gordon House Road, London NW5 1NE, UK.
Pennino Music Co, 6421 Industry Way, Westminster, Ca 92683, USA.
Allstate Music Supply Corporation, PO Box 6768, 1017 Westside Drive, Greensboro, NC 27405, USA.

WAL
Electric Wood, Sandown Works, Chairborough Road, High Wycombe, Bucks HP12 3HH, UK.

WASHBURN
Roland (UK) Ltd, Great West Trading Estate, 983 Great West Road, Brentford, Middlesex, UK.
Fretted Instruments Inc, 1415 Waukegan Road, Northbrook, IL 60062, USA.

WEM
Watkins Electric Music, 66 Offley Road, London SW9, UK.

WESTBURY
Rose-Morris & Co Ltd, 32-34 Gordon House Road, London NW5 1NE, UK.
Unicord, 89 Forst Street, Westbury, New York, NY 11590, USA.

WURLITZER
The Wurlitzer Company, 403 East Gurler Road, DeKalb, IL 60115, USA.
Wurlitzer UK, Industrial Estate, Parkgates Lane, Knutsford, Cheshire, UK.

YAMAHA
Nippon Gakki Co Ltd, 10-1 Nakazawa-cho, Hammamatsu, Shizuoka 430, Japan.
Yamaha Musical Instruments, Mount Avenue, Bletchley, Milton Keynes, MK1 1JE, UK.
Yamaha International Corporation, PO Box 6600, Buena Park, Ca 90622, USA.

ZILDJIAN
Avedis Zildjian Co, PO Box 198, Accord, MA 02018, USA.
Cymbals and Percussion Ltd, 68 Swithland Lane, Rothley, Leicestershire, UK.

3M
3M Magnetic Audio/Video Products, 3M Center, St Paul, Minnesota 55101, USA.
3M UK Ltd, PO Box 1, Bracknell, Berkshire RG12 1JU, UK.

GLOSSARY

A

Acoustic guitar *Classical:* Nylon-strung, small bodied guitar used for playing "classical" guitar music.
Dreadnought: Wide-waisted bodied guitar introduced in early twentieth century. Also called Jumbo.
Folk: Guitar with narrow waist and round shoulders, much used by folk accompanists.

Acoustic Piano General term used for grand and upright pianos, to distinguish them in rock from electric and electronic pianos.

Action *Guitar action:* The distance between the strings and the fingerboard.
Keyboard action: The sensitivity of the keys to the player's touch.
Piano action: The mechanical part of the instrument.

Active electronics Circuitry added to electric guitars and basses whereby a preamplifier enables the player to cut and boost tone settings by wider margins than possible with normal ("passive") guitars and basses.

ADT-automatic double tracking Electronic device designed to give the studio effect of overdubbing a second voice or instrument on to an existing track to create a thick, doubled effect.

Agogo Bells Brazilian percussion instrument consisting of two bells approximately a musical third apart, played with a variety of strikers.

Amplifier *Tube (valve) amp:* Amplifier using valve stages.
Combo amp: Abbreviation of combination amplifier – *ie* a combination of amplifier and speaker(s) in one unit.
Transistor amp: Amplifier using transistor stages.
Power amp: Amplifier without pre-amp; the main amplifier.

Amplitude The degree of change in a varying electrical signal, usually its loudness.

Attack The character of the very beginning of a musical note.

Attenuation Attenuation (the opposite of amplification) is the decreasing of the magnitude of a signal.

Audio Spectrum Audible sound. In theory people can hear over a range from 20Hz to 20kHz, though this varies from one person to another and in practice tends to be nearer 40Hz to 14kHz.

"Axe" Slang for electric guitar.

B

Backline The individual amplifiers and speaker cabinets behind each player on stage.

Bin and horn PAs typically consist of bass "bins" and treble "horns", components originally designed for cinema sound systems.

Bongos Small drum-like percussion instruments made from many different materials and usually played with the hands.

Brass 1. Metal commonly used for electric guitar hardware, based on the belief that it has special sustaining qualities.
2. General term for woodwind instruments made from brass, *eg* saxophone, trumpet and trombone – hence the term "brass section" for small team of brass instrument players augmenting rock band.

Bridge The bridge stops the sounding length of the strings on the body of the guitar. Bridge pins hold the body end of the strings secure on acoustic guitars.

Bug Slang for transducer or pickup attached to acoustic instrument, such as guitar or saxophone.

Bullet Small cover over end of truss rod on headstock of Stratocaster and similar electric guitars.

C

Cabasa Hand-held percussion instrument with stainless steel cylinder around which ball bearings are strung. It is shaken or played with the fingers.

Casework The usually wooden outer casing of an acoustic piano.

Chorus Electronic ensemble or multi-instrument sound involving short delay effects (usually between 5 and 30 milli-seconds) "swept" to produce slight deviations in pitch.

Clavichord Keyboard instrument dating from early fifteenth century, related to the piano but without its sustain facilities.

Coloration Any effect which degrades or distorts a sound.

Compression A process in which input signals are compressed or reduced by varying degrees, increasing the proportion of high-level signals and giving the impression of a louder resulting signal.
Compressor-limiter: A device which allows higher recording levels to be recorded on to tape, or provides overload protection in PA systems.

Course Pair of strings running closely together and tuned a particular interval apart, as on 12-string guitars.

Cowbell Metal percussion instrument: in rock usually mounted on the bass drum or played hand-held and struck with a drum stick.

Crossover Electronic device which splits sound into different frequency bands.
A passive crossover is wired between amplifier and speakers.
An active crossover is wired between mixed and amplifiers.

Cross-stringing The arrangement of piano strings in two different planes to reduce the size of the instrument.

Cutaway An incision into an electric guitar's body wood either side of the neck. A guitar with an incision both sides is a double cutaway instrument; with one, a single cutaway. Allows the player easier access to the upper frets.

Cymbals *Crash:* Usually thin or medium thickness, from 16in to 24in diameter.
Ride: Usually 18in to 24in diameter, for sustained rhythm keeping.
Hihat: Pair of cymbals opened and closed by special pedal and stand mechanism.
Swish: Usually 18in to 22in diameter, with upturned edge and rivets.
Pang: Sometimes with square-shaped bell, producing "pangier" tone, hence name.

D

Damping Any effect which deadens the sound of a musical note or sound – the palm of the hand on guitar strings, foam rubber under bass strings, or towels stuffed into the front of the bass drum.

Decay The "dying away" of a musical note – for synthesizers, the decay is the time immediately following attack.

Decibel (dB) A ratio of two values of power; used to measure sound pressure levels (SPLs) with a reference point at 0dB (the threshold of hearing) up to about 130dB (the loudest bearable sound and the threshold of pain).

Demo Abbreviation of "demonstration recording" – usually made for record companies or concert promoters to judge an artist or band's performance.

Delay The retardation of the time of arrival of a signal, after electronic treatment.

Direct injection Method of by passing microphones in the studio or stage, by plugging straight into the mixing desk by means of a direct injection (DI) box.

Distortion In electronics, an unwanted change or alteration to a signal. In rock, an often desired change giving a warm, thickened sound to the instrument's amplified characteristic.

Doppler shift A change in vibrational frequencies when a sound source moves relative to the ears or microphone.

Drawbar Control mechanism on Hammond or similar organ allowing the player to mix fundamental and harmonic notes to produce complex sounds.

Drum machine General term for

any device producing drum or percussion rhythms and sounds by mechanical, electronic or digital means.

Dynamic range The difference in decibels between a system's noise and overload levels.

E

Echo A distinct and separate repeat of a musical note or sound, repeating until it gradually dies away.

Electric/electronic An electric instrument transduces a mechanical phenomenon (*eg* a vibrating string) into an electrical signal, usually via a pickup. An electronic instrument produces sounds by purely electronic means.

Electric guitar *Semi-acoustic:* Hollow or semi-hollow bodied, sometimes called cello acoustic. *Solid:* Solid-bodied, usually wooden.

Envelope generator A module producing a voltage which changes as the envelope of a particular instrument's characteristics change. In synthesizers, these are generally the ADS (attack, decay, sustain) or ADSR (attack, decay, sustain, release) generators.

Equalizers Another term for tone control – increases or decreases various frequency components in a signal. A graphic equalizer has slide controls, each of which changes a particular frequency band's intensity, and in effect gives a graphic "read-out" of the frequency response of any given setting. A parametric equalizer is a more precise form of equalizer, enabling the user to pinpoint the frequency bands being modified.

Escapement *First escapement:* Piano action which allows the hammer to fall back after striking the string. *Second escapement:* Piano action which allows rapid repetition of notes.

F

Fader Sliding control on mixer, usually to increase or decrease

gain on one particular channel.

Feedback Howl produced when a pickup or microphone comes too near to a loudspeaker, thus picking up and amplifying its own signal.

Finger-style Playing guitar with fingers or nails rather than (more commonly in rock) with a plectrum.

Flanging A similar effect to phasing, but using time delay for filtering effect.

Flutter Small, rapid deviation in tape speed causing minor pitch variations.

Foldback Monitor speakers on stage enabling musicians to hear themselves and other members of the band via the PA mixer controls. In the studio, foldback is heard through headphones.

Frequency A flat frequency response is where apparent loudness is the same at all frequencies in the audio spectrum.

Fretless bass guitar Has a fingerboard without frets, so that the player can move more freely up and down the fingerboard and produce acoustic bass-like tones.

Frets Strips of wire placed at certain precise points on the fingerboard of a guitar to stop strings and produce notes of a specific scale. *Fretboard:* Another term for fingerboard. *Touch-activated frets:* Frets linked by some electronic means to another device on the instrument.

Fundamental The lowest frequency or note in a complex vibration or chord.

Fuzz Distortion effect produced by clipped waveforms: commonly brought about by electronic "fuzz boxes" plugged between instrument and amp.

G

Guiro Long, hollow, cylindrical percussion instrument with evenly spaced grooves which are scraped with a stick

H

Hammond organ Revolutionary keyboard instrument invented by Laurens Hammond in the 1930s.

Harmonics Oscillations with frequencies that are multiples of the fundamental.

Harpsichord Early keyboard instrument related to the piano in its use of a simple escapement system.

Headstock Area at the top of the guitar's neck which incorporates the machine heads, and usually bears the maker's logo.

Hertz (Hz) Unit of frequency equal to one cycle per second. One hundred Hertz equals one Kilohertz (kHz).

Horn Elongated projection on electric guitar's body either side of the cutaways (if any).

Hum Low pitched drone emanating from electrical equipment, usually originating in the mains supply.

J

Jack plug Mono or stereo signal connector, used on electric guitars and their amplifiers. *Jack lead:* Cord (lead) connecting two jack plugs. *Jackfield:* Series of jack plug sockets to allow interconnection of various devices in the studio, and in some modular synthesizers.

Joystick Control appearing as a vertical "stick" which can be rocked through various axes, sometimes used as performance control on synthesizers, or as a pan-pot on multi-speaker sound systems and PAs.

K

Keyboard The actual keys of a keyboard instrument, usually described as being of so many octaves, and as ranging from lowest note to highest note (*eg* the most suitable range for rock keyboards is from C to C).

L

"Log" Les Paul called his original electric guitar experiment the "log"

Lyrachord Brand name for fibreglass-like substance from which the backs of Ovation acoustic and acoustic-electric guitars are made.

M

Machine heads Gear mechanisms on the guitar's headstock around which the string ends are wound and by which they are brought into accurate tuning.

Manual Dual manual/single manual: Single manual keyboard instruments have one set of keys; dual manual instruments have two banks of keys, one above the other.

Mastering machine Stereo tape recorder on to which multitrack recordings are mixed, or mastered.

Miking up The process of placing microphones around instruments and speaker cabinets, both on stage and in the studio. Close miking is placing microphones near to instruments and speaker cabinets to achieve separation from other nearby sound sources.

Multicore Multiple core cable, used to carry many signals to or from the stage, and between the control room and the studio.

Multitracking Tape recording on anything from four to 32 tracks, with the facility of recording one or many at a time, and listening back to one or many previously recorded tracks at the same time – the basis of modern rock recording.

Mixdown The last stage of recording, where the multitrack tape is mixed down into two stereo tracks, the "final" version, where all equalization changes and additional effects are made and added.

Mixer A device which mixes

in-coming signals (usually from microphones or DI boxes) and balances the overall sound into one or more outputs.

N

Noise *White noise*: Noise containing equal amounts of all audio frequencies. *Pink noise*: Noise containing mostly low audio frequencies.

Noise generator Generator in synthesizer producing white noise for high frequency sound effects.

Noise reduction Literally a method of reducing noise in recording, enabling multitracking to exist. Most common type is made by Dolby Laboratories, which works by boosting high frequencies on recording and reducing them on replay, thus cutting down unwanted background hiss.

Nut A piece of bone, ivory, brass or plastic over which the strings pass from the fingerboard to the headstock's machine heads, providing the "stop" at this end of the guitar.

O

Octave Interval of twelve semi-tones, *eg* between middle C on the piano and the C 12 notes up the keys, or the distance between open E on a guitar and the E 12 frets up the same string.

Octave divider Electronic device for producing an additional note an octave apart from that being played.

Overdubbing Process in the recording studio for recording any additional parts "over" the backing or rhythm tracks, which is recorded first. These overdubs are typically instrumental fills or solos, and lead and backing vocals to replace the "guide" vocal which would have been recorded with the backing tack, and is subsequently wiped.

P

PA Public address system, or power amplification. In rock terms, the complete system of sound reinforcement: microphones, mixer, amplifiers and loudspeakers. The system amplifies the group's basic sound, to enable high sound levels to be accurately and powerfully communicated in live performance.

Pan pot Control on live or studio mixers for "panning" sound to the left or right of PA stacks or stereo mix.

Patch bay Area in recording studio or on modular synthesizer to link various sections together by means of cords called patch-cords. A particular configuration of connections on a synthesizer is called a "patch"

Performance control Synthesizer control for altering sound characteristics while note is still being played: pitchbend, low frequency modulation, release time, glide, volume, etc.

Phasing Effect produced mechanically by routing a signal to two tape recorders and recording the mixed off-tape input, while varying the speed of one machine to cause a slight delay difference. The phase cancellation and shift produced are copied electronically by using notch filters in the various phase effects pedals which have been available since the 1970s.

Pickup A pickup, or transducer, converts vibrations (*eg* of guitar strings) into electrical energy which can then be amplified. *Single-coil pickup*: Pickup based on a single-coil of wire – on the Stratocaster, for example, the coil is wound some 7,600 times around the bare magnets. *Humbucking pickup*: Pickup with two coils side by side, wound in opposite directions with reverse magnetic polarities and wired in parallel. *Pickup selector switch*: Control on electric guitar with more than one pickup to allow selection of various combinations of pickups. *PAF*: Original Gibson pickup, stamped "Patent Applied For"

Pinblock On the acoustic piano, carries the tuning pins which secure one end of the instrument's strings.

Pitch The relative depth or height of a musical note.

Pitchbend Performance control on synthesizer which literally bends the pitch of the note being played, usually by means of a lever, wheel or strip.

Plate The frame on a piano which resists the strings' tension.

Plectrum Small piece of tortoiseshell, plastic, metal etc, held between the thumb and first finger, used to pick or strum a guitar's strings.

Polepiece Small element of guitar pickup aligned under individual string and often screw-threaded to allow for vertical adjustment.

Position markers Inlays or applications to guitar's fingerboard giving octave point and other divisions for players' guidance.

Potentiometer Usually abbreviated to "pot". Control device – on the electric guitar altering volume and tone parameters.

Preamplifier Used in front of the main amplifier; amplifies low level sounds to a level which the power amplifier can deal with.

Presence Commonly a mid range tone control on instrument amplifiers.

R

Record head Device which imparts electrical signals to record information on to magnetic tape.

Replay head Device which senses recorded magnetic tape and produces an electrical signal from the recordings.

Replay keyboard Keyboard instrument using a system based on the recording and replay of original sounds, triggered by a standard keyboard. Examples include the Mellotron (now the Novatron), the Chamberlain, the Orchestron and the Binotron.

Resonwood Brand name for fiberglass-like substance used in body construction of Gibson's Sonex guitar range.

Reverberation Very short, randomly delayed repeat effects whose spacing gradually decreases as their level gradually decays.

Rim shot Drum beat played on snare drum with the stick hitting both the skin and drum rim at the same time, producing a distinctive sound.

Roadie Abbreviation of "road manager" – commonly any member of band's road crew who carry, set up, maintain, take apart and load up equipment at live performances.

S

Saddle Thin strip of hard material set into the bridge of a guitar over which the strings pass. The player usually has some degree of control over the relative position of the saddle – at least in the horizontal plane, allowing control of intonation.

Scratchplate Hard material, most commonly plastic, covering front of guitar to protect wood from scratches.

Sel-sync Abbreviation of "selective-synchronization". A tape recording process where the off-tape monitoring signal is taken from the record head itself rather than from the replay head, thus enabling existing and new recordings to be synchronized with one another.

Sequencer An analog or digital device providing control voltages and gate pulses for driving a synthesizer – programmed notes and sequences of notes can be replayed at will, making the sequencer something like a simple tape recorder linked to the synthesizer.

Shaker Percussion instrument (sometimes called a ka-me-so) similar to maracas but torpedo-shaped.

Shell The curved, cylindrical surround of a drum.

Signal An electrical impulse or "quantity" which conveys information by varying in some way: a microphone sends an electrical signal to a mixing desk; a guitar sends an electrical signal to an amplifier.

Snare *Throw-off snare:* A single lever device which releases the drum's snares in one movement. *Parallel action snare:* A snare mechanism that holds the snares parallel to the lower drum head.

Sound-on-sound The process of recording one musical performance on top of others by alternating between the left and right tracks of a stereo tape recorder.

Soundboard The part of a piano's internal construction on to which the bridges are fixed and which is responsible for much of the overall tone of the instrument.

Soundcheck Period of time before live performance when band and road crew adjust backline, PA and instruments to optimum for that particular venue.

Soundhole A hole in the top of an acoustic guitar that allows the tonal characteristic of the instrument to be projected.

Sound engineer Person in studio or at live performance who adjusts sound levels on the mixer and other equipment to aesthetic and technical optimum.

Speaker cabinet *Column speaker:* Direct radiator cabinet with loudspeakers arranged in vertical column. *Direct radiator:* Essentially a loudspeaker in an enclosed box – *eg* guitar speaker cabinet. *Flown speaker cabinets:* Those raised above the stage at large venues. *Horn:* A horn attached to a loudspeaker helps it couple more efficiently with the surrounding air.

Stack A "stack" of amplifiers – commonly British tube type – on top of several 4 x 12 direct radiator speaker cabinets, beloved by loud, heavy-rock bands.

Stage box Interconnection point in PA system where cables are routed to and from various components.

String *Ball end:* Small metal lump which enables the guitar string to be held securely at the bridge.

Sustain In synthesizers' ADSR envelopes, sustain level remains until the key being played is released. In other instruments, sustain is any elongation of a musical note, either by playing technique or artificial (*eg* electronic) means.

Synthesis *Additive synthesis:* Sound is built up from a series of sine waves, for example, to create a rich, complex sound. *Subtractive synthesis:* A harmonically rich sound has its unwanted frequencies filtered out to obtain the desired sound.

Synthesizers *Digital:* Instrument producing sounds from digital codes or via a computer using additive synthesis. *Fully polyphonic:* Instrument with pitch provided for every key, largely based on electric organ technology. *Monophonic:* Instrument where only one note can be sounded at a time. *Preset:* Instrument with switches which give preset imitative sounds. *String synthesizers:* Fully polyphonic instrument producing imitative string-section sounds.

T

Tailpiece The lower mounting point of the strings on a semi-acoustic guitar.

Tambourine Percussion instrument with a row of between four and 20 "jingles" (nickel, or other metal, discs) around a circular frame of plastic, metal or, more commonly, wood.

Tone wheel The Hammond Tone Wheel organ uses tone wheels to generate signals as they spin round at a fixed rate, their different shapes producing the various pitches required.

Top *Carved-top:* Guitar with wooden top "carved" into arched shape. *Flat-top:* Acoustic guitar with flat (*ie* non-arched) top. *Solid-top:* Acoustic guitar with solid (rather than laminated) top.

Track Four-track, 8-track *etc* refer to the number of parallel tracks which can be recorded on to a particular multitrack tape machine.

Transducer Device which converts one form of energy to another – most commonly in rock music, vibrations of strings into electrical energy capable of driving an instrument amplifier.

Transistor A semi-conductor device capable of providing amplification, with three or more electrodes. Used in many instrument amplifiers.

Tremolo arm More accurately a vibrato arm, though commonly called a tremolo arm. The device changes the pitch of an electric guitar's strings by mechanical means, thus introducing vibrato-type effects.

Truss rod Strengthening bar inserted into some guitar necks, enabling alteration of warped and bent necks.

Tube (valve) Electronic device in which electrons operate in a gas or vacuum inside a glass tube. Used in many instrument amplifiers.

Tuning pegs More usually called machine heads.

Twin-necked guitar Specially built guitar with two necks, usually to allow the player access to a six-string and 12-string guitar in one instrument.

V

Voice box Effects device which allows players to shape an instrument's amplified sound and tone with their mouths via a tube.

Voltage control The basis of musical synthesis – each note pressed on the instrument's keyboard or other form of controller produces a different voltage, and these voltages control all the synthesizer's functions.

Voltage controlled amplifier (VCA) Part of the synthesizer; shapes the sound of the resulting note or notes.

Voltage controlled filter (VCF) Part of the synthesizer; gives the resulting note (or notes) its tonal character.

Voltage controlled oscillator (VCO) Part of the synthesizer; sets the pitch of the note or notes played. The number of VCOs in a synthesizer determines the complexity of sound which can be built up by mixing the sounds of the oscillators.

Vibrato Regular "wavering" – *ie* vibrating – of a sound.

Voicing The instrumental sound chosen for a particular musical phrase, note or chord.

W

Wah-wah Effects pedal which changes the tonal characteristic of the modified instrument's sound from a dull, muted tone to a crisp, bright treble.

Wall of sound Term given to set-ups of amp and cabinet "stacks" – amplifiers atop two or more 4 x 12 cabinets.

Wow Slow deviation in tape speed causing long, slurring pitch variations.

INDEX

BIBLIOGRAPHY AND CREDITS

Magazines

Acme, rue des Sols 9, 1000 Bruxelles, Belgium.
Artist/Musiker, *Droste Verlag GmbH, Abt. Ed. Lintz Verlag,* Pressehaus am Martin-Luther-Platz, Postfach 11 22, D-4000 Düsseldorf 1, West Germany.
Contemporary Keyboard, *GPI Publications,* 20605 Lazaneo, Cupertino, Ca 95014, USA.
D.I.S.C. International, 60-62 avenue de Verdun, F-92320 Châtillon-s/s-Bagneux, France.
Electronics and Music Maker, *Maplin Publications,* 242 London Road, Westcliff-on-Sea, Essex.
Fachblatt, *JV-Journal Verlag GmbH,* Schillerstrasse 23a, D-8000 Munchen 2, West Germany.
Frets, *GPI Publications,* 20605 Lazaneo, Cupertino, Ca 95014, USA.
Fretwire Music, 36a Wheelock Street, Middlewich, Cheshire.
Guitar, *Musical New Services,* 20 Denmark Street, London WC2H 8NE.
Guitar Player, *GPI Publications,* 20605 Lazaneo, Cupertino, Ca 95014, USA.
International Musician, *Cover Publications,* Grosvenor House, 141-143 Drury Lane, London WC2 5TE.
Modern Drummer, 1000 Clifton Avenue, Clifton, NJ 07013, USA.
Music Maker, *Delta Magazines bv,* Postbus 16, NL-6500AA Nijmegen, Holland.

Music World, Central House, 42 Rayne Road, Braintree, Essex CM7 7QP.
Musician Player and Listener, *Amordian Press Inc,* PO Box 701, 42 Rogers Street, Gloucester, Mass 01930, USA.
Polyphony, PO Box 2030, Oklahoma City, OK 73156, USA.
Rock et Folk, 14 rue Chaptal, F-75009 Paris, France.
Sound International, Link House, Dingwall Avenue, Croydon CR9 2TA.
Studio Sound, Link House, Dingwall Avenue, Croydon CR9 2TA.

Books

Ken Achard **The Fender Guitar** *Musical New Services 1977*
Ken Achard **The History And Development Of The American Guitar** *Musical New Services 1979*
Craig Anderton **Home Recording For The Musician** *Guitar Player Books*
Ian C Bishop **The Gibson Guitar From 1950** *Musical New Services 1977*
Ian C Bishop **The Gibson Guitar From 1950 Volume Two** *Musical New Services 1979*
Donald Brosnac **The Electric Guitar – Its History And Construction** *Omnibus 1975*
Donald Brosnac **An Introduction To Scientific Guitar Design** *The Bold Strummer*

Paul Day **The Burns Book** *Sound Investments 1980*
Herbert E Deutsch **Synthesis** *Avfred Pub Co 1976*
Richard Dorf **Electronic Musical Instruments** *Plimpton 1968*
Tom & Mary Evans **The Guitar From Renaissance To Rock** *Facts On File*
Friend, Pearlman, Piggott **Learning Music With Synthesizers** *Hal Leonard 1974*
Karl Geiringer **Instruments In The History Of Western Music** *George Allen & Unwin 1978*
Guitar Player **The Guitar Player Book** *Guitar Player Books*
Guitar Player **Fix Your Axe** *Guitar Player Books*
F C Judd **Electronics In Music** *Neville Spearman 1972*
Mike Longworth **Martin Guitars** *Omnibus 1975*
Sibyl Marcuse **A Survey Of Musical Instruments** *David & Charles 1975*
Tony Mitchell **The Sounds Book Of The Electric Guitar** *Spotlight Publications 1980*
Walter Sear **A Guide To Electronic Music And Synthesizers** *Omnibus 1972*
Irving Sloane **Classic Guitar Construction** *Omnibus 1976*
Irving Sloane **Guitar Repair** *Omnibus 1973*
Maurice Summerfield **The Jazz Guitar** *Ashley Mark 1978*
Tom Wheeler **The Guitar Book** *Macdonald & Janes 1974*